KU-272-008

Child Welfare and Social Action in the Nineteenth and Twentieth Centuries: International Perspectives

Edited by
Jon Lawrence and Pat Starkey

FALKIRK COUNCIL
LIBRARY SUPPORT
FOR SCHOOLS

LIVERPOOL UNIVERSITY PRESS

First published 2001 by
Liverpool University Press
4 Cambridge Street
Liverpool
L69 7ZU

Copyright © Liverpool University Press 2001

All rights reserved. No part of this book may be reproduced, stored in a retrieval system, or transmitted, in any form or by any means, electronic, mechanical, photo-copying, recording or otherwise without the prior written permission of the publishers.

British Library Cataloguing-in-Publication Data
A British Library CIP Record is available

ISBN 0–85323–676–3 hardback
     0–85323–686–0 paperback

Typeset in Plantin by Koinonia, Bury
Printed and bound in Great Britain by Bookcraft Ltd, Midsomer Norton, Wilts.

313188

Child Welfare and Social Action in the Nineteenth and Twentieth Centuries

This book is to be returned on or before the last date stamped below.

EDUCATION

Library Services
Victoria Buildings
Queen Street
Falkirk
FK2 7AF

362
-7
CHI

Falkirk Council

Contents

FALKIRK COUNCIL
LIBRARY SUPPORT
FOR SCHOOLS

Acknowledgements

The editors would like to thank the British Academy, the Wellcome Institute for the History of Medicine, the Eleanor Rathbone Charitable Trust, the P.H. Holt Charitable Trust and the Friends of the University of Liverpool for their generous support of the 1998 conference on Child Welfare and Social Action out of which the present volume has grown. They would also like to thank Adrian Allan, Julie Grier, John Lansley and Simon Wilson for their help in organising the conference and ensuring its success.

The publishers are grateful to the following for permission to reproduce copyright material: Battye Library, Perth, for the photographs of the Fairbridge farm at Pinjarra (pages 58 and 66); Barnardo's Photographic Archive for the illustration of Barnardo's Girls' Village School (page 162); London Metropolitan Archives for the photograph of the North Surrey District School (page 152); University of Liverpool Special Collections and Archives for the photograph of child migrants bound for Australia on the *Otranto* (page 63).

Introduction:
Child Welfare and Social Action
Jon Lawrence and Pat Starkey

The essays published in this volume have been selected from over fifty papers presented at an international conference on Child Welfare and Social Action held at the University of Liverpool in July 1998. Organised by members of the departments of History, Special Collections and Archives, and Sociology, Social Policy and Social Work Studies, the conference marked the deposit of the records of NCH Action for Children (formerly the National Children's Homes) in the Special Collections and Archives Department of the University. There they joined an important voluntary social work collection, including the records of Barnardo's, the Fairbridge Trust, Family Service Units and the Simon Community. Liverpool is an appropriate home for them. The Social Science Department, founded in 1904 and perhaps inevitably associated with the name of Eleanor Rathbone, was one of the first in the country, and training for social workers has always been an important aspect of the work of its successor departments.

There is currently great academic and general interest in the question of child welfare. Recent historical work has done much to focus attention on changing conceptions of childhood and of children's rights during the nineteenth and twentieth centuries.[1] This has gone hand-in-hand with a rediscovery of the 'hidden histories' of childhood – shocking accounts of the physical and sexual abuse of children and of forced child migration, but also histories which seek to re-emphasise the importance of childhood as lived experience as well as discursive construction.[2] The present volume brings together a wide range of essays that engage with the major themes of this recent literature. The essays are organised into four thematic sections, each representing a key field of research into the history of childhood and child welfare. The first section brings together two essays that explore ways in which notions of 'delinquency' have been, and remain, heavily gendered. Tamara Myers' chapter on 'delinquent' teenage girls in inter-war Montreal neatly intertwines accounts of changing representations and changing policy frameworks with the lived experience of young women cut adrift in an exhilarating, but also frightening, city environment. Myers argues that, whereas in the late nineteenth century runaway girls (her 'deserting daughters') tended to be portrayed as defenceless victims of predatory adults, by the inter-war period they were widely viewed, and treated, as 'sex delinquents'. She shows how the courts were used to shore up parental authority, noting that their preoccupation with 'sex delinquency' often blinded them to the underlying reasons why girls chose to desert the family home. Myers offers a subtle reading of these 'tainted' court records, arguing that beneath the official obsession with girls' moral character and sexual history lies evidence that desertion could be motivated both by resistance to physical and sexual abuse, and by a defiant assertion of independence from the strictures of 'traditional' family life.

The essay by Jane Brown, Michelle Burman and Kay Tisdall takes a different tack by focusing on attitudes to violence among girls in urban Scotland today. But here too one finds the same determination to bring together *representations* and *experience* since the organising principle of this chapter is the tension between how 'experts' have categorised girls' violence, and how girls themselves understand violence within their own social worlds. The authors are rightly critical of the dominant paradigm which treats girls' violence as aberrant, 'masculinised' behaviour, arguing that by starting from this gendered standpoint researchers have been incapable of understanding how violence functions within girls' social worlds. They seek to overcome the shortcomings of such work by adopting an essentially ethnographic approach, using focus groups, participant observation and similar social methodologies to try to recover the meanings that girls themselves attach to violence in its different forms. The girls they studied are shown to use controlled violence ('rough and tumble') as an important aspect of group bonding. Crucially, they are also shown to conceptualise violence as something embedded in their own social relationships, and their own feminine identities, rather than as alien and male.

Section II focuses on child emigration. Anger that the migration of unaccompanied British children continued until as recently as the mid-1960s has made this an issue of great topical interest. People 'emigrated' as children, and their descendants, are increasingly vocal in their demands both for compensation for hardships suffered and for openness about the circumstances of their emigration. At the same time academics are increasingly alive to the major questions that forced emigration raises about the histories of childhood and of Empire in twentieth-century Britain. The longevity of child emigration would seem to question conventional understandings about the reconstruction (and growing idealisation) of childhood in twentieth-century Britain. Emigrant children appear to have been perceived primarily as economic 'units', rather than as the romanticised figures of contemporary literature or of the new child-centred thinking in the social sciences. Similarly, the emigration movement appears to have had little regard for influential new theories about child-rearing which, from the 1940s onwards, stressed the importance of family ties, and especially of 'healthy' bonding to the mother, to 'normal' child development. One might also argue that the rise and eventual fall of child emigration reveals much about the ideology of Empire in Britain, and especially about the stubborn persistence (as well as the inherent contradictions) of ideas of the British as a 'world race' with a global 'civilising' mission.

Members of Home Children Canada, who gave presentations about their activities at the conference, embody the legacy of child migration. This organisation, which represents the families of those sent to Canada as unaccompanied children, was in the UK to give evidence to the House of Commons Select Committee on emigration. Their trip was not in vain. The committee expressed unease about official involvement in what was acknowledged to be 'a bad, and in human terms, costly mistake'. Its inquiry has resulted in the establishment of a fund of £1m to enable descendants to make contact with families fragmented by the involuntary movement of their forebears to countries outside the UK.[3]

Patrick Dunae's essay discusses the activity of one society whose principal function was child migration. The Fairbridge Society originated in the activities of a small group of Rhodes scholars at Oxford in 1909. Motivated by an idealism which attempted to combine imperial ambition with child welfare, they founded the Society for the Furtherance of Child Emigration to the Colonies (later to become known as the Fairbridge Society, after the most active member of the group, Kingsley Fairbridge). Dunae's study of a Fairbridge project in

4   Child Welfare and Social Action

British Columbia shows the importance of both class and gender in its fortunes. Child migration to Canada was prohibited by Canadian government legislation in 1924. It is remarkable, therefore, that the establishment of the Fairbridge Farm School in Prince Edward Island was permitted ten years later, at a time of economic crisis and in the face of the growing conviction of the emerging social work profession that unaccompanied child migration was an evil. Dunae demonstrates the ability of a small group of male associates, sharing common class and educational experiences, to collude with the Canadian authorities not only to circumvent national legislation, but also to avoid local intervention by keeping the farm outside the health and welfare regulations which would normally have operated. Ultimately, child-welfare professionals (who were overwhelmingly female) were able to undermine the 'old boy' networks that sustained this arrangement, but not before allegations of sexual abuse by members of staff had been made, and proved. That such abuse should occur may not seem surprising in the light of the recent 'discovery' of widespread abuse in children's homes in the UK, but it has certainly contributed to the sense of outrage that governments should for so long have tolerated the movement of young children across the world.

Geoffrey Sherington's chapter also focuses on the work of the Fairbridge Society, which was responsible for about half of all child migrants who travelled to Australia. Sherington highlights some of the distortions that can creep into popular mythology as particular social issues become fashionably shocking. For example, he challenges some of the more alarming statistics popularly associated with emigration, particularly those contained in the joint BBC–ABC television series, *The Leaving of Liverpool*, screened in 1992 and reviewed in Australia as an account of 'philanthropic abduction'. For example, he argues that, in spite of the suggestions that 10,000 children – or even ten times that number – were sent as migrants to Australia after 1945, recent scholarship has shown that no more than a total of 6,000 were sent in the period 1912–1967, and that of those fewer than 3,000 were sent after the Second World War. Moreover, in spite of the popular perception that children were sent without parental consent, or even knowledge, he is able to demonstrate that, even during the inter-war period, families played an important role in the emigration of children, particularly in cases where the parents had originally placed their children in homes run by children's charities.

For example, almost one quarter of the 22 children sent to Australia by Fairbridge in 1935 had been nominated by their parents. Parents of nearly all the 21 children sailing in July 1949 had not only formally consented to their emigration, but had actively encouraged it.

Imperial ambitions, integral to the work of the Fairbridge Society but implicit in the whole notion of emigration, are discussed by Kathleen Paul. Her chapter largely concentrates on the complex relationships between British central and local government, the government of Australia and voluntary societies in the period after the Second World War. Each element in a complex equation had significantly different ambitions. Paul has shown that for the British government, 'emigrated' children were links in an imperial chain which bound the Dominions to the mother country and were intended to ensure attachments which would facilitate sustained British influence overseas. For Australia, on the other hand, such young immigrants were demographic assets, young enough to forget their past and to be moulded into the Australian way of life, helping in the work of populating an under-populated country and providing a welcome addition to the labour force. They also had white skins; black children were not accepted, nor were those with any defect, however minor – despite the traumas of the Second World War, these racist and eugenic agendas remained unvanquished. For the voluntary societies, largely responsible for organising the process of migration and mediating between the UK and Australia, the movement of children across the world allowed the portrayal of themselves as agents in the transformation of the 'problem' child into a worthy imperial citizen. This perception was not necessarily shared by the population of the receiving country. As Shurlee Swain has noted, many considered such youngsters as scum, exported from the chaotic netherworld of British urban poverty. Both Swain and Paul comment on the extent to which religious imperialism played its part, with the Roman Catholic church in both Australia and Britain intent on ensuring that Australia received its fair share of Catholics, while the Anglican church fought to ensure Anglican homes for Anglican migrants. Empire settlement and the older Fairbridge idea declined fast in the mid-1940s, and, as Sherington argues, the Society began to re-invent itself to adapt to changing views of welfare, leaving the field open to Barnardo's, which continued sending children to its homes in Australia until the late 1960s.

The impulse to rescue children from dangerous or morally

undesirable situations informed child migration as practised by all the major children's societies. In Australia, it also provided the rationale for the removal of Aboriginal children from their parents. Shurlee Swain positions the debate about the removal of children from their parents, whether migrant children from the Old Country or Aboriginal children wrested from their parents in an attempt to give them an 'improved' lifestyle, within a discourse which presented the parent as the enemy of the child. As she argues, recent media attention has focused on the final phase of child migration, which was an integral part of Australian post-war reconstruction. The authorities' belief that the country was under-populated, combined with the erroneous notion that British cities were full of unwanted war orphans, helped to place Australia in the position of petitioner, requesting at the highest levels of government that large numbers of white, healthy children should be sent to Australia. This mentality was not new: even before the war the Archbishop of Perth had argued for increased child migration to reduce the risk of exposure to 'the menace of the teeming millions of our neighbouring Asian races'.[4] But as Swain shows, this has to be seen as a function of racist ambitions, alongside the child removal policy within Australia, now impugned as genocide, which meant that from 1910 to 1970, between one in three and one in ten Aboriginal children were forcibly removed from their parents, who were deemed to be failing in the performance of their parental functions. Swain's conclusion makes two telling points, revealing her pessimism both about the use of history and about current child-care practice. First, she argues that the experience of child rescue in Australia shows the abusive potential of any institution which places adults in charge of vulnerable children. Second, she argues that individualistic ideologies – characteristic, she claims, of Australia, and, one might add, of most 'western' capitalist societies – abandon the cause of children by their failure to endorse a discourse of shared responsibility for community well-being and by their inability to listen and watch for signs of distress. Swain warns of the danger of using history to condemn the past in order to endorse complacency about the present.

Section III, 'Rethinking Philanthropy', brings together three essays that explore attempts to rethink the role of philanthropic effort in child welfare between the late nineteenth century and the Second World War. Emphasis is placed on the responses of children's charities and other voluntary agencies both to the late Victorian urge to celebrate (and prolong) the innocence of 'childhood', and to the growing willingness of the state to assume quasi-parental authority over children in the name of the 'national interest'. Lydia Murdoch offers a careful study of the movement to reform orphanages in later nineteenth-century Britain, showing how discourses on class and gender worked together to help construct the idealised view of the reformed orphanage as 'cottage home'. Female philanthropic reformers denounced both working-class homes and 'barrack-school' orphanages for brutalising children (especially girls) by submerging them in an undifferentiated mass of poor and degraded humanity. The smaller, 'family cottages', by contrast, allowed for the beneficent influence of the house 'mother' to foster the children's 'individuality' by teaching them skills and manners appropriate to their station in life. In this way, Murdoch argues, the movement for 'family cottages' combined an assault on the power and expertise of male officials and on the lifestyle and culture of the working-class families whose children it purported to 'save'.

John Stewart's essay on the politics of school meal provision in Scotland explores a fascinating instance of the tensions between advocates of state and voluntary provision of social services in Edwardian Britain. Stewart shows how groups hostile to state intervention were able to secure the exclusion of Scotland from the 1906 School Meals Act. Their argument was simple – voluntary provision was well established in Scotland, and was superior to state provision since it upheld the importance both of a philanthropic public spirit and of parental responsibility. However, Stewart's account goes on to trace the gradual undermining of the voluntarists' position in Scotland; a process that culminated, in 1908, in the enactment of legislation that gave Scottish local authorities far more extensive powers than their English counterparts. In short, Stewart's chapter convincingly demonstrates the importance of developing accounts of welfare legislation that eschew grand narratives in favour of a greater sensitivity to local socio-economic and political contexts. In this case, he shows that above all we must recognise that in Scotland, where the Lib–Lab pact held no sway, Liberal politicians had an especially keen sense of their need to out-bid Labour as champions both of welfare issues and of Scottish interests.

The final chapter in this section also focuses on an aspect of Scottish exceptionalism in child welfare policy. In a chapter that nicely complements Murdoch's work on the cottage home movement,

Lynn Abrams shows that in Scotland the boarding-out movement fulfilled a very similar function, both ideologically and practically. In Scotland child 'rescue' still involved the removal of working-class children from their 'unfit' parents, but rather than transfer them to a voluntary society's idealised pseudo-home, here most children were sent to live as boarders in remote parts of the Highlands and Western Isles. In essence, therefore, boarding out was a form of internal child migration policy. Impoverished children were taken from the poor streets of Glasgow and other Scottish cities to live new, supposedly healthier and more wholesome lives with crofting families. In the process, philanthropists and administrators could comfort themselves that they were 'saving' not just the pauper child, but also a fast disappearing (and culturally cherished) rural way of life. Just like the philanthropists who organised child emigration to the 'farm schools' of the Empire, these reformers believed that rural life provided the perfect context for the realisation of an idealised, and intensely romanticised, childhood for the poor child saved from the horrors of the urban slum. However, Abrams' principal interest in this chapter is not to elaborate the discourses that legitimated this policy, but rather to explore the cruelties it inflicted upon many of the children who underwent 'boarding out' in the first half of the twentieth century. Abrams uses in-depth interviews and a 'child-centred perspective' to explore the psychological legacy of forced separation from blood family. She charts the struggle, in later life, to reconstruct an ideal- ised blood family, and shows how discovering the truth about the past often does little to solve the problems of a fractured identity. Too many former boarded-outs, she argues, remain haunted as adults by the same sense of not 'belonging' that cursed their childhoods.

Section IV, '"Welfare States" and Child Welfare', explores further the issue of state intervention in family life, and hence in child welfare, during the twentieth century. The chapters focus on two main issues: first, how changing perceptions of the nature of 'childhood' and 'the family' have influenced the development and execution of state policies and, secondly, how voluntary agencies have continually redefined their role in child welfare in response to shifts both in state policy and in the perception of what child 'welfare' actually means. Both issues are clearly of immense contemporary relevance. As Shurlee Swain has done, Molly Ladd-Taylor demonstrates the prevalence of a view which sees the parent, and especially the 'bad mother', as the enemy of the child. She argues that for most of the twentieth century, United States welfare policy has viewed family problems as the consequence of parental, most often maternal, failure. Appropriate remedies, therefore, have concentrated on remedying parental defect, by providing education and training to impoverished parents, rather than addressing environmental problems and delivering medical care and financial resources. Ladd-Taylor discusses the ease with which the Minnesotan sterilisation law of 1925 defined some women as feeble-minded and, therefore, bad or potentially bad mothers. Such women, it was believed, should be prevented from becoming pregnant. In Minnesota, the eugenic 'advantages' of compulsory sterilisation – fewer congenitally mentally incapable children – were championed alongside its sociological ones – fewer poorly parented children – in an attempt to solve the seemingly endless cycle of family poverty, dysfunction and delinquency. However, the consequences for some women were tragic and, furthermore, the policy made little impression on wider social problems. Moreover, as Ladd-Taylor argues, although surgical sterilisation is no longer seen as a simple and cost-effective solution to perplexing social problems, the fiscal, social and eugenic impulses underpinning it still colour US welfare policy.

The persistence of eugenic explanations for family problems, and the consequent failure to develop an adequate critique of economic and social conditions, is also explored by Pat Starkey. She examines the work of Pacifist Service Units and its successor organisation, Family Service Units, in England during and immediately after the Second World War. She examines the close relationship which developed in many areas between FSU and the local Medical Officers of Health and argues that this was the result of the creation of a tripartite structure for the National Health Service, vesting responsibility for environmental health problems with local departments of public health. In consequence the poor family ran the risk of being treated as a medical problem. Grubby children became evidence of parental failure and an element in a syndrome – the problem family – often assumed in public health circles to have hereditary elements and a defined aetiology and prognosis. The professionalisation of social work from the mid-1950s and the large increase in numbers of social workers eventually weakened the influence of public health doctors. Newly confident of their role, and supported by new structures, social workers wrested from public health doctors the care of families deemed to be at risk because of parental incompetence or neglect.[5] But although the dominance of the medical model began to fade from about the middle of the 1950s, it was largely replaced by psychodynamic social work which also saw the causation of family problems as internal to the family, albeit to their relationships rather than their standards of domestic hygiene. To some extent, therefore, changes in methods of dealing with poorly functioning families may be understood as a function of the rise and fall – the working out of struggles and ambitions – of two professions, medicine and social work.[6] In this process, children were almost invisible, except in their function as victims or as evidence of parental failure.

Julie Grier also considers relationships between the voluntary and the statutory sectors and examines the complex pattern of relationships that developed between erstwhile child rescue societies and central and local government in the UK during the 1940s and early 1950s. She is able to show how large voluntary organisations, specifically National Children's Homes and Barnardo's, were able to manipulate situations and to take advantage of the untidiness which resulted from the post-war introduction of measures which left such societies straddling the responsibilities of a number of different government departments. The ministries of Health and Education and the Home Office all had an interest in aspects of child welfare, and the skill of the voluntary societies – either individually or together – in playing one department off against another made nonsense of the 'spirit of friendly rivalry' which the Curtis committee had suggested in 1946 should characterise relationships between the voluntary and statutory sectors. However, as Grier notes, in spite of the tensions generated by such complex, and sometimes strained, relationships, both NCH and Barnardo's actively contributed to the shaping of post-war child-care provision.

In conclusion, while the twelve chapters offer substantial historical contributions in their own right, taken together they represent an important contribution to the understanding of child welfare and social action in the nineteenth and twentieth centuries. The chapters brought together in this volume challenge many assumptions about the history of childhood and child welfare policy. We are asked to look again at the discourses that constructed and legitimated interventions in children's lives, from child emigration and child 'rescue' schemes, to the policing both of 'delinquency' and of 'unfit' families. But the chapters are not concerned solely with deconstructing mythic histories. On the contrary, there is a recurring insistence that histories of childhood and child welfare must not lose sight of children themselves, nor of their experiences at the sharp end of state and philanthropic 'interventions'.

Notes

1. For instance, Hugh Cunningham, *The Children of the Poor: Representations of Childhood Since the Seventeenth Century*, Oxford, Blackwell, 1991; Harry Hendrick, *Child Welfare: England, 1872–1989*, London, Routledge, 1994; Carolyn Steedman, *Strange Dislocations: Childhood and the Idea of Human Interiority, 1780–1930*, London, Virago, 1995.

2. For instance, J. S. La Fontaine, *Child Sexual Abuse*, Cambridge, Polity Press, 1990; M. Chesterman, *Child Sexual Abuse and Social Work*, Norwich, University of East Anglia Press, 1985; Linda Gordon, *Heroes of their Own Lives*, London, Virago, 1988; Philip Bean, *Lost Children of the Empire*, London, Unwin Hyman, 1989; K. Paul, *Whitewashing Britain: Race and Citizenship in the Post-War Era*, Ithaca, NY, Cornell University Press, 1997; G. Sherington and C. Jeffrey, *Fairbridge: Empire and Child Migration*, London, Woburn Press, 1998; B. Coldrey, *Good British Stock: Child and Youth Migration to Australia*, Canberra, National Archives of Australia, 1999; Anna Davin, *Growing Up Poor: Home, School and Street in London, 1870–1914*, London, Rivers Oram Press, 1996.

3. Health Committee, *Third Report on the Welfare of Former British Child Migrants*, Vol. 1 (Report and Proceedings of the Committee), House of Commons, Session 1997–98.

4. Quoted in W. Webster, *Imagining Home: Gender, 'Race' and National Identity, 1945–64*, London, UCL Press, 1998, p. 30.

5. J. Welshman, 'In Search of the "Problem Family": Public Health and Social Work in England and Wales 1940–1970', *Social History of Medicine* 9, 1996, p. 465.

6. Hendrick, *Child Welfare*, p. 242.

I
Gender and 'Delinquency'

1

Deserting Daughters: Runaways and the Red-Light District of Montreal before 1945

Tamara Myers

In the middle of an April night in 1924, Germaine C. slipped out of her family home through an open window. Across Montreal she travelled to meet her boyfriend at 188 Boulevard St Laurent where they rented a room as 'husband and wife'.[1] Not two months earlier, Alice M. also deserted her home, to escape the physical abuse of her father. While on the run she and a girlfriend similarly rented a room at 188 Boulevard St Laurent.[2] Both girls were caught, hauled into the Juvenile Delinquents' Court (*Cour des jeunes délinquants*) and punished.

This chapter is about girls who ran away from home and were subsequently caught in the web of the emergent juvenile justice system in early twentieth-century Montreal. The juxtaposition of the above two cases suggests that a range of reasons caused girls to desert their family homes; it also hints at the potentially central role played by the social geography of the city – not to mention the reputation of certain streets such as Boulevard St Laurent – in girls' desertions. The intention of this study is to reveal the significance of girls' desertions by shedding light on their experiences on the streets of Montreal and reviewing the competing discourses generated to explain why girls left home without permission.

Since the late nineteenth century, disappearing daughters had commanded considerable popular attention in Montreal due to widespread fears about international rings of prostitution and the existence of white slavers in the city. Prostitution and fallen womanhood appeared to be emblematic of the vulnerability of all young women in modern industrialised cities. The panic over missing girls led to the creation of laws and protective social agencies to safeguard female chastity and regulate the social lives of young, single women.[3] In the early twentieth century, however, the archetypal deserting daughter shifted from defenceless victim to sex delinquent. Sex delinquents, or 'problem' girls, willingly ventured into the city's commercial amusement arenas and wilfully pushed boundaries of acceptable social and sexual behaviour. A major target of the modern juvenile justice movement – the sex delinquent – could be found daily in the nation's new juvenile courts.

The Montreal Juvenile Delinquents' Court opened in 1912. In this new court, girls' misbehaviour was largely interpreted in sexual terms, but it was not sexual behaviour alone that concerned the court and parents: desertion of the family home was as critical to determining if a girl would end up in court as the suggestion of promiscuity. Defined as habitual or multiple nights spent away from home, desertion meant far more than a threat to female chastity, for it signified daughters' abdication of their subordinate yet integral role within the family hierarchy.

Records of the juvenile court reveal diverse reasons and competing explanations for desertion. For their part, court officers and parents accused girls of sexual misconduct. Most court cases focused on the issue of a girl's virginity but this was only part of the story. Some of the very common female desertion cases heard in the Montreal juvenile court tell a more complex story of violent homes and daughters' determination to escape them. Others suggest that desertion was a means of resisting familial expectations regarding work. Ethnicity and class frequently dictated the kind of work a daughter would perform; some girls rejected unpaid labour in their homes and deserted to take up paid positions in the city's thriving industrial sector. As a result of the complexity of desertion cases, runaway daughters simultaneously elicited compassion and alarm from the new juvenile court which was increasingly troubled by the problem of runaway girls.

Girls' attempts at running away were often eventually thwarted by parents and the juvenile justice authorities, but the social geography of Montreal in the early twentieth century permitted them at least a temporary refuge and anonymity. If one accepts the warnings of social reformers, the city's vibrant, cosmopolitan, industrial and commercial centre devoured unsuspecting young women. Yet these perambulating adolescents managed, with some effort, to negotiate their days and nights on Montreal's streets thanks mainly to support networks of female (and to a lesser extent male) friends, and to the proliferation of cheap rented accommodation.

This study is based on more than 200 cases of female desertion that came before the court between 1912 and 1945. In the first decades of the court's operation, it annually processed more than one thousand formal cases of delinquency and neglect. Girls made up approximately one-fifth of these cases. As many as three-quarters of Montreal female delinquents were French Canadian and born in Quebec. The other 25 per cent consisted of Protestants of English and Scottish backgrounds, Irish Catholics, and European Jews. (Aboriginal girls were absent from this court largely due to the fact that reserves lay off the island of Montreal and were outside the jurisdiction of the court.) Female delinquents typically came to the Juvenile Delinquents' Court when they were between the ages of 14 and 16. Most girls came from working-class areas of Montreal and had had at least some experience earning an income. With compulsory schooling laws not introduced in Quebec until the 1940s, these girls had generally had little education past their eleventh birthdays.[4]

Montreal Female Delinquents

The federal Juvenile Delinquents Act of 1908 (JDA) introduced juvenile courts to Canada. The act contained a hazy definition of delinquency, specifying merely that a delinquent was a child under 16 who committed an offence against the Criminal Code, provincial statutes or municipal by-laws. While the juvenile offence of desertion cannot be found in the 1908 legislation, juvenile courts regularly policed this errant behaviour. The first judge of Montreal's Juvenile Delinquents' Court, François-Xavier Choquet, publicly argued for desertion to be entrenched in the federal JDA. He criticised the federal law for lacking the necessary explicitness regarding juvenile delinquency, including immoral conduct, frequenting moving pictures and pool rooms, and desertion. In a national civic affairs magazine he provided his understanding of delinquency: 'A Juvenile delinquent means also any child who is incorrigible or ... absents itself from or deserts its home or place of abode ...'[5]

In his court, Judge Choquet was able to put into practice his support for the inclusion of desertion in the Canadian juvenile justice system because provincial legislation in Quebec had specified desertion as a juvenile offence. Since the 1870s, provincial reform and industrial schools had been established to incarcerate youths separately from adults. Girls, then, who exhibited 'bad or vicious habits' were placed in these institutions by the lower criminal courts. In 1912, the year the juvenile court opened, provincial legislation specified that a child could be sent to a reform facility for having 'deserted or abandoned the home of the person who is in charge of him [sic] without permission or sufficient reason ...'[6] Choquet used this definition of delinquency in his courtroom.

Girls who deserted their family homes became a major preoccupation of the Montreal juvenile court. By 1918, 25 per cent of female delinquents came before the court for desertion, while many cases of 'incorrigibility' and 'vagrancy' also involved desertions. By 1924, more than half of female court cases centred on desertion. Statistics of the Montreal Police Department from the 1920s reveal that between one-third and one-half of *fillettes* were arrested for *'déserter ses parents'*.[7] Considered a far more serious offence when committed by a girl than a boy, female desertion was policed vigorously. In 1924, for example, 102 girls were arrested for deserting compared to 61 boys. However, the overall ratio of girls to boys arrested that year was 192:834.[8]

The involvement of the police and juvenile court in tracking down deserters began with parental complaints. Because of the nature of delinquency – often reducible to generational conflict in the home in the case of girls – the court relied upon parents to bring forward complaints. [9] In many cases, their daughter's desertion was the last straw. The threshold for tolerance of a daughter's bad behaviour varied from household to household, as two cases of desertion in the 1920s illustrate. Minnie D. and Tilly F. both deserted and were brought to court by their mothers.[10] Minnie was brought in after spending just one night out while Tilly had been gone for three months before her parents made a complaint. There are similarities in the profile of the girls: the girls were 15 and 16; both girls were immigrants, having come with their parents from England and Scotland, respectively; and both mothers were widows. The different reactions to their daughters' desertions may have to do with contrasting attitudes towards state involvement in private matters. It might also have to do with family situations and the role that the girls played. Minnie D.'s widowed mother was out of work and expected her daughter to work and contribute her wages to the family budget. At the time of the desertion, she was refusing to work and was spending nights at dance halls. On the other hand, Tilly's mother had remarried and the family does not seem to have been dependent on her wages. When she left home she worked as a live-in domestic servant. While Tilly's parents did not know where she was it is possible that she had threatened to work and live elsewhere. Generally, parents turned to the juvenile court only when a pattern of deserting had been established.

In attempting to make sense of the high percentage of female desertion cases in the Montreal juvenile tribunal, it is important to place them on a continuum of behaviour that attracted the court's attention. The typical early-twentieth-century delinquent daughter was described as being '*sorteuse*' [in the habit of going out on the town] or having '*découcher*' [spent nights away from home]. Desertions, then, could consist of habitual nights out over a period of time as well as an extended period away from the family home. Some adolescent girls intended to return home, while others did not.

Once girls were brought to court the suggestive sexual nature of 'spending the night out' or running away took on great significance at the juvenile tribunal. Court-ordered gynaecological examinations functioned as the centrepiece of evidence in these cases.[11] The loss of virginity (suggested by a ruptured hymen) and venereal disease in effect defined girls as delinquents. Premarital sex, as Andrée Lévesque has observed, was condemned by the Catholic church in Quebec at this time and girls who got pregnant out of wedlock were encouraged to wait out their pregnancies in religious institutions where they were forced to use pseudonyms and place their children in orphanages.[12] The conflation of girls' delinquencies with sexual precocity has given scholars reason to proclaim the gendered nature of juvenile offences.[13] In the case of Montreal most girls accused of desertion had had some sexual experience but their desertions were often about much more than having sex. Details from the juvenile court illuminate the sexual histories of deserting daughters but should not obscure the girls' reasons for leaving.

Resistance and Control

The juvenile court tended to focus on girls' sexual experience during their desertion but the reasons why girls deserted are as numerous as the girls themselves. According to probation officers, what led girls down this path of 'debauchery' was a combination of the girls' weakness for the modern city and a lack of rigour in parenting.

Although the court may have assumed that single mothers and derelict parents produced these undisciplined adolescents, it was the girls who were brought to court. In their defence, girls provided diverse answers as to why they ran away. Girls' explanations are tales of resistance: at times eloquently, and in detail, they reveal what they perceived to be unfair treatment at home. Girls often justified their behaviour in terms of a once mutually advantageous familial relationship now gone awry. Besides wanting to work on their own terms, they ran away because their leisure activities strained family life, or they had chosen inappropriate boyfriends and were prevented from dating, or family members had physically and sexually abused them.

According to both parents and the juvenile court, daughters' desertions were particularly menacing (beyond the threat of pregnancy and disgrace) because they had absented themselves from the family. In Catholic French Canadian families, girls owed respect and obedience to their fathers, and were obliged to aid their mothers in the home. In working-class and immigrant families teenage daughters were expected to make meals, clean the house, care for dependent siblings and parents, and contribute to the family economy. The family determined what kind of job they might have, the style of clothing they wore, and if, when and whom daughters could date. In return for being part of this family order they received food, shelter and protection. However, the equilibrium in the family sometimes broke down during adolescence. Intergenerational tension between adolescents and adults was exacerbated in the early twentieth century amid immense social and economic change.[14] Working-class families depended on daughters to maintain their roles within the family, while the girls were drawn increasingly out of the home into Montreal's wage economy and new forms of leisure independent from their families and communities.

Young women working for pay proved to be a source of economic relief but also of intergenerational tension within families. The abundance of factory work and increasingly plentiful service sector jobs in Montreal gave adolescent girls just enough cash to permit them some independence. While all girls would be required to contribute to the management and upkeep of the home, working for wages depended on individual family situations.[15] For example, some recent immigrants refused to allow their daughters to engage in readily available paid work. Yetta H., a Russian Jew, told the probation officer that she desired the 'freedom and independence' one obtained through earning a living. Her desertion was justified, she believed, because her parents prevented her from working. Upon running away, she secured a job first in a candy factory, then in a hotel washing dishes for $5 per week plus her board.[16] It was in the hotel that she was arrested for deserting her family. An Italian family that had come to Montreal just months before the outbreak of the First World War also resisted their daughter's aspirations to work outside the home. Sixteen-year-old Leontine deserted in 1918, she claimed, because she wanted to work in downtown Montreal and her father's house was simply too far away. Like Yetta, she easily found employment (at the American Can Company factory) and was soon caught.[17]

Immigrant families used the juvenile court to stop girls from engaging in paid employment, even though the court supported adolescent girls developing a strong work ethic in the decades before compulsory education in Quebec. The perils of this city clearly gave migrant and immigrant families cause for concern. Linda Gordon notes in her research on Boston that familial conflict was heightened among new families because of parents' anxiety over the teenagers' independence on the streets, especially once they had access to paid employment.[18]

Adolescent girls in working-class families were extremely important in replacing mothers when necessary. The death or illness of a mother often meant that an adolescent daughter assumed the responsibilities of raising younger siblings and maintaining the household. Fleurette C., a 17-year-old French Canadian, was told to look after her siblings when her mother was taken ill in December 1923. The demands of eight siblings, a working father and an ill mother fell on her shoulders. No doubt this was arduous work that afforded her little independence. For a month she coped, then deserted. She did not leave to avoid work; indeed she deserted to find more acceptable work outside the home. In the city's red-light district she easily found herself a job as a domestic servant.[19]

Other girls claimed they deserted because they feared a reprimand from parents regarding their lack of work. Dorothy E., a 15-year-old English immigrant, failed to come home because she was afraid to return without a job. Brought to court by her parents, Dorothy was eventually sent home on probation. She would return within six months, however, in an attempt to escape a hostile family environment. Her mother begged the court to place her in reform school to protect her from her father whose quick temper flared over his daughter's continuing failure to find work. For a combination of her own wilfulness (illustrated by her desertion) and a need to safeguard her, the court incarcerated Dorothy for two years.[20]

In deserting, some girls gained the freedom they needed to pursue their love interests. Parental objections to girls' choices stemmed from their belief that their daughter was too young to be courted or that the young man's religious, ethnic, or racial background was unacceptable. When daughters professed their love for, and intention to marry, the boyfriend with whom they had deserted, parents revealed that they had no intention of permitting unacceptable liaisons to continue. Although families may have feared the consequences resulting from a daughter's desertion with a lover, at times they preferred to face disgrace rather than allow an 'inappropriate' marriage to occur.

During the First World War, 16-year-old Aurore M. dutifully worked in a munitions factory. However, she and her younger sister were much more interested in the local theatre and turned their attention to acting. Aurore landed a job with a touring company and went on the road. At this time she met an African-American man whom she alleged was responsible for her pregnancy. Although he proved to be single and Catholic her parents refused to allow them to marry and filed a complaint against her for desertion.[21] At this time in Quebec, being pregnant on one's wedding day was not uncommon; however, interracial marriage in this case was forbidden. Aurore was sent home and placed on probation.

English–French tensions also ran very high when it came to daughters dating, although linguistic and religious differences may not have been as insurmountable as race. When Gladys G., an English Anglican girl, began dating Leo P., a French Canadian Catholic boy, it created tremendous difficulty at home. Gladys and Leo attended dances once a week. This so provoked her father that he kicked her out of his house and threatened to shoot her. As the probation officer noted, it was the father who brought the complaint against the daughter for desertion but clearly he had told her to leave.[22] The father's behaviour was seen as irrational in this case and, in an unusual twist, Leo was portrayed as her saviour. The probation officer recommended that she live apart from her family until the couple married. In another case, Vita O., a 13-year-old Montreal-born daughter of immigrants, pleaded with her parents to accept her boyfriend, Alfred. Her father protested against the relationship because of the boyfriend's French Canadian heritage – he told the probation officer, 'the French Canadians beat their wives'. The acrimony over her boyfriend escalated to the point that Vita was beaten by her father and deserted. Alfred and Vita spent one week in a rented room in the red-light district. News of her damaged reputation and ruptured hymen forced Vita's parents to overlook their original objections to Alfred and to concede to a prompt Catholic wedding.[23]

In desertion cases, probation officers recorded countless stories of physical violence in families. Mothers and fathers, and sometimes brothers and sisters, punched and kicked girls, threw them on the floor, threatened to shoot them and banished them from their homes. Many working-class families whose lives intersected with the Montreal juvenile court were familiar with violence, including corporal punishment of adolescents. It is unlikely that at this time parents would conceptualise violence as abuse, notwithstanding the North American child protection movement.[24] Discipline was a common excuse for violence; indeed, it was often seen as justifiable by juvenile justice authorities as much as parents in the early twentieth century. Gordon has attempted to explain the abuse of children in working-class Boston as discipline – a result of the limited ability of parents to protect their children from the dangerous city streets.[25] The court concurred with parents that girls were risking their reputations and their future as wives and mothers through unchaperoned (i.e. immoral) lifestyles.

In Montreal some parents claimed that they were correcting their children for refusing to obey, especially daughters who refused to come home before midnight or who stayed out all night. When 14-year-old Ida D. deserted she claimed that she had been hit repeatedly by her parents who justified the violence as a response to their daughter's habit of spending nights on the streets. The probation officer emphasised in her report that Ida liked the streets and boys too much for her own good and investigated her sexual experience; the escalation of physical violence in the home, which Ida claimed prompted her desertion, became secondary to her indiscretions.[26]

Girls sometimes admitted that tensions over their night-time adventures provoked violence that led, in turn, to desertion. In 1924 Adrienne C. deserted her family home to join her boyfriend. When asked to explain her actions, she cited the brutality of her father: rather than being motivated by lust as her parents would have it, she was attempting to escape a beating. Her parents did not deny it but rather claimed the violence was justified because the father was attempting to break her habit of staying out until midnight. This family felt severe corporal punishment was necessary given the danger the city presented to their 17-year-old daughter. She, however, felt that the father's actions were indefensible and that it was she who had been wronged.[27]

In some situations probation officers recognised habitual violence as abusive and attempted to protect the adolescent victim. For example, 15-year-old Lilian D. was brought to court because her behaviour had been 'bad' in the past year; according to her mother, she did not come home at night and was in the habit of frequenting moving picture houses. Lilian retorted that her mother had frequently beaten her since she was young: the report described daily cuffs to the head, kicks and punches. Because Lilian was culpable of sexual transgressions she did not garner the full support of the court. Though her mother's bad reputation led the court to reject its favoured programme of probation, it determined instead to send Lilian to reform school for a minimum of two years for 'protection'.[28]

Girls whose medical examinations were not 'against them' fared better in getting the court to deal with violent family situations. In a 1928 case of desertion, an Italian-born girl ran away because she was terrified of her brother and father. Ida B. had left home because she had broken the gramophone and was afraid of being beaten by her brother who frequently hit her. The father constantly scolded the girl. The probation officer wrote that the mother backed up her daughter's story, saying the father was *'comme un diable'* [like a devil] and that *'la vie est enfer chez son père'* [life is hell at her father's home].[29] In this case the girl was examined and found to be a virgin. That, along with the lack of evidence that Ida had attended the cinema or smoked cigarettes, and the fact that she had sought out her sister and her godmother during her desertion, brought her the sympathy of the court. In another case, 10-year-old Marie-Jeanne had deserted because her father beat her. She, like Ida, found an older married woman to care for her. Because she was also a virgin, she was pitied and placed in an industrial school for her own protection.[30]

A father's right to discipline a child was reflected in the laws and customs of Quebec: the province's Civil Code and the Roman Catholic tradition conferred power and authority upon male heads of households. In extreme, but not infrequent, cases this structure of power led to the physical and sexual abuse of girls at the hands of fathers (or social fathers).[31] In her study of incest cases in Quebec from 1858 to 1938, Marie-Aimée Cliche has argued that the authority of Quebec fathers to physically discipline their children 'for their own good' opened the door to abuse.[32] Such domestic abuse occasionally met with resistance in the form of desertion which ironically led to the girl's appearance before the court. In the context of the juvenile court, girls were asked to explain their actions and in the course of doing so, revealed how they had been abused. Desertion represented an attempt on the part of girls to escape cycles of abuse. Girls were not always believed, but occasionally the probation officers condemned the home. In such cases, criticism of the father's actions was framed not as a comment on patriarchal power but as the result of alcoholism, poverty or desperation.

In cases involving incest, girls often felt that they had nothing to lose by leaving home.[33] Anne G.'s mother brought her to the juvenile court for desertion in early December 1918. The oldest of five children, Anne was sent out to work at a glove factory, adding $5.50 to the weekly family income. Anne's parents did not get along, especially when her father drank: earlier that autumn he had locked his wife out of the family home. During his wife's absence, the father raped Anne. Anne seemed to lack the paralysing shame that often accompanied incest and prevented girls from escaping abusive situations: Anne had her father arrested. From jail he wrote and asked that she rescind her allegation. After three months in jail he was released on bail, and again he insisted she take back her story, threatening her to the point that she was forced to make an escape through a window. Anne was then arrested for desertion. The charges against Anne were only dismissed once the father was found guilty of incest.[34]

In the case of sisters Gabrielle and Germaine, desertion was the chosen mode of resistance to a very abusive situation. Their rebellious acts were policed whereas their father's criminal acts were not. This is outlined by the fact that the father, a perpetrator of incest, was the one who brought forward the complaint of desertion against his daughters who, he claimed, no longer submitted to his will. In 1924 these girls were 16 and 18. Their mother had died when the girls were very young and subsequently they had been sent to various relatives and institutions. For the previous four years, however, they had lived with their father. Germaine, the older girl, kept house for her father while Gabrielle worked outside the home as a domestic. The father had the girls charged with desertion because they came and went as they pleased and he had evidence that they were involved sexually with boys. The probation officer made up a long list of the girls' lovers. However, what was also revealed in the juvenile court was that from the ages of 10 and 12 these girls had been sexually and physically abused. Germaine spent entire nights with her father; when she attempted to leave to find sanctuary at an aunt's, he beat her. She told the court that he had told her she had to serve him as a wife. Gabrielle claimed to have caught the two 'in the act'.

Both sisters were sexually abused by the father but responded to it differently: Germaine the older daughter almost always obliged him and was rewarded with clothes and money; Gabrielle on the other hand resisted her father and was denied the necessities of life. Gabrielle managed to escape for short periods, taking up work outside the home. Germaine's situation exhibited what Gordon labels as the classic traits of domestic incest – where the eldest daughter replaces a wife. The father was committed to, and dependent upon, the eldest daughter as manager of his household and as sexual partner. By the autumn of 1924 the power dynamic in the household was breaking down and the father was losing control of his daughters. It was then that he sought the help of the juvenile court to discipline them. The evidence of sexual abuse led the probation officer to criticise the father's behaviour, but the evidence of 'sex delinquency' caused her to recommend that the younger sister be placed in the reform school with the nuns of the Bon-Pasteur for rehabilitation. Because the girls were acting out as sex delinquents they were not constructed as victims of a sexual predator – their desertion was not understood as a response to an abusive home life, and they were denied the protection and sympathy of the court.[35] The records are unclear as to whether the father was ever prosecuted.

Runaways on the Streets of Montreal

In early twentieth-century Montreal, young women who ventured onto the streets at night without chaperones provoked fear, anxiety and alarm. Much has been written about how the quintessential industrialising city was constructed as a menace to virtuous womanhood. However, experiences of runaways have been little explored except by sociologists and criminologists working since the 1970s on the perceived problem of homeless youth.[36] Early twentieth-century deserting daughters found jobs and temporary lodgings, and spent evenings with lovers and friends at dance halls, moving picture houses and even in brothels. They encountered both danger and pleasure. In the following section I examine the kinds of experiences girls acquired while running away – experiences which involved both adventure and survival.

In the early twentieth century, Montreal was an important commercial and industrial centre that drew people both from the Quebec countryside and from around the world. A predominantly French-speaking and Catholic city, it was home to nearly one million people from a diversity of ethnic backgrounds. It contained many of the contradictions of large cities at the time: fabulous wealth, striking architecture, monuments to the Church on the one hand, and poverty, slums, and depravity on the other. Often touted as 'modern and progressive, historic and romantic' it also earned a reputation as the 'Sodom of North America'.[37] Ranked as a major port of entry for white slavers,[38] Montreal had an established and well-known red-light district that attracted Montrealers and visitors alike. So thoroughly defined as a centre of prostitution in the popular imagination it seems to have existed in spatial isolation, yet, as we will see, its boundaries were fluid. This red-light district was centrally located, nestling in and around hospitals, schools and neighbourhoods settled by recent immigrants.[39]

From the late nineteenth century, Montreal's darker side had earned a reputation for victimising unsuspecting young women. Women alone in the city were at particular risk: the Women's Christian Temperance Union, the Soeurs du Bon-Pasteur, the Montreal Local Council of Women and the Fédération nationale St-Jean-Baptiste[40] worked to protect these women, while the sensationalist press propagated stories of young women disappearing. By the end of the First World War anti-vice campaigns and 'moral surveys' had shown that young women were agents of their own peril; working in the city by day, 'modern girls' indulged in 'immoral' activities often in the red-light district at night. Working-class girls' susceptibility to moral ruin, according to anti-vice reformers, was directly related to their weakness for luxury: girls from 'respectable homes, but who want to dress as well and have as "good time" as their more wealthy sisters, have fallen too easy victims to the wiles of the scoundrelly "pimps"'.[41] The Fédération nationale St-Jean-Baptiste labelled these women '*jeunes filles modernes*' who were responsible for weakening Christian morality and family bonds.[42] A perceived need to prevent girls from becoming 'modern' led to the establishment of an array of social control mechanisms from policewomen in the First World War to curfew laws in the Second World War.

Girls did not heed the warnings of the social reformers regarding the risks of the red-light district. Rather, they chose to go there when they ran away. This is not to suggest that these adolescents were prostitutes; rather, they found this area provided them with the adventure and anonymity that most neighbourhoods did not. These girls were part of what Cynthia Comacchio suggests was an emergent 'youth culture expressed through leisure activity'.[43] By the 1910s 'modern girls' were seen 'unattended, promenading up and down' at the intersection of St Laurent Boulevard and St Catherine Street – in the heart of the red-light district.[44] New patterns of work and leisure coupled with the rise of the commercial amusement industry facilitated adolescent girls' pursuit of movies, dancing, and restaurants. This lifestyle, what one probation officer called '*la vie légère*', was a rejection of the work ethic, discipline, and authority.[45] Where reformers saw brothels, disease and depravity, girls who came of age during and after the First World War saw a compelling world defined by youth and defiance of authority, be it parental, Church or state.

Through delinquent girls' confessions to probation officers, the Montreal Juvenile Delinquents' Court probed the city's unsavoury downtown core. The probation officers' reports consistently point to a thriving Montreal nightlife. One girl, Irène C., left home one night in February 1918 to go dancing and did not come home for three days.[46] Another girl admitted to going out to the Jardin de Danse on St Catherine Street where she did the fox-trot, the one-step and the waltz with young men she met there.[47] In cases from the 1920s and 1930s girls as young as 13 sought out movies, dance halls and restaurants, concluding their evenings in the cheap rooms located within the boundaries of the red-light district.[48] By the 1940s cabarets and theatres similarly drew young women into the downtown areas at night.[49] During the Second World War, Lucy G., a 15-year-old daughter of Polish immigrants, deserted with a girlfriend for a skiing trip. She was found in downtown Montreal in a house full of contraband coffee, sugar and butter. She told her probation officer that she wanted glamour and excitement, and preferred to wear slinky black clothing rather than the simple clothes her mother bought for her.[50]

In response to the rising number of single wage-earners in the city, rental accommodation boomed in the early twentieth century. The proliferation of cheap rooms rented by the day caught the attention of many girls wanting to slip anonymously into the city. Establishments offering '*chambres à louer*' [rooms to let] ranged from makeshift brothels to respectable boarding houses, a point not lost on women reformers hoping to control the moral environment of the city.[51] These rooms proved to be an effective short-term solution for runaways: inexpensive enough to be attractive yet too costly to become a permanent residence. During the First World War a room on rue St Justin in the red-light district cost $2.50 per week, about half an adolescent girl's salary. Irène J., the fox-trotting delinquent mentioned above, solved her financial difficulties by doubling up with another girl at a boarding house on rue St Justin. In the 1920s a room could be had for a weekly rate of $4, still a considerable portion of a girl's $7 salary.[52] Rates for rooms did not change substantially, for by 1944, Jeannette L. was still able to rent a room with her girlfriend for $4 a week.[53]

Most girls found rooms at establishments that did not question their age, their company or their activities. To the consternation of the probation officer investigating the case of Marie-Rose C., the boarding house keeper did not object when the adolescent received her boyfriend in the room during her two-week stay.[54] This was not always the case, however – as Irène J. found out, not all keepers permitted female tenants to have men in their rooms.[55]

Independence for adolescent girls did not mean negotiating Montreal by night on their own: networks of girlfriends encouraged and sustained their desertions. Many deserting daughters slept at the homes of relatives or friends when they could. Girls relayed stories of meeting girlfriends, venturing to dance halls or cinemas and together finding a place to spend the night. For instance, Alice M. spent one week at a girlfriend's home, and then with another friend she went 'en chambre' at 188 St Laurent Boulevard.[56] Similarly, Mary R. met her friend Sadie F. and together they spent the night at another girl's home.[57] Married girlfriends, often themselves still teenagers, offered runaways a place to stay.[58]

In hearing girls' tales, probation officers frequently concluded that relationships between girls were at the root of delinquent acts.

Primarily, these relationships interfered with parents' ability to discipline, and even replaced familial bonds. Critical of girls' friendships, probation officers rejected the notion of mutual relationships among teenage girls, insisting instead on a hierarchical model where there were leaders and followers. A common refrain of probation officer Rose Henderson was that girlfriends were not 'desirable companion[s]'.[59] Girls such as Sadie F., mentioned above, who had already come before the court, were automatically blamed for leading Mary R. down the wrong path.[60] Older girls were singled out as particularly bad influences. Rita R., one of the few girls before the court to have made it to business college, deserted, according to the probation officer, because of the influence of 'sophisticated' girls she had met at school.[61] Probation officers were frequently suspicious of girlfriends because of the seeming ease with which they lied to protect one another. When mothers went looking for daughters who had not returned home, girlfriends were known to cover for them.[62]

Distrust of girlfriends speaks directly to the fear that the traditional family had lost its power to control adolescent girls. Gordon writes, 'Weakened family and community networks meant that adolescents relied on peer approval and companionship, and often came to disdain their parents, while parents could not trust these peers to protect children and orient them toward secure futures.'[63] Rather than see girlfriends as safer company than the wily men so often described in the press, probation officers worked to separate girlfriends in the long term.

Parents' and probation officers' anxieties about girls on the town in Montreal were not necessarily unfounded, for girls were frequently sexually active with boyfriends, and were occasionally forced by circumstance to exchange sex for accommodation or meals. Undoubtedly some girls entered the city's thriving sex trade. The story Eva L. told of her desertion confirmed the worst fears of probation officers. She claimed to have been coaxed into deserting by her friend Rita S. After work one Saturday they met at a house of prostitution on La Gauchetière where Eva made $3–4 dollars. From there two men took them to St Elizabeth Street where they lived for two weeks in a room paid for by the men. Then they went back to another brothel on La Gauchetière where Eva paid $1.50 a week for a room and earned 50 cents profit on each 'trick'. At this last place Rita's mother caught up with the girls and had them arrested.[64]

Scholars now recognise the close connection between physical and sexual abuse at home and prostitution.[65] Having few economic options in the first half of the twentieth century, it is not at all surprising to find girls escaping dysfunctional family situations only to find themselves victimised by men on the streets. Irène M.'s drunken father habitually hit his four daughters and their mother. In the middle of winter, 1924, he threw all of them out of the house onto the street. Irène chose not to return and wound up at '*mauvaises maisons*' (a euphemistic term for brothels) where she stayed for four weeks. She came home on her own recognisance but departed again. Eventually she was arrested for being found in a disorderly house.[66] She had been supporting herself through prostitution.

Cases of runaway girls entering prostitution are extreme examples; more common were the cases of girls going to rooms with young men they knew and exchanging sex with them for the price of the room. When 14-year-old Simonne T. deserted she rented a room with Paul D. who paid for the room. Although they had dated for months before the desertion, according to Simonne it was when they went 'en chambre' that he seduced her.[67] Mary Odem has suggested that California runaways in this time period traded on their sexuality in their struggle to survive on their own.[68] Recent research has found that many runaway girls become involved in prostitution (or an exchange of sexual activity for food, shelter or money)[69] in order to survive. Exchanging sex for shelter or food speaks to the material reality of life for these girls who could not earn enough to be independent of their families.

Adolescent female desertion was threatening because of the perceived danger the city presented to unchaperoned young women; it was also threatening because of the independence and self-sufficiency exhibited by girls in the face of their alleged peril. In some cases the girls' desertions reveal their keen ability to survive away from their families. Others illustrate the social and economic disadvantage of being adolescent and female. Considering the tremendous risk involved, it is perhaps surprising that so many girls chose to run away. It is for this reason that it is important to examine why they left.

Girls who ran away from home were violating familial order. Their reasons for deserting involved the desire for freedom to pursue paid employment on their own terms and their choice of love interest. Sometimes they retorted with stories of violent homes which put their delinquent actions into a different light. Sexual encounters were often part of a runaway's experience but do not alone explain their motivations. The kind of experience they had was shaped by their gender and age but also the particular moment in the development of the city.

Conclusion

At the beginning of the twentieth century, deserting daughters were problematic because they symbolised the weakening of traditional structures of Quebec society: the family and the Church. New state institutions such as the juvenile court in Montreal were founded to combat this problem and simultaneously police and protect adolescent girls. Early in the history of the Montreal Juvenile Delinquents' Court, desertion became an important part of its work with girls.

Girls who spent nights away from home were labelled sex delinquents. The juvenile court's obsession with sexual delinquency has meant for historians that its files present apparently thorough records of these girls' sexual histories. The challenge for us is to read beyond the details of girls' sexual experience towards a more thorough understanding of their motivation in disobeying parents. These cases were rarely simple and cannot be reduced to daughters' sexual precocity. Sexual experience was often combined with dereliction of duties at home, general disobedience to parents, and failure to contribute earnings to the family budget or help with the housework. Deserting daughters who asserted their independence and resisted violent and unhappy homes were extremely threatening to parents. They left their homes and ventured on to the streets of Montreal where they found pleasure and danger, where they were rarely alone, and where the social geography of Montreal aided them in their journey.

Notes

1. Ministère de la Justice du Québec (Montréal), Centre de Pré-Archivage, Montreal Juvenile Delinquents' Court [hereafter MJDC], 3 April 1924, Case #284. All names have been shortened to protect the privacy of the individuals.

2. MJDC, 2 April 1924, #235.

3. K. Dubinsky, *Improper Advances: Rape and Heterosexual Conflict in Ontario,*

1880–1929, Chicago, University of Chicago Press, 1993; C. Backhouse, *Petticoats and Prejudice*, Toronto, Osgoode Society, 1991; M. Odem, *Delinquent Daughters: Protecting and Policing Adolescent Female Sexuality in the United States, 1885–1920*, Chapel Hill, NC, University of North Carolina Press, 1995, p. 50.

4. Based on a larger project on female delinquents before the Montreal Juvenile Delinquents' Court, 1912–46 which has been funded through a Social Sciences and Humanities Research Council Postdoctoral Fellowship.

5. Judge Choquet, 'The Juvenile Court', *The Canadian Municipal Journal* June 1914, p. 233.

6. An Act to Amend the Revised Statutes, 1909, respecting Juvenile Delinquency, 3 George V, Chap. 39, Article 4036.

7. Archives municipales de Montréal, Département de Police, *Rapports annuels*, 'Statistics des Crimes et Délits', 1923–26.

8. Archives municipales de Montréal, Département de Police, *Rapports annuels*, 'Statistics des Crimes et Délits', 1924, pp. 33–35 and 39.

9. On parents' roles in generating a clientele for juvenile courts, see T. Myers, 'The Voluntary Delinquent: Parents, Daughters, and the Montreal Juvenile Delinquents' Court', *Canadian Historical Review* 80(2), June 1999, pp. 242–68.

10. MJDC, 4 August 1924, #632, and 3 October 1924, #921.

11. T. Myers, 'Qui t'a débauchée? Female Adolescent Sexuality and the Juvenile Delinquents' Court in Early Twentieth Century Montreal', in *Family Matters: Papers in Post-Confederation Canadian Family History*, ed. E. Montigny and L. Chambers, Toronto, Canadian Scholars Press, 1998, pp. 377–94; F. Iacovetta, 'Stretched but not Ruptured: Delinquent Girls, Working-Class Parents and the Family Court', Paper Presented to the Third Carleton Conference on the History of the Family, Ottawa, Canada, 15–17 May 1997.

12. A. Lévesque, *Making and Breaking the Rules: Women in Quebec, 1919–1939*, Toronto, McClelland and Stewart, 1994, p. 54.

13. Odem, *Delinquent Daughters*; C. Strange, *Toronto's Girl Problem: The Perils and Pleasures of the City, 1880–1930*, Toronto, University of Toronto Press, 1995; R. Alexander, *The 'Girl Problem': Female Sexual Delinquency in New York, 1900–1930*, Ithaca, NY, Cornell University Press, 1995; M. Chesney-Lind, *Girls, Delinquency and Juvenile Justice*, Belmont, CA, Brooks/Cole Pub. Co., 1992; J. Sangster, 'Incarcerating "Bad" Girls: The Regulation of Sexuality through the Female Refuges Act in Ontario, 1920–1945', *Journal of the History of Sexuality* 7(2), October 1996; S. Schlossman and S. Wallach, 'The Crime of Precocious Sexuality: Female Juvenile Delinquency in the Progressive Era', *Harvard Educational Review* 48(1), February 1978; L. Mahood, *Policing Gender, Class and Family: Britain, 1850–1940*, London, UCL Press, 1995.

14. L. Gordon, *Heroes of their Own Lives: The Politics and History of Family Violence*, Boston, Penguin Books, 1988, p. 188.

15. On this subject see B. Bradbury, *Working Families: Age, Gender and Daily Survival in Industrializing Montreal*, Toronto, McClelland and Stewart, 1993, Chapter 4, and J. Sangster, *Earning Respect: The Lives of Working Women in Small-Town Ontario, 1920–1960*, Toronto, University of Toronto Press, 1995, Chapter 2.

16. MJDC, 31 May 1918, #4975.

17. MJDC, 4 July 1924, #459. In this case, the probation officer pointed to

Leontine's respectable parents and sided with her mother who wanted her at home, not at the factory.

18. Gordon, *Heroes of their Own Lives*, pp. 188–89.

19. MJDC, 8 February 1924, #93.

20. MJDC, 4 January 1924, #1. This case illustrates how the juvenile court's mandates – to police and protect youth – overlapped. The father, for his part, stated that he agreed to Dorothy's confinement not because of his menacing behaviour but rather because she 'a deserté mon toit sans permission et de plus est incorrigible et incontrolable'.

21. MJDC, 12 September 1918, #5339.

22. MJDC, 13 August 1924, #671.

23. MJDC, 13 January 1928, # 1508.

24. See Gordon, *Heroes of their Own Lives*; E. Pleck, *Domestic Tyranny: The Making of American Social Policy Against Family Violence*, New York, Oxford University Press, 1987. On family violence in Quebec see M.-A.Cliche, 'Un secret bien gardé: L'inceste dans la société traditionelle Québécoise, 1858–1938', *Revue d'histoire de l'Amérique français* 50(2), Autumn 1996; K. Harvey, 'To Love, Honour and Obey: Wife-Battering in Working Class Montreal, 1869–79', *Urban History Review* 2, October 1990, pp. 128–40; P. Gossage, 'La marâtre: Marie-Anne Houde and the Myth of the Wicked Stepmother in Quebec', *Canadian Historical Review* 76(4), December 1995, pp. 563–97.

25. Gordon, *Heroes of their Own Lives*, p. 179.

26. MJDC, 19 August 1918, #5254.

27. MJDC, 14 April 1924, #303.

28. MJDC, 8 June 1928, #1982.

29. MJDC, 30 June 1928, #1978.

30. MJDC, 27 June 1928, #2060.

31. Social fathers include step-fathers and mothers' boyfriends.

32. Cliché, 'Un secret bien gardé', p. 205.

33. In recent sociological literature on homeless youths (runaways) it has been determined that 'youths are unlikely to run away and stay away from home when the decision means loss of valued rewards from family relationships': L.B. Whitbeck and R.L. Simons, 'Life on the Streets: The Victimization of Runaway and Homeless Adolescents', *Youth and Society* 22(1), September 1990, p. 109.

34. MJDC, 9 December 1918, #5590.

35. MJDC, 9 October 1924, #867.

36. This literature begins in the 1960s but really explodes in the 1970s when runaways become an international concern. For a recent study on the experiences of youths on the streets in Canadian cities, see J. Hagan and B. McCarthy, *Mean Streets: Youth Crime and Homelessness*, Cambridge, Cambridge University Press, 1997.

37. *Montreal: Historic, Romantic* (1932); Montreal, *Recorder's Court Annual Report* (1923), p. 12.

38. R. Rosen, *The Lost Sisterhood: Prostitution in America, 1900–1918*, Baltimore, MD, Johns Hopkins University Press, 1982, p. 120.

39. The red-light district was bordered by St Laurent Street in the west, St Denis Street in the east, Sherbrooke Street to the north and Craig Street to the south.

40. Beginning in the 1880s women's organisations worked through their churches

to ameliorate conditions in urban centres in Canada. At the century's turn women had organised around a host of social reform measures including temperance, child welfare and sanitary reform. Their lobbying efforts were often directed at the implementation of legislation that would control human behaviour; for example anti-prostitution and age of consent laws.

41. 'The Social Evil', *Canadian Municipal Journal* March 1919, p. 74.

42. 'Obstacles au développement de l'esprit familial', *La Bonne Parole* April 1930, p. 6.

43. C. Comacchio, 'Dancing to Perdition: Adolescence and Leisure in Interwar English Canada', *Journal of Canadian Studies*, Autumn 1997, p. 6.

44. As cited in Comacchio, 'Dancing to Perdition', p. 7.

45. MJDC, 14 January 1924, #34.

46. MJDC, 23 February 1918, #4673.

47. MJDC, 24 September 1918, #5396.

48. MJDC, 13 January 1928, #1508; 11 January 1930 #12.

49. MJDC, 10 January 1944, #5640; 24 January 1944, #5743.

50. MJDC, 12 January 1944, #5653.

51. Increasingly, wage-earning women sought out accommodation, resulting in a rash of boarding house openings. Religious orders and women's organisations attempted to meet the demand and direct women into respectable lodgings but demand far outstripped availability. During the First World War, the Montreal Local Council of Women protested against the uncontrolled spread of boarding houses and mounted a campaign to have these establishments licensed. National Archives of Canada, Montreal Local Council of Women, MG 28, I 164, Vol. 6, Projects, 'Plan to License and Supervise all Boarding and Rooming Houses.'

52. MJDC, 24 March 1924, #246. Rose Anna M., a 15-year-old, made $7 a week and rented a room with her boyfriend at 146 rue Ste Elizabeth for $4.

53. MJDC, 24 January 1944, #5743.

54. MJDC, 1 February 1924, #78.

55. MJDC, 24 September 1918, #5396.

56. MJDC, 3 April 1924, #235.

57. MJDC, 23 March 1918 #4749; 3 January 1918, #4580.

58. MJDC, 22 April, 1924, #301.

59. MJDC, 31 May 1918, #4975.

60. MJDC, 22 March 1924, #231.

61. MJDC, 2 May, 1924, #347.

62. MJDC, 25 April 1924, #295.

63. Gordon, *Heroes of their Own Lives*, p. 188.

64. MJDC, 17 April 1918, #4816.

65. R. L. Simons and L. B. Whitebeck, 'Sexual Abuse as a Precursor to Prostitution and Victimization Among Adolescent and Adult Homeless Women', *Journal of Family Issues* 12(3), September 1991, pp. 361–79; M. Chesney-Lind and R. S. Shelden, *Girls, Delinquency, and Juvenile Justice*, Pacific Grove, CA, Brooks/Cole Pub. Co., 1992, p. 35.

66. MJDC, 18 February 1924, #130.

67. MJDC, 7 January 1932, #11.

68. Odem, *Delinquent Daughters*, p. 56.

69. Chesney-Lind and Sheldon, *Girls, Delinquency and Juvenile Justice*, p. 35.

2

'Just Trying to be Men'? Violence, Girls and their Social Worlds

J. A. Brown, M. Burman and K. Tisdall

In Britain, in recent years, violent and aggressive behaviour by teenage girls has received considerable media attention. In 1996, the attack on actress Elizabeth Hurley by four girls in the West End of London received extensive coverage.[1] Other reports followed, highlighting girl gangs, bullying and the torturing of victims by girls.[2] Indeed, some writers maintain that violence by girls constitutes a new 'moral panic'.[3] Media reportage invariably links this 'new phenomenon' with more established concerns about the rise in youth crime, increased social disorder and a decline in social and moral values. What is of particular interest, however, is the shift in focus from 'dangerous' young men to 'dangerous' young women and the highly gendered ways in which violence by girls is popularly depicted and explained.

With some notable exceptions girls' violence has, until recently, attracted relatively little academic interest and thus little is known about the role of violence in girls' lives.[4] Violence by young men has been explicitly and extensively considered – indeed, sociological theorisations of violence and anti-social behaviour have been based almost exclusively on *male* behaviour. This is as true for the earlier subcultural explanations focusing on the activities of working-class (male) youth,[5] and social learning explanations that stress the importance of boys' peer groups,[6] as it is for more recent research on individual-level predictors stressing personality, genetic and/or social characteristics.[7] In more general studies of crime and criminal behaviour women and girls have been similarly overlooked.[8]

The psychological literature on violence – although vast – has a history of being similarly gender-blind.[9] This is most marked in relation to psychological studies of childhood aggression.[10] Developmental accounts of violence and aggression in childhood subsume and hide girls through the frequent use of homogeneous and gender-neutral categories.[11] Undifferentiated and over-generalised concepts, such as 'child' and 'children', obscure the fact that the focus is invariably on boys.

Some psychological literature, however, has concentrated on *differences* between boys' and girls' aggression. It is boys who are regularly described as 'acting out', who exhibit 'conduct disorders', and who are said to engage in extreme acts of violence. The expression of anger in girls and young women is conceptualised as very 'different' from that of males. Recent work by such researchers as Rys and Bear and Björkqvist, Osterman and Kaukiainen, for example, has extended definitions of 'aggression' to include what is termed 'indirect social aggression' which involves manipulation of social relationships.[12] This form of behaviour is more frequently reported for girls. Other studies, however, suggest that girls are more likely to direct their aggression inwards. Swaffer and Hollis said of the young women in their study that 'it was easier to direct their anger upon themselves than upon others. Self-directed anger manifested itself in self-injurious behaviour such as self-cutting and self-strangulation.'[13]

The image of introspective and self-injurious girls can be found elsewhere in studies of violent offenders and their backgrounds, where girls tend towards 'internalised' responses in the form of psychiatric conditions whereas boys 'act out' and externalise their responses.[14] Campbell also argues that there are fundamental gender differences in perceptions of aggressiveness: males view aggression primarily in terms of gaining control whereas females tend to see it as a loss of control.[15]

Some of the reasons for the exclusion of women and girls from empirical studies and theoretical development in the area of violence may seem obvious, and have been defended on four main grounds. First, females are considered much more passive than males and are seen as posing far less risk in terms of their potential for violence. Second, females are much less involved in violent behaviour than males, and hence are considered less of a 'problem'. Third, females rarely participate in extreme forms of physical violence that may result in serious bodily harm, suicide or homicide and, as a result, their violence is seen as less harmful, and therefore less worthy of investigation. Fourth, as we have seen, female violence is explained as qualitatively different from male violence: it is socially manipulative and indirect, it is expressive rather than instrumental, and it is more likely to be internalised and to include self-harm behaviours.[16]

The marginalisation of women and girls in theorising around violence has had several far-reaching (and, at times, rather contradictory) implications which, in turn, have further obscured female violence. One set of implications cohere around what may be called the 'repudiation' of female violence. Because of the implicit lack of acknowledgment, women and girls' ability to behave in ways that can be categorised as 'violent' has been ignored or minimised.[17] A second set of implications concern the presumption that, when it does occur, female violence is pathological behaviour. In other words, violent females are crazy, deranged, unbalanced. Perhaps the most pervasive set of implications arise from developing theories of violence largely in relation to young men and thus basing the theories on masculinist presumptions. These theories have then been proposed as having universal applicability – when they are, in fact, highly gendered accounts. So, although theories were developed to explain the violent behaviour of young men, some contend that they can be adapted to explain the behaviour of women and girls.[18] As a result, not only is violence by females often described and understood in relation to the male paradigm, but there is also a tendency to proclaim that violent females must be 'trying to be men'.[19]

Overall, this has led to the deployment and perpetuation of gender-stereotypical conceptualisations of female violence, namely the 'hidden' violent female, the 'pathological' violent female, the 'self-injurious' violent female, and the 'masculine' violent female. None of these conceptualisations of female behaviour are new, nor are they exclusive to the theorisation of violence. Indeed they are typologies that can be found elsewhere, particularly in relation to conceptions of female offending behaviour. For example, the 'masculine' female offender has long been a stereotype in criminology,[20] as has the 'mad not bad' pathological female offender.[21] While offending was thought of as normal and natural for young men – part of growing up, of adolescence – offending for women was seen as unusual and unnatural. Research demonstrates the historical relevance of these stereotypes, and their continuing influence today on practice in penal institutions.[22]

Girls' participation in gangs is one area in which these entrenched images of young women have been challenged. In much of the early literature on 'gangs', girls were largely absent.[23] When girls were mentioned, their role in male gangs tended either to be sexualised – as providing services for gang members – or they were portrayed as 'tomboys', unfeminine and 'more like boys'.[24] The most notable exceptions to this are the American studies on 'girl gangs' conducted by Campbell, Chesney-Lind and, more recently, Miller. Campbell highlights the sexuality of girls and their role in gangs, maintaining that their gendered experience 'inside' gangs mirrors their everyday lives and that gang membership is one answer to other problems revolving around safety, racism and poverty.[25] Chesney-Lind argues for a more complex picture than the current demonisation of girl gangs in the American media, maintaining that there is meagre evidence to support the idea of a new, violent female offender.[26] Chesney-Lind argues forcefully that the violence and offending of girls needs to be understood in its social, material and gendered contexts: 'efforts to construct a feminist model of delinquency must first and foremost be sensitive to the situations of girls. Failure to consider the existing empirical evidence on girls' lives and behaviour can quickly lead to stereotypical thinking and theoretical dead ends.'[27]

Redressing the Balance: Feminist-Influenced Ethnographic Studies

What do we know about girls' lives? McRobbie's work in the 1970s made a significant contribution to our understanding of the social worlds of girls, with her examinations of girls' investment in popular culture, including popular music and magazines.[28] Given the theoretical neglect of gender in early British youth studies,[29] McRobbie's work challenged existing androcentric models of youth culture where girls featured as victims or hangers-on.[30] She addressed the issue of gender at a time when the dominant paradigms available for theorising class and culture were Marxist and masculine in orientation, and generally neglected issues of gender.

McRobbie argued that girls were to be found in different spatial locations to boys, such as their bedrooms, and highlighted their creative use of these domestic spaces. Stressing the agency rather than the passivity of girls, she explained their involvement in 'teeny bopper' subcultures as a 'way of buying time within the commercial mainstream, from the real world of sexual encounters'.[31] Her work has been important because she paved the way for subsequent ethnographic studies which aimed to redress the earlier marginalisation and neglect of girls.[32]

These later studies were conducted at a time when theoretical sensitivity towards gender and ethnicity was well developed, and the 'compulsory' nature of heterosexuality was theorised as the dominant discourse regarding sexuality.[33] Significantly, these studies focus on the minutiae of girls' lives and shed light on the interpersonal dynamics of girls' friendships and the ways in which sharing, trust and the keeping of secrets are rated highly in the intimate relationships of girls. Also apparent is researchers' critical awareness of stereotypical representations of girls. Griffith, for example, questions and re-evaluates teachers' perceptions (as well as some girls' views), that their behaviour tended towards 'cattiness' and that relationships among girls were perceived as 'synonymous with falling out'.[34] Griffith questions such assumptions regarding the dynamics of female relationships, arguing that the regularity with which some girls appear to 'fall out' is more fruitfully understood in terms of 'manoeuvres within friendships', rather than evidence of shallow and transient relationships among girls.

Girls' Friendships and Social Worlds as a Context for Understanding Violence

The focus on girls' social worlds, and in particular, the emotional importance of girls' friendships, informed our approach to studying girls and violent behaviour. We undertook a small-scale exploratory study with girls from four localities within a major Scottish city, examining their understandings and perceptions of violence.[35] Twenty-three girls aged 10–15 years took part in a series of small group discussions and completed self-report questionnaires on their experiences of violence.[36]

Our research had two interrelated objectives. First we sought to explore girls' own accounts of the meaning of violence – what 'counts' as violence and their views about violence. We did not want to identify, in advance, any particular aspect of violence because our intention was to provide the opportunity for girls to discuss what 'counts' as violence for them. Second, we aimed to explore how violence fitted into their social worlds and how it may affect them in their daily lives.

A central aim, therefore, was to examine girls' conceptualisations of violence. One of the initial ways we did this was to ask girls in small groups to participate in a brainstorming session as to what types of action or behaviour they considered 'violent'. This proved to be an illuminating exercise: not only did it provide a comprehensive and diverse list, but it also gave us insight into the interrelationships between actions, motive and the relevance of intentionality. Further, it also enabled us to compare girls' conceptualisations with traditional definitions of 'violence' which tend to privilege intentional and interpersonal forms of violence.[37] This was important since studies of bullying, for example, found that young people's views about what constituted bullying differed in some significant respects from those found in the established literature on the subject. La Fontaine found that young people's accounts emphasised the emotional impact of bullying. Overall, she found that young people identified a greater variety of behaviours as bullying, ranging from teasing to what is described as 'serious physical harm'.[38]

Intentionally harmful behaviour, such as pushing, pinching, pulling hair and kicking were all identified as common acts of violence used by girls, and furthermore, were viewed as acceptable actions within certain contexts. This reiterates Campbell's finding that over 70 per cent of teenage girls in her sample viewed kicking in a fight as acceptable behaviour.[39] This questions existing stereotypes regarding female 'violence' evident in the literature where intimidatory behaviour tends to be framed in terms of girls' 'bitchiness' and their reliance on verbal forms of aggression.[40]

The girls who participated in our study also spoke of more subtle and coercive kinds of behaviour, which often did not involve physical contact but which carried violent intent, which they identified as 'peer pressure', 'scaring people', 'threats' and 'bullying'. This kind of intimidatory behaviour and forms of verbal aggression, such as 'name-calling', 'slagging' and 'spreading rumours', were termed 'violence' by most girls. Unsurprisingly, the intention to harm was pertinent to girls' evaluation. However, girls also viewed the emotional impact (i.e. 'hurt feelings') as an important factor in their considerations of what 'counts' as violence.

Again somewhat unsurprisingly, girls' experiences of violence shaped their understanding of it. In two different locations, where racial and religious tensions were part of local cultures and social landscapes, girls demonstrated a heightened consciousness of racial and sectarian violence and these themes tended to dominate discussions. A group of older girls (i.e. 14- and 15-year-olds), who sometimes ventured into the city to access leisure facilities, identified these locations, especially 'the dancing', as places of violence.

A common theme related to girls' use of non-verbal and symbolic forms of aggression towards other girls within the context of friendships. A consistent feature in their stories of disputes and fall-outs included the use of symbolic forms of aggression in 'hostile looks'. What they termed 'growling', 'drawing daggers', 'binging' or giving 'dirty looks' were described as common occurrences, and a key feature of their interactional repertoires. Studies of non-verbal communication have shown that prolonged staring between strangers, particularly in public places, provokes uneasiness and is often interpreted as threatening.[41] This finding was confirmed in girls' accounts of feeling vulnerable when walking past other groups of young people who congregated in local streets and play areas. Interestingly, prolonged gazes given in this kind of public situation were more likely to be identified as 'violent' and menacing by teenage girls. Yet in the more private world of the home environment, and in the context of kin and intimate relationships, 'growling' at family members was presented as a 'normal' and acceptable part of everyday interactions. One girl laughed when she said that 'I do it to my ma every two minutes' (Focus Group, Area Four). This latter example provides an illuminating contrast with psychoanalytic explanations which pathologise 'critical looks' as 'dysfunctional interactions'.[42] Our initial findings, however, suggest that girls attached a range of meanings and intentions to 'dirty looks' and these could shift depending on the nature of social relationships and the particular socio-situational context in which they take place.

Some overtly 'violent' acts that girls describe being involved in were assessed as playful, 'less serious' or accidental. In other words, they were devoid of harmful intent. This was borne out in one unanticipated research issue which emerged both from the focus groups and from periods of overt observation with girls, namely the character of play-fighting and other games engaged in by teenage girls. Frequently we were struck by the physicality of girls' relationships: they would preen each other, use each others' bodies as resting posts and frequently link arms.[43] Midway through the research, each girls' group was given a disposable camera in order to photograph themselves with their friends, 'hanging out' in their local area. A striking theme of the resultant images was 'intertwined bodies': girls in a variety of poses, across a range of locations in their bedrooms, local play areas and streets. This tactile component of their relationships included a lot of play-fighting, dead-arm punching and games that generally involved some test of strength and endurance. Often these games were offshoots of exuberant and routinised joking interchanges which we observed regularly in girls' social groups. One particular contest we witnessed was a game girls called 'scaggs', or 'knucklie', alternatively known as 'knuckles' in England.[44] In this game one player holds out their clenched fist while the opponent strikes the other's knuckles as hard as they can with their own fist. Each player then takes a turn to strike their partner.

Here Opie and Opie's important observational studies of children's cultures are helpful. Their work, conducted across Britain in the 1950s and 1960s, detailed the games children played in both streets and school playgrounds. Their work, however, embodies stereo-typical gender-role assumptions about appropriate masculine and feminine behaviour. In their consideration of childhood games, the behaviour of girls was confined to specific types of physical aggression such as hair-pulling. Primarily the behaviour of girls was aligned with indirect and covert forms of aggression which aimed socially to exclude other children – an emphasis now formalised in psychological explanations of female aggression.[45] Collective non-speaking or what was described as sending someone 'to Coventry' was attributed to girls, while all the competitive and overtly aggressive games were associated with the active male gender. Further evidence of this kind of gender stereotyping is evident in early psychological texts which address the topic of play-fighting in childhood. Again, girls are portrayed as passive and 'less vigorous' than boys. While it is acknowledged that girls occasionally engage in play-fighting, it is argued that when they do so they assume a subordinate position: 'Girls almost never wrestle for superior position … If a girl is on the bottom, she usually just lies there passively.'[46]

Our preliminary findings, however, challenge some of these comparative stereotypes in the literature. Today very little is known about teenage girls' participation in 'rough and tumble' type games. More specifically, a gap exists in how girls' views about such games may connect with their conceptualisations of 'violence'. Not only did we find that girls actively engaged in play-fighting in their friendship groups, but within the context of 'play-fighting', aggressive actions such as punching, squeezing, lying on top of the other person, and name-calling were regarded as acceptable and often humorous ('good for a laugh') by participating girls. These findings illuminate the ways in which humour and the notion of 'play' serve to dilute girls' assessments of 'violence' and, as such, inform our understanding of what types of behaviour are socially acceptable to girls. When questioned about the meaning of play-fighting girls responded by making comments such as, 'It's just a carry on' or 'It's just kidding around'. As a result, within the relatively safe framework of the rules of a 'game', and in the context of what was viewed as 'a good laugh', 'violent' actions were evaluated as permissible and acceptable forms of behaviour. Social scientists have long recognised the importance of humour as a mechanism for managing aggression in social relationships.[47] In a similar way girls' participation in competitive games was said to provide a legitimate outlet for managing irritation and anger in social relationships. As one of the girls noted about the game of knucklies,

> Some people play it right after they are annoyed with somebody – like they just say right we'll get a game of this. Right. And nobody's going to turn round and say no 'cos you get called chicken. So, like, fine and that, and you just hope you get the highest card so you can smack them as hard as anything. (Individual Interview, Area One)

Girls' use of 'violence' in games and play-fighting is multi-functional. In the context of a game, shared signals operated, investing participants with a degree of safety. These rules provided opt-out clauses for players and appeared to defuse escalating tension and aggression. For example, one friendship group of girls with whom we had protracted contact interspersed their wrestling games ('dummy fighting') with mutually agreed rest periods which they called 'time out'. This could serve a number of purposes: it provided rest periods for tired participants or it could be used as a tactic in order to trick the opponent and catch them off guard. 'Pleading for mercy', begging or simply screaming were other devices used to signal a request for a break.

We found a surprising degree of moral consensus in girls' accounts, specifically with regard to the kinds of circumstances where 'violent' behaviour could be viewed as wholly justified or could be excused. Agreement was evident in the types of behaviour girls viewed as provocative. Generally, name-calling and verbal criticism, especially of the 'underhand' kind, were cited as prime sources of anger, particularly when someone was talked about 'behind my back'. 'Nasty' and critical comments about body shape, namely deviations from the culturally valued ideal (being too thin – 'an anorexic bitch', or too fat – 'a fat cow'), were raised as common verbal criticisms made by peers of both sexes. These were regarded as offensive and annoying, as were other comments about appearance, particularly clothing and dress styles. Clothing could lead to being excluded by peers because wearing what was regarded as unfashion-able or 'uncool' clothes with 'cheap labels' was offered as an explanation for ignoring and socially rejecting other young people. Alternatively, wearing clothes with a 'good name' (e.g. designer brands such as Calvin Klein or Tommy Hilfiger) was collectively prized, and thus represented a powerful symbol of inclusion, group identity and confidence.[48] Sometimes, this outward sign of conformity, and what was observed, literally, as a 'uniform identity', was followed through in other aspects of girls' dress, including accessories (gold signet rings and drop earrings) as well as hairstyles.

Importantly, however, the most intensely expressed source of anger among girls related to another facet of girls' collective identities which were rooted in familial relationships. Threats to what could be termed 'family honour' were the most serious form of insult from the point of view of girls. Making derogatory and critical remarks about family members, especially mothers, was regarded as the ultimate provocative insult by the majority of girls – something that has been found as a relevant source of provocation among teenage girls in other studies.[49] Abusive name-calling which conferred 'outsider' and 'low' status (e.g. 'druggie' or 'alky'), racial abuse, as well as religious and sexualised taunts, were the most offensive types of comments mentioned by girls. One girl highlighted the emotional impact of this verbal form of violence: 'If they call you a name like cow or something, right, that's no very hurtful. But if they call your mum a cow that is very hurtful' (Focus Group, Area Three). In contrast, another girl described a different response in her 'violent' physical reaction: 'She kept talking about me behind my back and everything and kept saying I was a bitch and stuff. But I mean I just let it go. But then she started talking about my mum and I just went mental – I just turned round and walloped her' (Focus Group, Area Three).

Such responses were regarded as perfectly legitimate given the serious nature of this kind of insult. Paradoxically, while girls considered defending 'family honour' important, relationships with close family members, particularly siblings, were identified as a perpetual source of annoyance, irritation and anger. Other studies have found that girls are more likely than boys to cite siblings and parents as agents of anger.[50] Typical sources of conflict with siblings were reported as arguments about television viewing preferences, possessions, and the 'fair' distribution of domestic chores. Power struggles and fights were portrayed as ordinary and acceptable dimensions of intimate family relationships. Girls' social lives provided a key site for investigating these 'ambivalences'. Disagreements and fall-outs with friends were similarly viewed as part and parcel of intimate relationships; occurrences that constituted an integral feature of girls' friendship groups. In the following example, a member of a long-established girls' group elaborated on everyday interactions within the group: 'We always contradict each other, like if somebody says something, I go: "Oh, he never says that". Right. And then it always ends in a big argument' (Focus Group, Area Four). Nevertheless, girls' perceptions of aggression between siblings appeared to be qualitatively different from other forms of verbal and physical 'violence' reported in other non-kin relationships. In relation to the domestic sphere, girls appeared to have a rather relaxed attitude towards 'violent' actions towards siblings and this was presented as an everyday or routinised kind of 'violence'.[51] This is an area requiring further investigation.

Concluding Remarks

Rarely is girls' and women's violence described in the literature without comparison to boys' and men's violence; the comparison itself underlines the 'naturalisation' of male violence and its gendered theorisation. Our initial findings can be used both to challenge some of the stereotypes of girls' 'violence', and to question current models of understanding violence in the social science literature.

The 'violence' girls described was often connected with their femininities and embedded in social relationships, especially their friendships and peer relationships. We found very little evidence to suggest that girls were simply 'mimicking the males', or 'trying to be men' as some have suggested.[52] These preliminary findings, while certainly requiring further investigation, clearly question the comparative distinctions made by Campbell and others. Fundamentally, the findings demonstrate a level of everyday and routinised 'violence', sometimes of considerable physical and emotional harm, that directly contradicts the identification of female violence as hidden, pathological, abnormal or particularly masculinised.

Girls' descriptions did not indicate 'a loss of control' when they were 'violent', but demonstrated a range of responses across social contexts and relationships. Moreover, our initial findings suggest that girls' use of violence was multi-functional. Within their friendship groups, the girls' violence, and most particularly its use in games, demonstrated a form of 'instrumental violence' involving the girls' position and relationship with other girls. While boys' team games and 'rough and tumble' have been presented as 'natural' and socially acceptable diversionary paths for boys' aggression, the literature has neglected the physicality of girls' interactions. This facet of girls' relationships was evident in our research in their use of games to patrol relationships and provide a (relatively) safe framework for 'violence', complete with rules and limits.

In short, this preliminary study provides a challenge to the dismissal of girls' violence either as being so infrequent as to be unworthy of consideration, or as some extreme form of pathology or abnormality, or as a response to forms of gendered victimisation. Rather, it points to a more complex picture of girls' use of violence and intentionally harmful behaviour which insists that this behaviour must be placed within the context of girls' everyday lives.[53]

Notes

1. For instance, *Daily Mail*, 12 October 1996 ('Rising Tide of Female Violence').

2. For instance, *Evening Times*, 4 May 1998 ('Subway Gangs Terror'); *The Scotsman*, 30 September 1997 ('Police to question youths after bullied teenager kills herself'); *The Scotsman*, 4 March 1997 ('Girl laughed in recreation of stabbing').

3. K. Thompson, *Moral Panics*, London, Routledge, 1998.

4. But see A. Campbell, 'Self-Report Fighting by Females: A Preliminary Study', *British Journal of Criminology* 26, 1986, pp. 28–46; 'Female Participation in Gangs', in *Gangs in America*, ed. C. P. Huff, Newbury Park, Sage, 1990, pp. 163–82; *The Girls in the Gang*, Cambridge, Blackwell, 2nd edn 1991; and finally, *Out of Control: Men, Women and Aggression*, London, Pandora Books, 1993. Also M. Chesney-Lind, 'Girls, Gangs and Violence: Reinventing the Liberated Female Crook', *Humanity and Society* 17, 1993, pp. 321–44.

5. M. Wolfgang and F. Ferracuti, *The Subculture of Violence*, London, Tavistock, 1967.

6. G. R. Patterson, B. D. DeBaryshe and E. Ramsey, 'A Developmental Perspective on Anti-Social Behaviour', *American Psychologist* 44, 1989, pp. 329–35.

7. J. Wilson and R. Hernstein, *Crime and Human Nature*, New York, Simon and Schuster, 1994; D. Farrington, 'Criminal Career Research in the United Kingdom', *British Journal of Criminology* 32(4), 1992, pp. 521–36.

8. See the discussion by C. Smart, *Women, Crime and Criminology*, London, Routledge and Kegan Paul, 1977; F. Heidensohn, *Women and Crime*, Oxford, Oxford University Press, 1985.

9. P. Pearson, *When She was Bad*, London, Virago, 1998.

10. J. D. Pepler and K. H. Ruben (eds), *The Development and Treatment of Aggression*, Hove and London, Lawrence Eribaum Associates, 1991.

11. E. Burman, *Deconstructing Developmental Psychology*, London, Routledge, 1994.

12. G. S. Rys and G. G. Bear, 'Relational Aggression and Peer Relations: Gender and Developmental Issues', *Merrill-Palmer Quarterly* 43(1), 1997, pp. 87–106; K. Björkqvist, K.Osterman and A. Kaukiainen, 'Do Girls Manipulate and Boys Fight?', *Aggressive Behaviour* 18, 1992, pp. 117–27.

13. T. Swaffer and C. R. Hollis, 'Adolescent Anger', *Journal of Adolescence* 20, 1997, pp. 567–75 (572).

14. G. Boswell, 'The Background of Violent Offenders', in *Violence in Children and Adolescence*, ed. V. Varma, London, Jessica Kingsley, 1996, pp. 22–36 (31).

15. Campbell, *Out of Control*.

16. Campbell, *Out of Control*; Boswell, 'Background of Violent Offenders'.

17. J.W. White and R. Kowalski, 'Deconstructing the Myth of the Non-Aggressive Woman', *Psychology of Women Quarterly* 18, 1994, pp. 487–508.

18. Though see the argument of Chesney-Lind, 'Girls, Gangs and Violence', pp. 321–44.

19. Campbell, *Out of Control*, p. 144.

20. C. Lombroso and W. Ferrero, *The Female Offender*, London, T. Fisher Unwin, 1895; W.I. Thomas, *The Unadjusted Girl*, Boston, Little, Brown and Co., 1923; O. Pollak, *The Criminality of Women*, Philadelphia, University of Pennsylvania Press, 1950.

21. See the discussion in Heidensohn, *Women and Crime*.

22. M. J. Wiener, 'The Criminalization of Victorian Men', in *Men and Violence: Gender, Honor and Rituals in Modern Europe*, ed. P. Spierenburg, Columbus, OH, Ohio State University Press, 1998; R. P. Dobash, R. E. Dobash and S. Gutteridge, *The Imprisonment of Women*, Oxford, Basil Blackwell, 1986; J. Kersten, 'A Gender Specific Look at Patterns of Violence in Juvenile Institutions', *International Journal of the Sociology of the Law* 18, 1990, pp. 473–93.

23. For example, F. M. Thrasher, *The Gang: A Study of 1,313 Gangs in Chicago*, London, Phoenix, 1927.

24. C. S. Taylor, *Girl Gangs, Women and Drugs*, East Lansing, MI, Michigan State University Press, 1993.

25. Campbell, *Girls in the Gang*.

26. Chesney-Lind, 'Girls, Gangs and Violence'.

27. M. Chesney-Lind, 'Girls' Crime and Woman's Place: Toward a Feminist

Model of Female Delinquency', *Crime & Delinquency* 35(1), 1989, pp. 5–29 (19). See also Jody Miller, *One of the Guys: Girls, Gangs and Gender*, Oxford, Oxford University Press, 2001.

28. A. McRobbie, *Feminism and Youth Culture from Jackie to Just Seventeen*, Basingstoke, Macmillan, 1991.

29. P. Willis, *Learning to Labour*, London, Gower, 1977; D. Hebdige, *Sub-Culture: The Meaning of Style*, London, Methuen, 1979.

30. Thompson, *Moral Panics*.

31. McRobbie, *Feminism and Youth Culture*, p. 14.

32. See especially S. Lees, *Sugar and Spice: Sexuality and Adolescent Girls*, London, Penguin, 1993; H. Wuiff, 'Inter-Racial Friendship: Consuming Youth Styles, Ethnicity and Teenage Femininity in South London', in *Youth Cultures: A Cross-Cultural Perspective*, ed. V. Amit-Talai and H. Wuiff, London, Routledge, 1995, pp. 63–80; V. Griffith, *Adolescent Girls and their Friends: A Feminist Ethnography*, Aldershot, Avebury, 1995; V. Hey, *The Company She Keeps: An Ethnography of Girls' Friendships*, Buckingham, Open University Press, 1997.

33. See G. Hawkes, *The Sociology of Sex and Sexuality*, Buckingham, Open University Press, 1996.

34. Griffith, *Adolescent Girls and their Friends*, p. 75.

35. We are grateful to the Calouste Gulbenkian Foundation for funding a part-time research post (March–September 1997), and to the girls and youth organisations who participated, for enabling us to carry out this work.

36. All participants were guaranteed anonymity, hence the decision not to discuss the location of the research project. See P. Alderson, *Listening to Children: Children, Social Research and Ethics*, Ilford, Barnardos, 1995 for a discussion of ethical considerations in social research with young people.

37. H. Bradby (ed.), *Defining Violence*, Aldershot, Avebury, 1996; J. C. Smith and S. Bailey, 'One Hundred Girls in Care Referred to an Adolescent Forensic Mental Health Service', *Journal of Adolescence* 21, 1998, pp. 555–68.

38. J. La Fontaine, *Bullying: The Child's View*, London, Calouste Gulbenkian Foundation, 1991.

39. Campbell, 'Self-Report Fighting'.

40. For instance, C. Keise, *Sugar and Spice? Bullying in Single Sex Schools*, Stoke on Trent, Trentham Books, 1992; D. Olweus, *Bullying at School: What We Know and What We Can Do*, Oxford, Blackwell, 1993.

41. M. Argyle, *Bodily Communication*, London, Methuen, 1988.

42. A. Miller, *Thou Shall Not be Aware: Society's Betrayal of the Child*, New York, Collins, 1984.

43. See Griffith, *Adolescent Girls and their Friends*.

44. I. Opie and P. Opie, *Children's Games in Street and Playground*, Oxford, The Clarendon Press, 1969, p. 223.

45. Björkqvist et al., 'Do Girls Manipulate?'.

46. O. Aldis, *Play Fighting*, New York, Academic Press, 1975, p.196.

47. A. R. Radcliffe-Brown, *Structure and Function in Primitive Society*, London, Cohen West, 1949; I. Goffman, *Asylums*, New York, Doubleday Anchor, 1961.

48. See A. Furlong and F. Cartmel, *Young People and Social Change*, Buckingham, Open University Press, 1997.

49. Campbell, 'Self-Report Fighting'; E. Anderson, 'Violence and the Inner-City Street Code', in *Violence and Childhood in the Inner City*, ed. J. McCord, Cambridge, Cambridge University Press, 1997.

50. S. Feshbach, N. D. Feshbach, R. S. Cohen and M. Hoffman, 'The Antecedents of Anger: A Developmental Approach', in *Aggression in Children and Youth*, ed. R. M. Kaplan, The Hague, Martinus Hijhoff, 1984, pp. 162–75.

51. E. A. Stanko, *Everyday Violence: How Women and Men Experience Physical and Sexual Danger*, London, Pandora, 1990.

52. Anderson, 'Violence and the Inner-City', p. 25; Campbell, *Out of Control*, p. 144.

53. Since this chapter was written, the authors have been awarded a grant by the Economic and Social Research Council under their Violence Research Programme to carry out a larger study of girls and violence. Details of 'A View From The Girls: Exploring Violence and Violent Behaviour', award number L133251018 can be found at http://www.gla.ac.uk/girlsandviolence.

II
Child Emigration

3

Fairbridge Child Migrants

Geoffrey Sherington

In recent years, the media and governments have focused on the history of British child migration. The children sent to the former British Dominions have been seen as *The Lost Children of Empire* separated from family and home and exiled across the oceans to hardship.[1] There has been a specific concern with the child migrants sent to Australia and especially the child migrants of the period immediately after the Second World War. These children have been portrayed as victims not only in the press but in such dramatic fiction as the joint BBC–ABC four-hour mini-series *The Leaving of Liverpool*, which was reviewed in Australia as an account of 'philanthropic abduction'.[2] In 1996, the Parliament of Western Australia, where most twentieth-century child migrants had been sent, established a Select Committee of Enquiry.[3] In 1998, the Health Committee of the House of Commons presented its own report on the welfare of former British child migrants. Its conclusion was that 'Child migration was a bad and, in human terms, costly mistake', which had been based on deceit and abuse of the children who had been caught up in the various schemes.[4] Accepting this report, the British Labour government, noting that child migration was 'a misguided policy' which had left a legacy of problems and suffering, agreed to establish a £1 million fund to enable former child migrants to reunite with any surviving kith and kin.[5] In 2001 the Senate of the Australian Parliament also established its own enquiry which would produce a further extensive report 'regretting the psychological, social and economic harm caused to the children'.[6]

Earlier scholarship has already analysed the nature of child migration to Canada in the late nineteenth and early twentieth centuries. The work of Joy Parr and others revealed the interaction between working-class parents and a number of the voluntary societies which led first to children being placed in institutions and then to their emigration, sometimes without, but often with parental consent.[7] The current critique of child migration, as particularly detailed and summarised in the House of Commons' Health Committee report, has focused on three related areas. First, it has been claimed that the vast majority of child migrants had been attracted by images of opportunity in Australia and then sent overseas without consent or knowledge of their family. Secondly, it is suggested that in Australia, the child migrants were subjected to both physical and sexual abuse. Finally, it is argued that the effect of migration and experiences in Australia has had a devastating effect on the former child migrants particularly in terms of personal and cultural identity.[8]

There have been exaggerated suggestions that up to 10,000 child migrants came to Australia after 1945 although recent scholarship based on official figures suggests no more than 3,000 postwar arrivals with a total of 6,000 in the years from 1912 to 1967 when child migration virtually ceased.[9] Even the critics have accepted that perhaps a majority of the child migrants benefited from the experience but the general representation is still negative.[10] Much of the current criticism in Australia is directed principally against Catholic child migration and is partly substantiated by both scholarship and the acceptance by Catholic authorities (including out of court settlements) that abuse did occur in a number of its institutions in Western Australia.[11]

Whatever the case against Catholic child migration, it is important to recognise that there were a number of different child migration schemes. Approximately half of all child migrants to Australia came under the auspices of the Fairbridge Society, which was the best-known child migration scheme between Britain and Australia. Founded as the Child Emigration Society (CES) in 1909 but later named after its founder Kingsley Fairbridge, the Fairbridge Society became the most celebrated of the new imperial-minded child-saving organisations that emerged in the early twentieth century. By the 1920s the Society was so well established that the Colonial Secretary, Leopold Amery, could describe the original farm at Pinjarra, Western Australia, as the 'finest institution for human regeneration that ever existed', a view now far removed from most contemporary perspectives.[12]

The general history of Fairbridge child migration, including a detailed analysis of the life and ideals of Kingsley Fairbridge, is the subject of a recently released study.[13] This particular research is based more specifically on the case files which the Fairbridge Society compiled on each child sent out from Britain. In contrast to both Catholic child migration and also to such organisations as Barnardo's, which sent so many child migrants to Canada and then also to Australia, the Fairbridge Society had none of its own homes or institutions in Britain upon which to draw for the child emigrants. From its beginning the Society became a recruiting agency, depending upon state institutions, voluntary agencies and private nominations for child emigrants. This particular context of recruitment meant that the origins of Fairbridge children were very diverse. This study examines the background of the children and then attempts to reconstruct parts of their lives in Australia. In the process it tries to address a number of the issues that have been raised by the current critique of child migration schemes.

The focus of research is on four groups of Fairbridge child migrants who came to Pinjarra which was the original Fairbridge farm. The specific groups are the 35 boys who came out in 1913 as the 'original' Fairbridge child emigrants; the two parties of 58 boys and girls who arrived in 1921, the year when child migration revived after the First World War; and two selected samples of later sailing parties, one of 22 children arriving in 1935 in the context of the Depression of the 1930s and the second of 21 children arriving in 1949 in the context of the revival of Fairbridge migration after the Second World War. This total of 136 child migrants represents about ten per cent of the overall numbers sent from Britain to Pinjarra during these years. When set within the context of the overall Fairbridge migration scheme, an examination of their background and experiences should thus enable us to provide some conclusions regarding such matters as parental involvement in child migration as well as the treatment of the children in Australia.

The first part of the chapter examines the process by which the Fairbridge Society recruited the children it sent overseas. The emphasis here is thematic, looking at three major ways that the children came to the Fairbridge Society: through Poor Law and local authority institutions; via the Children's Homes of the voluntary sector; and by parents directly enrolling their children with the Society. The second part of the chapter is essentially chronological, examining the lives of the children in Australia and comparing the experiences of those who arrived at different points of time. By looking at both recruitment patterns and experiences, the discussion tries to reveal a history which has its own human dimension but which is set within the changing contexts of the social and economic history of Britain and Australia over the twentieth century.

Children from Poor Law and Local Authority Institutions

Under the 1834 Poor Law, local Boards of Guardians had assumed formal responsibility for the care and education of children of the poor. By the early 1900s it has been estimated that there were between 70,000 and 80,000 children under the jurisdiction of the Poor Law. Most of these children were either in workhouses with adults or in specific Poor Law homes for children while about one-fifth were either boarded out or in the various homes of the voluntary organisations such as Barnardo's which had emerged during the nineteenth century with the specific aim of 'child rescue'.[14]

With the establishment of the CES, Kingsley Fairbridge had his own campaign to 'rescue' children from the Poor Law homes which he saw as having provided no benefits to their inmates.[15] In the period just prior to the First World War, he was able to recruit a number of Poor Law children principally in the London area even though there was growing opposition to child emigration from a number of Boards of Guardians associated with the Labour Party. Overall about two-thirds of the original parties of 35 boys arriving in 1912–13 had been nominated through Poor Law Boards of Guardians.

As suggested above, much of the current controversy over child migration has revolved around the suggestion that many of the child migrants were not really orphans and therefore parental consent should have been sought before the children were sent overseas. In effect, the surviving documentation suggests that the majority of the Fairbridge Poor Law boys in 1912–13 had apparently lost all contact with relatives. Fourteen of the boys were technically orphans with both parents either dead or not known and all had been in Poor Law institutions for much of their early lives, sometimes for as long as five or six years and often along with their generally younger siblings. Having been in Poor Law homes meant that many of these original Fairbridge migrants had come from the poorest stratum of the working class. In all these cases the Boards of Guardians had become legal guardians of the children and had given permission for their emigration.[16]

A few of the original Fairbridge children still had known living relatives but some of these were also in Poor Law homes. One boy from Islington Guardians' School in London still had both parents living: the address of his mother was unknown; his father, aged 42, was in the workhouse.[17] More common was the pattern of one parent still living. One widow, a charwoman, had been forced to place her two sons in the workhouse in Taunton, Somerset; after six years in institutional life the two boys were sent together to Western Australia.[18]

The role of the Poor Law homes and local government authorities in the recruitment of Fairbridge children would remain an important feature in the history of the Fairbridge migration scheme, although these state institutions would never be as prominent as they were in the origins of the first parties of children. After the First World War some Poor Law Unions nominated young emigrants. But in the wake of the Poor Law Royal Commission of 1905–09, the administration of the Poor Law was in a process of transition. By 1929 the powers of the local Boards of Guardians would be transferred to Public Assistance Committees of local councils.[19]

When Fairbridge child migration revived after the First World War, the context of state-controlled child welfare had thus changed. The passage of the Maternity and Child Welfare Act and creation of the Ministry of Health in 1918 provided a new focus on the well-being of all infants and children. During the war the illegitimacy rate had risen to six per cent of all births, but this had actually strengthened the movement for support of unmarried mothers with the formation in 1918 of the National Council for the Unmarried Mother and her Child.[20] The Adoption Act of 1920 and its successor of 1926 and the provision of allowances to single mothers helped reduce the numbers of deserted or abandoned children who might have become candidates for emigration. By 1920 the overall numbers of children in the care of the state had fallen by over 20,000 from the pre-war years; the downward trend would continue throughout the 1920s and 1930s.[21]

In contrast therefore to the first parties of Fairbridge children, only about a quarter of those arriving in 1921 had been in Poor Law institutions. Some of them were technically 'war orphans' and had then been 'coerced' into emigration. The father of one boy had been killed in the war in 1915 and his mother had died of tuberculosis in 1917. He had two elder sisters aged 18 and 16. One of his sisters tried to look after six-year-old George and his three elder brothers aged eight, 11 and 14. He has recalled that 'One day she found out

Figure 1: Four brothers from London sent out to Pinjarra in 1921 by the Paddington Board of Guardians. Source: Battye Library, Perth, BA 311/2.

somebody was coming to take us away, so she took us to the picture theatre, hoping to hide us from these people. Turned out to be the police. The police came to the theatre … they just took us away from our sister, where we went I could not tell you, nor does she know where we went.'[22] In April 1921, nominated by the Paddington Board of Guardians, the four boys were put on board the *S.S. Ormonde* bound for the farm at Pinjarra.

Poverty in inter-war Britain continued to have an impact on Fairbridge recruitment of children from local authority homes. The studies of Seebohm Rowntree and others confirmed that in certain British cities half the children were living in poverty affecting their health and well-being. Even the doubling of the provision of school meals and milk in the 1930s could not overcome childhood mal-nutrition.[23] With continuing state support for child emigration as a form of social welfare, the British government encouraged the Society to open offices in areas of high unemployment such as Wales and Newcastle-upon-Tyne.

Among the party of 16 boys and six girls who sailed for Western Australia on the *Otranto* in August 1935, Public Assistance Authorities had nominated half. Most of these had come from the Midlands. They included a set of five siblings nominated by the Public Assistance Committee of Warwickshire County Council. Their mother had died of pneumonia in 1929 and her second husband had then deserted his family. A 16-year-old daughter from the mother's first marriage had been placed in a children's home in 1932 along with two girls aged 13 and eight and two boys aged nine and 11 from the second marriage. The Fairbridge Society eventually agreed to all five emigrating even though the eldest girl at age 16 was one of the oldest children ever sent out.[24]

The Society's recruitment of children in the care of local authorities was transformed with the Second World War and the emergence of the welfare state. While the Australian government remained committed to the revival of the pre-war child migration schemes, even encouraging new ventures, under the 1948 Children Act children in the care of local authorities could only be sent overseas with the express agreement of the Home Office.[25] In the period 1948–54, less than one-fifth of the more than 300 Fairbridge children arriving in Australia had been nominated by local authorities.[26] In the Fairbridge party of July 1949, selected here as a sample for study, none of the 21 children had been in the care of local authorities.

Children from Voluntary Societies

While significant numbers of Fairbridge children had been in the care of the Poor Law and later local authorities, many others had been in the homes of the 'voluntary' sector. As in the case of child migration to Canada in the late nineteenth century, large numbers of these children had been placed in these church and other institutions as a result of a family crisis. Significantly, the surviving records suggest that parents or other relatives of these children not only agreed to but had even encouraged and directly supported the emigration of their children, sometimes in the obvious interests of the child, but often because of new family circumstances such as a father or mother re-marrying.

Among the original parties of 1912–13, one-third had been in voluntary homes or had been nominated by private individuals. The variety of family and social circumstances was very marked and not all the boys came from the poor working class. The mother of one boy was already aged 55. Her husband, a clerk in holy orders, had died in 1905, leaving his wife with a family of three sons and three daughters. This young emigrant had already spent three years in All Saints Boys Orphanage in Lewisham, London.[27] It would seem that emigration was also often the solution to the problem of children from an earlier marriage. Thus at least two widows among the parents of these first arrivals had married again and had apparently then chosen to allow their sons to emigrate.[28]

A family or personal crisis thus often lay behind a parental decision to allow children to emigrate. Of the 58 children who emigrated in 1921, the fathers of ten, including three sets of siblings, had been apparently killed in the First World War. Not all these children were born into poverty. The father of one boy who came out in January 1921 was a French field doctor killed in the war. His mother was a professional singer. Born in Paris but then living in England, he remembers residing in a large house but then being sent to other homes before ending up in Swanleigh Boys Orphanage in Kent, which was a naval orphanage for prospective naval cadets. A woman in Pinner, Middlesex, took an interest in him and eventually he was nominated for the first party of children that left England in January 1921.[29]

Almost half the children emigrating in 1921 (a total of 26, including 11 sets of siblings) had lost their mother rather than their father. Among this latter group it would seem that it was the inability of widowers to sustain their children that had led to them agreeing to emigration. The numbers of siblings emigrating together was suggestive of the effect on families of the death of a mother and wife. Among the children leaving in January 1921 were six-year-old twin girls whose father was unemployed. In the July 1921 party were three girls aged four-and-a-half, eight and 12 whose mother had died in 1917 from septic poisoning and whose father was a machine hand in Kent.[30] There were also an 11-year-old with his five-year-old brother whose father was an ex-soldier widowed and on an army pension after 21 years' service.[31]

The dependence of the Fairbridge Society upon the voluntary sector is also seen in a number of special relationships. In 1921, following a visit to Pinjarra by its chief emigration officer, Barnardo's decided to send many of its children to the farm. By the mid-1920s, almost half the Fairbridge children arriving in Western Australia were sent by Barnardo's.[32] In the party of May 1928 all but 13 of the 115 arrivals had been with Barnardo's. Among them was a ten-year-old who had been left with Barnardo's at the age of five, following the death of his father; after five years living with two separate stepmothers, his mother ageed to him being sent to Pinjarra, this being his second trip to Australia as he and his parents had already come as migrants to New South Wales in 1922–23.[33]

When Barnardo's established its own farm school in New South Wales in 1929, the Fairbridge Society formed a close relationship with Middlemore Emigration Homes. Many of the parties of children were based briefly with Middlemore in Birmingham, before sailing to Australia or Canada. Middlemore also had its own longer-term residents, some of whom were sent out as Fairbridge emigrants.[34]

Four of the party of 22 sailing for Australia in July 1935 had been long-term residents of Middlemore. One 13-year-old boy had been in Middlemore since 1929 following the death of his mother from flu.[35] Another five-year-old girl had been placed there from the age of two after her parents had deserted their family; her five elder sisters and brother had already gone to Pinjarra. Even though she was formally 'under age', it had been decided to send her as the Superintendent of Middlemore would accompany the party.[36] Finally, there was a girl aged 11 and her nine-year-old brother who had been in Middlemore for 18 months following the death of their mother.[37]

Children Enrolled by Parents

The discussion above suggests that families often played an important role in the emigration of children, particularly where the parents had originally placed their children in homes run by the voluntary sector. More specifically, there were also many parents who actively sought to enrol children into what they saw as an imperial emigration scheme.

The actual 'enrolment' of children with the Fairbridge Society is seen from the beginning of the scheme. One boy, who arrived in July 1913, came from a family in Oxford and was still residing with both his parents and four younger siblings. He also had his mother's uncle and his father's cousin in Australia. His father was a tailor and it would appear that his parents saw the CES scheme as providing a new opportunity in the Empire.[38] Another was the son of a gardener at Petersfield, whose mother had died in 1910; the boy emigrated leaving behind his father, two elder brothers, two elder sisters and three younger sisters.[39] This first party of boys in January 1913 also included Mrs Wickham, a widow who came out as 'matron' on the ship bringing her four sons with her.[40] And perhaps hope in the Empire also resided in the motives of the widower aged 51 who worked in the Royal Arsenal in London and who had placed his son in a children's home in Bristol. He had only seen his son once in six years but was actually paying his passage fare to Australia and hoped to see him off at the dockside.[41]

This faith in Empire settlement was even more marked after the First World War when the Fairbridge Society received official support from the British and Australian governments. In 1921 ten of the child emigrants, almost one-sixth of the total number in that year, actually had both parents living. Some of the children were virtually part of family migration with their parents also going to Australia under Empire settlement schemes. The secretary of the Society indicated in June 1921 that, despite Kingsley Fairbridge's objections to parental interference, it was often necessary to encourage families to go with their children, while the government-sponsored Oversea Settlement Committee was anxious to assist family migration where possible. A brother and a sister had been sponsored by the Western Australian Emigration Department and two brothers by the Oversea Settlement Committee. All these four children came out in July 1921 but would eventually leave Pinjarra; the mother of the first two went

Figure 2: The party of children who sailed in July 1935 on the *Otranto* bound for Western Australia. The older boy on the right of the group was a former Fairbridge child migrant returning to Australia. Source: University of Liverpool Special Collections and Archives 97/3791.

to the farm in 1925 to demand their return and the other two simply went back home with their parents.[42]

By the mid-1930s, as the reputation of the Fairbridge Society grew, parental involvement became more obvious. Almost one-quarter of the 22 Fairbridge children sailing for Australia in July 1935 had been nominated by parents. Included among these were a 12-year-old boy still living with his parents in County Durham. There was also an adopted ten-year-old child of an obviously middle-class family in Devon which felt that it could no longer cope with the 'backwardness' of the boy. The case had been referred to the Fairbridge Society by the London Child Guidance Clinic, an indication of the growing significance of the child guidance movement in the 1930s. Finally there were three brothers aged six, eight and nine, the children of a female Roman Catholic divorcee living in West London. This latter group of three brothers in particular revealed what would become a new pattern in the background of Fairbridge children: the effect of family separation upon middle-class and professional families. Deserted by her husband, the mother of the three boys had sought support from a barrister in London in approaching the Fairbridge Society to enrol her sons on the understanding that she would hope to put aside a trust fund to help establish them as farmers in Western Australia.[43]

The effect of family crisis and marriage breakdown was even more prominent in the background of Fairbridge children after the Second World War when the divorce rate increased fivefold from 1936–40 to 1946–50.[44] Eleven of the 21 children leaving in July 1949 had been nominated by organisations or individuals other than their parents, although in almost all cases parents had not only formally consented to the emigration of their children but often encouraged such a move because of marriage or family crisis. Three children, two of whom were a brother and a sister, had been in Middlemore homes because of a family separation.[45] Another four children were nominated to Fairbridge through child guidance clinics. In one family, a four-year-old girl had remained at home while her seven-year-old half-sister and her ten-year-old brother were in a hostel. The mother was apparently agreeable for them all to go to Australia after they had been rejected by the man with whom she was living.[46] A 13-year-old boy had been placed in a hostel because he was unable to get on with his step-mother; he was apparently anxious to escape his home situation and was looking forward to Australia.[47] There was also an eight-year-old illegitimate boy who had been fostered out by his mother since he was three; the Berkshire clinic had nominated him although his foster parents also wanted to maintain contact as they were intending to migrate to Australia.[48]

Only in the case of one young emigrant in July 1949 does it appear that a parent had definitely not consented to emigration. This was a girl, the illegitimate daughter of a French Canadian soldier and a married woman whose husband would not accept responsibility for the child. A local branch of the Fairbridge Society itself had lodged the girl with a 'foster mother' but without arranging formal adoption. Eventually, and without the knowledge of her natural mother, the Society decided to send the child overseas once she reached five. Although the 'foster mother' apparently agreed to this action she later wrote to the Queen requesting that the Society return the young girl. The case caused controversy in the press but the Fairbridge Society refused to consider repatriating the young girl.[49]

With the new Children Act of 1948 restricting the emigration of children in the care of local authorities, the Fairbridge Society actually became more dependent on direct approaches from parents. At least ten of the party of 21 leaving in July 1949 had been directly nominated by their parents. Thus, a 28-year-old bus driver in London, an ex-serviceman deserted by his wife, after trying to make various domestic arrangements for his eight- and seven-year-old sons, decided that the best opportunity for all would be to send them to Australia with the Fairbridge Society.[50] The most notable case of 'voluntary enrolment' among the July 1949 party was that of a truck driver and his wife from Tottenham. Their family of nine children had been disrupted during the Second World War. With the mother in work, a number of the girls had been evacuated outside London while one of the sons was still suffering shell shock. The parents wanted to emigrate to Australia along with seven of the children but felt that they could not all go until the question of housing shortages in Australia was resolved. One son aged 17 was enrolled in the Big Brother scheme (a youth migration scheme between Britain and Australia first formed in 1925 and revived after the Second World War). Having first written to the Australian prime minister Ben Chifley, the mother now approached the Fairbridge Society seeking help on grounds of 'abject poverty'. She persuaded the Society to take five of her children: two boys aged ten and eight and three girls aged 15, 13 and 12. The parents indicated that they would probably follow their children in three to four years' time.[51] Eventually the whole family did emigrate to Australia, arriving at Pinjarra seeking work and then demanding their children back from Fairbridge, so causing problems for the Society (for further discussion see below).

Life in Australia

The current image of child emigration, particularly as represented in such television productions as *The Leaving of Liverpool*, is of British children, and specifically boys, being, not 'saved' from their past, but rather put to labour on arrival in Australia. The reality in the Fairbridge scheme was more complex. Kingsley Fairbridge aimed to turn boys from British cities into either farm labourers or small farmers who could help develop the Empire. When girls arrived at Pinjarra after 1921, he expected that they would become domestics or the wives of

Figure 3: Kingsley Fairbridge teaching agricultural skills to some members of the first parties of child migrants to arrive in Western Australia. Source: Battye Library, Perth, 5709B.

farm labourers or small farmers. The Fairbridge system operated on these premises until the Second World War. The scheme was founded on a conservative philosophy of child-saving and imperialism but it would be wrong to assume that it was created as a system of child labour and abuse.

Kingsley Fairbridge conceived of his young emigrants as imperial citizens in the making, placing emphasis on both physical and moral development and material well-being to be developed through contact with the soil. With an average age of about ten on arrival, most of the young emigrants of 1912–13 spent up to five or six years on the Pinjarra farm working alongside Fairbridge but also extending their formal education. Still only in his thirties, he undoubtedly developed a strong rapport with these first parties of children. As his wife and a later commentator have suggested, it was during the First World War that a community almost like an extended family developed at Pinjarra, albeit governed by Fairbridge's own values and sense of imperial mission.[52]

As with the pre-war parties of boys, most of those who arrived in 1921 spent their early period in Australia on the original farm at Pinjarra before moving to a new larger site purchased with the support of the British government. Kingsley Fairbridge had less opportunity than previously to influence the values of these post-war arrivals before his death at the early age of 39 in 1924, but he did leave a lasting impression. One of the arrivals in 1921 remembers that it was only after he moved to the new farm that he came into personal contact with Fairbridge:

> Well, we had only heard of Kingsley Fairbridge as sort of distant figurehead, you know, up to those days, at our age, we hadn't met him. But then, apparently after we'd been at the school a few months, Kingsley Fairbridge organised groups to go up to his new house then...as soon as he had a room that he could congregate the children in, he used to have certain evenings, certain groups would go up and he'd have talks with them. He'd tell them all about South Africa and his life as a boy and the hardships he went through ... My impression of him was that we looked upon him as a father, he had a natural way with children. You felt really comfortable with him and at ease with him. He only had to raise his voice just a slight semitone when he spoke to you, for you to know that he meant business if you misbehaved.[53]

Following the death of Fairbridge, the administration of the Society fell into crisis with a conflict between the central body in London and the local organisation in Perth. The conflict was not resolved until the appointment in 1928 of Colonel S.J. Heath who was a former Grenadier Guardsman and then commandant of a detention centre for the training and discipline of young soldiers. As in the later case of the Fairbridge farm on Vancouver Island, the Society's choice of a former senior soldier had consequences for the administration of the farm and the lives of the children. Heath changed the atmosphere of the Pinjarra farm, turning it into a combination of a military barracks and the image if not the substance of an English boarding school. Whereas much had previously depended upon a close relationship between Kingsley Fairbridge and the young emigrants, Heath was a rather remote figure. The day-to-day lives of the children were now governed by the 'cottage mothers', the women in charge of the system of residential cottages that Fairbridge had created on the new farm school site in the period just before his death.The education and training of the children was also systematised. All received an elementary education until age 14 when the boys became farm trainees and the girls received instruction in domestic work.[54]

By 1935, there were almost 300 on the farm at Pinjarra. The older intimacy of Fairbridge's relations with children had become ossified. There was also a crisis in administration of the farm after Colonel Heath retired in 1936. As in the wake of the death of Kingsley Fairbridge in 1924, instability reigned, with disputes between the Fairbridge Society in London and the local committee in Perth. This had a major impact on the administration of the farm. Eventually, the Society in London instituted an enquiry carried out by the British High Commission in Australia in 1944.[55] In the wake of that enquiry and in the context of the new concerns over child welfare in Britain, the Fairbridge Society sought to re-invent itself, attempting to pay much more attention to modern methods of child care.

In effect, the Fairbridge system that was created in the climate of early twentieth-century imperialism had become increasingly redundant and irrelevant, even by the 1930s when the Pinjarra experiment was most celebrated. Life on the farm during the inter-war years was often physically tough, although in material terms most children were probably better off than if they had remained in an institution in Britain. Where the system often failed was in the lack of training and understanding of child care. Many of the staff were ill-equipped to deal with children who had often suffered both physical and emotional deprivation in their early lives. As the published memoirs of former Fairbridge children suggest, the role of the cottage mothers was crucial in these respects. A caring if ill-trained cottage mother could make a difference in helping the children adjust to life on the farm and in Australia; others were sometimes cruel if not sadistic in behaviour.[56]

It was not that the Society was unaware of its obligations to the children. Kingsley Fairbridge had created a system of 'after-care', sending boys out for employment with the local farmers and maintaining records on their movements. In 1924, the Society resolved that there should be an inspection of all those in work during the first two years of their employment. By 1928, Miss Mary Dennehy, who had become an employee at Pinjarra in 1916, became the first after-care officer. Under the direction of Miss Dennehy, who remained in employment until the 1930s and continued contact with many former Fairbridge children well beyond that period, the Fairbridge after-care system attempted to maintain close records on all former Fairbridge children until they reached the age of at least 21.

With a shortage of young rural workers in Western Australia by the 1930s former Fairbridge boys and girls were in demand, and were being sent even to the remote northwest of the state. With more than 600 former child migrants now in employment, the system of after-care began to break down. In 1936, Dallas Paterson, who briefly replaced Colonel Heath as principal at Pinjarra, provided a report on the problems with a number of former Fairbridge children, with boys becoming criminals and girls falling pregnant.[57] By the early 1940s there were complaints reaching the Fairbridge Society in London that children were being put into employment without proper care. Such complaints eventually led to reforms in methods and postwar changes in the administration at Pinjarra.[58]

What the surviving after-care records do reveal is the futility of Fairbridge's hopes that child migrants could simply become new successful rural settlers. This was particularly so for the parties of children who arrived before the First World War and during the 1920s. The general failure of the Fairbridge system must be seen in the context of the early twentieth century when governments in Western Australia encouraged agricultural development including schemes to settle British adult migrants in groups to clear the land in the southwest of the state.[59] In effect, agricultural development and group settlement collapsed in the Depression of the 1930s. Large numbers of emigrant farmers simply left their properties with debts unpaid, embittered by the expectations of prosperity which governments had created over the previous decade.[60]

A similar pattern is seen among the early Fairbridge arrivals, many of whom made consistent efforts to become property owners, taking up land during the 1920s only to abandon their farms in the 1930s. The most famous farmer among the early arrivals was one who had arrived as a nine-year-old in July 1913. One of ten boys sent out by the Board of Guardians from the children's home at Kingston-on-Thames, where he had been resident for six years, by the age of 18 he had been given a block of 960 acres by the Western Australian government. His story was recounted in the press when Fairbridge journeyed to England in 1922 to encourage financial support for his child migration scheme.[61] By the mid-1920s he had acquired a further 1,000 acres and was employing boys from the Pinjarra farm. But he could not escape the harsh realities of the Depression and related personal crises. The 1930s brought a financial and personal crisis. He had married in 1929 but his wife became ill and died in 1931. He had to give up his land. He served in the Australian Home Forces during the Second World War but his second wife deserted him after the war and he was left to care for four young children. By 1958, in his mid-fifties, he was in hospital. It would seem that even the early training he had received under Kingsley Fairbridge was no protection from the problems of adult life.[62]

Related personal and financial crises are also revealed in the file notes on a number of the other early Fairbridge arrivals. One boy worked in the northwest of Western Australia but could not adapt to the harsh climate and died of pneumonia in 1929 in his late twenties.[63] Two brothers who had arrived in the second party in July 1913 tried to become small farmers in the 1920s but suffered serious mental breakdowns in the 1930s. One of these was hospitalised in 1935 and died in 1940 in his mid-thirties; his brother was in an old men's home at the age of 38 in 1941 and died six years later. How far their crises related to issues of upbringing remains hard to determine, but perhaps the ultimate lack of a network of family and other support may be significant.[64]

This pattern of economic difficulties and personal crises appears throughout the surviving case notes on many of the early Fairbridge arrivals. By the 1950s none of the original arrivals owned farms and few were working on the land. Now well into middle age, and generally without formal qualifications, except what they may have acquired in war service, most of Kingsley Fairbridge's first parties of emigrant children were employed in unskilled or semi-skilled work in the growing economy of Western Australia. Those who maintained contact with the farm school at Pinjarra, even remaining committed to Fairbridge's ideals, were now in occupations not imagined when they arrived.

In this respect the experiences of one, while not necessarily typical, provide some insight into a life cycle influenced by the patterns of migration and changing opportunities. The boy who had arrived in 1913 as an eight-year-old from Oxford, and whose parents had seen the scheme as a form of Empire settlement, left the farm school in 1920 aged 15, and went to work on wheat farms in the southwest of Western Australia where he remained until the late 1930s as a 'keen supporter' of Fairbridge and what had been done for him. By 1949 he was married and living in a small rural settlement in Western Australia. Three years later he was working there with his family as a telephone lineman at a 'lucrative wage' which 'gives him great satisfaction'.[65] Not all his fellow immigrants of 1912–13 had been so fortunate.

There were similar problems for the arrivals of 1921. They generally went out to jobs in the late 1920s on the eve of the Depression. In their early to mid-twenties by the 1930s, they confronted a deteriorating labour market. As with the majority of pre-war arrivals, most of the boys found itinerant work on farms. The girls were employed helping farmers' wives or in local country towns. Only a small minority, not more than four of the 58 arrivals of 1921, even attempted to become property-owners. One girl married a former Fairbridge boy in 1929 and they became settlers in the southwest of the state. By 1935, they had four children and were struggling to survive, owing a large debt to the state Agricultural Bank. A year later they had abandoned their block and the husband was working on the roads under a sustenance scheme.[66] Another boy, who had arrived at Pinjarra aged 13, and was therefore older than most of the other child migrants, had left the farm in 1922 and within five years had experience in orchard work, on a dairy farm and sheep farming. By the early 1930s he had bought a property but had to give it up when the price of wheat collapsed. At one time he claimed that he had walked 2,000 miles in search of work.[67] His brother who had come as a child migrant died of pneumonia in 1932 aged 19 after suffering ill-health for a number of years.[68]

At least three of the children who arrived in 1921 returned to

Britain. After two attempts to find her employment, the Fairbridge Society repatriated one girl on grounds of mental health.[69] Her sister, who had come with her, remained in Australia under difficult circumstances, unable to keep a job, being placed in a Catholic home and becoming an unmarried mother in her early twenties.[70] Two brothers, aged eight and ten on their arrival in 1921, had gone out to work in the mid to late 1920s. By 1931, they were anxious to return home to their mother and step-father but in order to avoid any controversy with the Fairbridge authorities, which assumed legal responsibilities for all the children until the age of majority, they delayed their return until 1934 by which time they had turned 21.[71]

For most of the 1921 arrivals the 1930s Depression had a major effect. The surviving case notes suggest a pattern of ill-health and personal crisis for at least one-fifth. Four of the 58 suffered a mental or physical breakdown while still in their twenties. During the economic crisis of the Depression, others went through major personal traumas including one boy being convicted and imprisoned and another fathering a child with a girl aged 14.

It would seem that the major change in the lives of those who had come to Pinjarra in the inter-war years was the direct result of the outbreak of the Second World War. More than 600 of the former children from Pinjarra, or at least 60 per cent who had arrived at the farm in the 1920s and 1930s, joined the military forces (539 males and 56 females) of whom 50 were killed and 39 became prisoners of war.[72] Ironically, the only one among the arrivals of 1921 who appears to have made a successful transition to farming was an ex-serviceman who was able to purchase a property of 1,500 acres through a war service settlement scheme.[73]

In contrast to the Fairbridge children who came in 1912–13 and 1921, the experiences of the arrivals in 1935 and 1949 seem to have been far less traumatic. While most of the arrivals of 1935 initially became farm labourers or domestic servants, post-war prosperity benefited many of them. One boy nominated through the Devon Public Assistance Authority, and aged 12 on his arrival, left Pinjarra in 1939. By 1957 he was a sheep shearer and contractor, married with two children and apparently well settled: 'I will never regret coming out under the Fairbridge scheme. I have married an Australian girl and am very happy.'[74] At least two of the August 1935 party were able to return to Britain after the Second World War, although one boy, who had failed to keep contact with his mother, returned home to find that his family now rejected him. By 1949, he was trying to get the Fairbridge Society to help him go back to Australia.[75] Another boy returned to England and helped his parents, who had apparently deserted him as a child, to buy a house in Devon. Within a few years he had become a wool classer, followed by a period as a long-distance lorry driver.[76]

Of those nominated privately among the 1935 arrivals, the boy sent out by his adopted parents in Devon originally found problems of identity particularly as he believed that they had rejected him. By the early 1950s, however, then in his mid-twenties, he was using his original surname and making a career for himself in the Solomon Islands as a plantation manager. He was also eager to keep contact with the Fairbridge Society and his previous cottage mother.[77] Even more notable was the fate of the three brothers enrolled by their mother following her divorce. Maintaining contact with her sons and dissatisfied with the training in farming that they were receiving at Pinjarra, in 1942 the mother of these three boys arranged for them to be transferred to the Catholic farm Tardun. The Fairbridge Society agreed willingly to this transfer particularly as the two younger brothers were regarded as 'mentally defective'. After the Second World War all three boys went to work and received the trust funds that their mother had invested for them. The eldest son later went to a plantation in New Guinea; one of his younger brothers served in the Australian Army after the Second World War and then became a painter; the other brother eventually came to own a lead mine. In later life the eldest son wrote to the Fairbridge Society expressing his appreciation of his years on the farm (in contrast to his years at Tardun) and noting that the earlier prejudice against his two younger brothers was the result of the views of one cottage mother. He concluded 'All my skills, standards for living, dedication to duty, had their roots at Fairbridge.'[78]

Not all who came in 1935 had such success in later life. A 13-year-old who had been in Middlemore following the death of his mother was regarded on his arrival in Western Australia as a 'semi-invalid'. He was not well throughout much of his work as a farm labourer. He did join the military but after the war became a plasterer. By 1979, only in his late fifties, he was in a 'a home of sick and elderly men' when his brother, who remained in Britain, was able to contact him.[79]

Despite the current critique of child migration from Britain after the Second World War, the surviving after-care records suggest that the arrivals at Pinjarra in 1949 may have had the least traumatic experiences of all the groups considered here. The July 1949 party arrived in Australia at a time when the nature of Fairbridge education and care had been transformed. The new administration at Pinjarra in the 1940s and 1950s still maintained a focus on the older ideals of Fairbridge but now agreed that the children should be given a variety of possible opportunities beyond rural work and domestic service. From the early 1950s many of the children on the farm were even provided with the opportunity to go on to the local high school. In 1955, the Pinjarra authorities reported to the Society in London that just over half the boys leaving the farm after the war had gone into rural work, with the remainder entering skilled trades, the military or going on to further education; three-quarters of the girls had gone into nursing, secretarial or commercial occupations with only a minority being in domestic service.[80]

Of those 11 children in the July 1949 party nominated by organisations, the case records are not always complete, but very few appear to have gone into the traditional pre-war patterns of rural work or domestic service. Of the three siblings from the Berkshire Child Guidance Clinic, the older girl had married at 17, her sister went to work as a domestic help and her older brother worked on farms and then on the railways until being killed in a road accident at the age of 25.[81] Another boy who had agreed to emigration to escape his step-mother went to high school and eventually became a primary school teacher.[82] Of the three children from Middlemore, one girl had become a nursing assistant by 1960, her brother began an apprenticeship and applied to join the Navy, while the boy who had arrived as a seven-year-old had by the age of 17 joined the Public Works Department and was saving to buy a car; by 1967, still only in his mid-twenties, he had become a trade union official.[83]

What the case files also reveal is the continuing efforts of many of the post-war child emigrants, even those nominated through organisations, to maintain contact with parents, generally with the support but sometimes without the approval of the Fairbridge Society. Much to the concern of the Society, the mother of the three siblings nominated though the Berkshire clinic continued an active correspondence and eventually migrated to be with one of her daughters.[84] Another of the boys from Berkshire corresponded with both his mother and also his foster parents who had now migrated to Adelaide. The foster parents were initially anxious to adopt him but nothing eventuated. Significantly the case file reveals that the boy's mother kept in contact with both the Society and her son until he reached the age of majority.[85] A seven-year-old child migrant from Newcastle, nominated through the National Society for the Prevention of Cruelty to Children, had by 1960 started a career in modelling. This girl had remained anxious to maintain contact with her mother, but despite considerable efforts on the part of the Fairbridge Society over a number of years there was no trace of her mother's whereabouts.[86]

Among the children directly enrolled by their parents there is even clearer evidence of continuing and even very close contact. Thus in 1951, after unsuccessfully seeking help from Fairbridge in an application for emigration, the parents of the five Tottenham children arrived in Western Australia seeking employment. By mid-1951 the mother had written to the Duke of Gloucester, the President of Fairbridge, complaining that her two elder daughters had been 'pushed off into service' and demanding the return of the younger children. The Fairbridge Society denied the charges about the older girls and on grounds of legal guardianship (granted to the Society under the Australian 1946 Immigration (Guardianship of Children) Act) refused to allow the younger children to join their parents while also denying one of the older girls, now aged 17, the right to marry. The dispute dragged on until at least 1953 by which time the case files suggest that the younger boy and youngest girl, then aged respectively 12 and 15, were more content to stay at Pinjarra than to join their parents.[87]

While the surviving records do not provide full details beyond the 1950s there is less evidence of personal crises than was the case earlier, although one child migrant in the 1949 party, after a period of difficulties in employment, walked out on his employer and in his early twenties came under the care of the state mental health service.[88] One final case from the party of July 1949 reveals, however, the futility of even considering emigration for some of these post-war arrivals. One boy from Staffordshire underwent a brief but traumatic experience in Australia. His mother, a female textile worker in Staffordshire, whose husband had died of tuberculosis contracted while on war service, had agonised over the future of her eldest boy, aged 11. Even though her son had been awarded a scholarship to secondary school she eventually decided that Australia would offer the opportunity to pursue a farming career.[89] He was unhappy even on the voyage out to Australia. Once at Pinjarra he ran away on a number of occasions. In mid-1951, despite the fact that he had already passed a scholarship examination in England, the authorities in Australia classified him as 'sub-normal', a commentary more on the nature of mental testing at the time than on the boy's abilities. The Fairbridge Society decided to repatriate him to England. But this story at least had its own happy postscript. In 1957, the headmaster of Leek High School in Staffordshire informed the Fairbridge Society that this former emigrant had now completed a shortened three-year GCE course and was attending Loughborough Training College studying chemical engineering.[90] Such a case was a reflection of how the whole context of child emigration had changed since Fairbridge founded his Society almost 50 years previously.

Conclusions

This history of the case studies of Fairbridge child migrants tends to challenge some of the assumptions of the current critique of child emigration. This is particularly so in relation to questions of the patterns of emigration. Over almost four decades from 1913 to 1949 public authorities, voluntary societies, parents and even the potential emigrants were all involved in the process which would send Fairbridge children to Australia. The major change in the pattern of recruitment probably occurred between the pre-1939 parties of children and those sent out after the Second World War. Particularly noticeable is the growing influence of parents in these decisions and the continuing contact that many parents maintained with their children. Already some recent research has suggested that in the post-Second World War period, the voluntary organisations with residential homes in Britain, such as Barnardo's and the National Children's Homes, were very particular in seeking parental consent and approval for the emigration of children.[91] In the case of the Fairbridge Society, which used nominations from parents from the outset, the popular view of 'philanthropic abduction' certainly requires major qualification.

What then of the experiences of the child migrants in Australia? The critics have suggested that once they left Britain the child migrants lost contact with home and family, in the process even 'losing' their own self-identity. In effect, Kingsley Fairbridge believed that he was recreating a new life, new opportunities and perhaps new identities

for the children he had 'saved'. Much of this ideal failed to materialise but it would be a mistake to suggest that life at Pinjarra for these
Fairbridge childen was one of systematic abuse. Rather, their overall
experiences related to the changing context of opportunities in Australia
over the twentieth century. The Fairbridge Society intended the
children to become Empire settlers but this was never really achieved.
The early arrivals were given expectations of a rural life which soon
dissipated in the crisis of the 1930s Depression; the latter arrivals
entered occupations which were not all that different to those
generally taken up by the Australian-born population or even to what
they might have been able to achieve had they remained in Britain.
What had been a celebrated Empire settlement scheme in the inter-
war years became just one of a number of schemes of migration to
Australia in the period after the Second World War.

Rather than seeking to condemn child migration as either a 'costly
mistake' or 'misguided' it should be understood as, first, reflecting
changing views of childhood and child welfare in Britain and,
secondly, as a barometer of the changing relations between Britain and
Australia. The Fairbridge scheme was formed in the context of both
philanthropic child-saving and British Empire settlement. Not only
did these related images of child rescue and Empire sustain the
Society until at least the 1940s but they also held a strong appeal for
many of those nominating children. Child migration and education
on a farm in the Empire seemed to be not only a better alternative
than the barrack-life of residential institutions, but also a solution to the
problems of material poverty. Undoubtedly all associated with Fairbridge were over-confident that the lives of these children could be
re-made. Moreover, while the death of Fairbridge created a myth of
an ideal to be achieved, the Fairbridge farm itself became far more
institutionalised and even ossified in its methods and approaches.
Not only did the Depression of the 1930s end any hope of the former
Fairbridge emigrants becoming modest rural yeomanry, but for
some the trauma of their lives, both before Fairbridge and then as
young emigrants, may have become too much, leading to personal
crisis. Even by the end of the 1930s, both the hopes of Empire
settlement and the older Fairbridge ideal were in decline. By the mid-
1940s, while the Fairbridge Society had re-invented itself to adapt to
changing views of welfare, the family and childhood, the whole
rationale for its existence was disappearing. At the same time, the British
government had long abandoned any hopes in Empire settlement,

although the Australian authorities were still willing to accept child migrants not so much for the earlier ideals of land settlement but as part of an overall aim of increasing population through migration. Nevertheless, despite the increasing irrelevance of the Fairbridge scheme, we should still recognise that many of the families of the children, and particularly those who came after the Second World War, may have still seen hope in the old vision of Empire even though a later generation may now raise questions as to whether it might have been better for the children if they had never been sent to Australia.

Notes

1. Philip Bean and Joy Melville, *Lost Children of the Empire*, London, Unwin Hyman, 1989. This was produced in conjunction with a video of the same title. For a similar account but focusing solely on child migration to Australia, see Alan Gill, *Orphans of Empire: The Shocking Story of Child Migration to Australia*, Sydney, Millennium Books, 1997.

2. *Financial Review*, 3 July 1992. The brochure for the launch of the TV series had a photo of a boy and girl coming down a gangplank with the caption, 'Is this the unwanted trash of Britain's glory?'. The height of press interest occurred in the mid-1980s but has continued. For some early and influential examples see 'Lost Children of Empire', *The Observer Review*, 19 and 26 July 1989; 'Reluctant Pioneers', *The Times Educational Supplement*, 21 April 1989; 'The forgotten children they fed to the Empire', *The Guardian*, 6 May 1989.

3. Western Australian Legislative Assembly, *Select Committee into Child Migration*, 1996.

4. Health Committee, *Third Report: The Welfare of Former British Child Migrants*, Vol. 1, Report and Proceedings of the Committee, House of Commons Session 1997–98, p. xxviii.

5. Department of Health, *The Welfare of Former British Child Migrants*, Government Response to the Third Report from the Health Committee, 1997–98, Cm 4182.

6. Australian Parliament, Senate, Community Affairs Reference Committee, *Lost Innocents: Righting the Record*, http://www.aph.gov.au/senate/committee/clac_ctee/child_migrant/contents.htm

7. Joy Parr, *Labouring Children: British Immigrant Apprentices to Canada, 1869–1924*, London, Croom Helm, 1980. See also Gillian Wagner, *Children of the Empire*, London, Weidenfeld and Nicolson, 1982.

8. Health Committee, *The Welfare of Former British Child Migrants*, passim.

9. The total figure of approximately 6,000 child migrants is based upon

research in the British and Australian government archives for *An Encyclopedia of the Australian Nation, its People and their Origins*, ed. J. Jupp, forthcoming 2001. For the post-war figures see Barry Coldrey, 'Child Migrants from Post-War Britain', *History* (magazine of the Royal Australian Historical Society) 53, September 1997, pp. 20–23. It has been claimed without any substantiation that in the post-1945 period the main child migrant agencies 'packed off some 10,000 British children to Australia' (Bean and Melville, *Lost Children of the Empire*, p. 110). This claim has been accepted almost as fact by the opponents of child migration even though the question of numbers is complicated by the aggregation of child and youth migration, while after 1957 many child migrants migrated with their parents as part of approved schemes.

10. Health Committee, *The Welfare of Former British Child Migrants*, p. xxiii and Gill, *Orphans of Empire*, p. 9.

11. Barry Coldrey, *The Scheme: The Christian Brothers and Childcare in Western Australia*, Perth, Pacific Argyle Press, 1993.

12. Child Emigration Society, *Fairbridge Farm Schools*, Report for 1927, p. 7 cited in Alex G. Scholes, *Education for Empire Settlement*, London, Longmans Green, 1932, p. 151.

13. Geoffrey Sherington and Chris Jeffery, *Fairbridge: Empire and Child Migration*, London, Woburn Press, 1998.

14. Harry Hendrik, *Child Welfare: England 1872–1989*, London, Routledge and Kegan Paul, 1994, p. 76, and Jean S. Heywood, *Children in Care: The Development of the Service for the Deprived Child*, London, Routledge and Kegan Paul, 1965, p. 90.

15. 'The Emigration of Poor Children to the Colonies', speech read before the Colonial Club at Oxford, reprinted by the Child Emigration Society, Fairbridge Archives (FA), D296 A2, University of Liverpool (UL).

16. Child Migrant Files, Parties A and B, FA D296 E1/1, UL. The later references draw upon this source supplemented by after-care files in FA D296 E2, UL.

17. Child Migrant File A9/1.

18. Child Migrant Files B7/1 and B7/2.

19. Heywood, *Children in Care*, pp. 119-27.

20. Heywood, *Children in Care*, p. 115. See also Deborah Dwork, *War is Good for Babies and Other Young Children*, London, Tavistock, 1987, pp. 208–20.

21. R. S. Parker, *Away From Home: A Short History of Provision for Separated Children*, London, Barnardos, 1990, p. 61.

22. Interview with Mr George and Mrs Lily Snellin, 11 July 1985, OH1876, Battye Library Perth (BL) and Child Migrant Files 2/15/1-4.

23. See Seebohm Rowntree, *Poverty and Progress. A Second Social Survey*, London, Longmans Green, 1941, pp. 155–60; and Hendrik, *Child Welfare*, pp. 133–48.

24. Child Migrant Files 988, 987, 986, 971 and 970.

25. For fuller discussion see Sherington and Jeffery, *Fairbridge*, pp. 197–219.

26. Sherington and Jeffery, *Fairbridge*, p. 233.

27. Child Migrant File B2/1.

28. Child Migrant Files B10/1 and B12/1.

29. Interview with Mr Jack Maude, 13 September 1985, OH 1875, BL.

30. Child Migrant Files 3/24/1, 2 and 3.

31. Child Migrant Files 3/33/1 and 2.

32. Sherington and Jeffery, *Fairbridge*, pp. 109, 128–32.

33. Sherington and Jeffery, *Fairbridge*, pp. 131–32.

34. Sherington and Jeffery, *Fairbridge*, pp. 134–35.

35. Child Migrant File 979.

36. Child Migrant File 985.

37. Child Migrant Files 983 and 989.

38. Child Migrant File B1/1.

39. Child Migrant File A6/1. This boy was drowned within his first year in Australia. See *The West Australian*, 1 September 1913.

40. The press report of the arrival of the first party suggested that the 13 boys had been under 'the charge' of Mrs Wickham while on the ship. *The West Australian*, 22 January 1913.

41. Child Migrant File A2/1.

42. Child Migrant Files 3/30/1 and 2, and 3/31/1 and 2.

43. Child Migrant Files 974, 975, 976.

44. O. R. McGregor, *Divorce in England: A Centenary Study*, London, Heinemann, 1957, p. 6.

45. Child Migrant Files 1134, 1146 and 1147.

46. Child Migrant Files 1131, 1132 and 1143.

47. Child Migrant File 1148.

48. Child Migrant File 1145.

49. Child Migrant File 1133.

50. Child Migrant Files 1136 and 1137.

51. Child Migrant Files 1140, 1139, 1130, 1129 and 1128.

52. Ruby Fairbridge, *Pinjarra*, London, Oxford University Press in association with Humphrey Milford, 1937, pp. 131–66; Mabel Creeman, 'A Surrogate Parent Approach to Child Emigration: The First Kingsley Fairbridge Farm School 1912–1924', in *Childhood and Society in Western Australia*, ed. Penelope Hetherington, Nedlands, University of Western Australia Press with the Centre for Western Australia History, University of Western Australia, 1988, pp. 127-43.

53. Interview with Mr Jack Maude, 13 September 1985, OH1875, BL.

54. For fuller discussion, see Sherington and Jeffery, *Fairbridge*, pp. 120–51.

55. Sherington and Jeffery, *Fairbridge*, Chapters 5 and 6.

56. For contrasting accounts of Pinjarra in the inter-war years see John Lane, *Fairbridge Kid*, Fremantle, Fremantle Arts Press, 1990, and Flo Hickson, *Flo: Migrant Child from Liverpool*, Warwick, Plowright Press, 1998.

57. Sherington and Jeffery, *Fairbridge*, pp. 145–47.

58. Sherington and Jeffery, *Fairbridge*, pp. 200–03.

59. G. D. Snooks, 'Development in Adversity 1913 to 1946', in *A New History of Western Australia*, ed. C. T. Stannage, Nedlands, University of Western Australia Press, 1981, pp. 237–66; J. P. Gabbedy, *Group Settlement: Its Origins, Politics and Administration*, Parts 1 and 2, Nedlands, University of Western Australia Press, 1988.

60. Geoffrey Bolton, *A Fine Country to Starve In*, Nedlands, University of Western Australia Press in association with Edith Cowan University, 1994.

61. *Surbiton Times*, 1 December 1922, press cutting, Fairbridge Society Records, 3028A/44, BL.

62. Child Migrant File B17/1.
63. Child Migrant File B14/1.
64. Child Migrants Files B/6/1 and 2.
65. Child Migrant File B1/1.
66. Child Migrant File 2/13/1.
67. Child Migrant File 2/16/2.
68. Child Migrant File 2/16/1
69. Child Migrant File 2/14/2.
70. Child Migrant File 2/14/1.
71. Child Migrant Files 3/321 and 3/32/2.
72. *The Fairbridgian*, June 1950, vol. viii, no. 42, pp. 19-20, BL.
73. Child Migrant File 2/17/1.
74. Child Migrant File 982.
75. Child Migrant File 981.
76. Child Migrant File 968.
77. Child Migrant File 978.
78. Child Migrant File 974.
79. Child Migrant File 979.
80. Statistics relating to children who have come to Pinjarra and Molong since the Second World War, FA, D296, UL.
81. Child Migrant Files 1132, 1131 and 1143.
82. Child Migrant File 1148.
83. Child Migrant File 1146.
84. Child Migrant File 1132.
85. Child Migrant File 1145.
86. Child Migrant File 1135.
87. Child Migrant Files 1140, 1139 and 1130.
88. Child Migrant File 1141.
89. Child Migrant File 1142.
90. Child Migrant File 1142.
91. A. McVeigh, 'Child Migration in the Post-War Period', in *New Directions in Social and Economic History*, ed. I. Blanchard, Avonbridge, Newless Press, 1995; and Gerry Urey, 'Child Migration: 1950–1955' (report for National Children's Homes and copy in Department of Archives and Special Collections, University of Liverpool).

4

Gender, Generations and Social Class: The Fairbridge Society and British Child Migration to Canada, 1930–1960

Patrick A. Dunae

From the mid-1930s to the early 1950s, the Fairbridge Society operated a unique residential training centre for underprivileged British children in Canada. The Prince of Wales Fairbridge Farm School was located on Vancouver Island, in Canada's most westerly province, British Columbia. The Fairbridge Farm School was a remarkable community and is significant to the history of child welfare and social action in several respects.

The very fact of its existence is remarkable, because the Fairbridge enterprise was established several years after British child migration to Canada had officially ended. From the 1860s onwards nearly 100,000 dependent children were sent to Canada by organisations such as Barnardo's.[1] Resettlement schemes involving British 'home children' had always been controversial, but after the First World War child migration was discredited as a means of Empire settlement and as a child welfare strategy. Accordingly, in the mid-1920s the Canadian government enacted regulations that were supposed to put an end to the trans-Atlantic child migration movement. The Fairbridge Society, however, managed to circumvent these regulations in the early 1930s.

The Fairbridge Farm School was remarkable because it was located in British Columbia, a province that had had no experience with British home children, and because it was established in the early years of the Depression, a time when many Canadians were opposed to immigration of any kind. The Fairbridge enterprise was also notable because of its overtly imperial complexion and its quintessentially masculine character.

No less striking is the fact that the Fairbridge initiative in Canada began at a time when Canadian social workers were defining their profession. Members of this ascendant profession were young, university-trained women who were opposed to child migration and institutionalised child care. They collided with representatives of the Fairbridge Society, most of whom were middle-aged, Empire-minded males.

At the risk of oversimplifying matters, the Prince of Wales Fairbridge Farm School on Vancouver Island was contested terrain between opposing camps of child welfare advocates. The two camps – gentlemen and players, a fraternity and a sorority – were defined by ideology, age, gender and social class. As this chapter will show, the sorority ultimately triumphed in the struggle for control of Fairbridge. In the process, the sorority helped to affirm the status of social work as a profession and to establish a distinctive character for child welfare programmes in Western Canada after the Second World War.

The Fairbridge Society developed out of an organisation known as the Society for the Furtherance of Child Migration, formed at Oxford University in 1909 by Kingsley Ogilvie Fairbridge.[2] Born in South Africa in 1885, Fairbridge was raised in Southern Rhodesia where his father worked as a surveyor for Cecil Rhodes' British South Africa Company. As Kathryn Tendrick has remarked, Rhodes had an 'intoxicating effect' on certain types of men – men who were 'young, intelligent, athletic, patriotic, unattached, and in need of a purpose in life'.[3] Kingsley Fairbridge was one of those bedazzled young men.[4]

Years later, Fairbridge recalled an occasion when, at the age of 11 years, he had spent an afternoon with Rhodes. Looking back on that afternoon, he regretted that he had not offered himself unreservedly to the Colossus. 'If I might go back again to that one day! If only I had had then even the little wit that I have now! I should have said "Take me, take me, and let me serve you!"'[5] Fairbridge would honour the memory of Rhodes and contribute to the cause of Empire through his child settlement scheme.

Fairbridge's interest in child migration sprang out of his first visit to England in 1903. The 18-year-old colonial had not expected to see widespread poverty and unsanitary slums in the Empire's metropolis. He was appalled at some of the scenes he witnessed – men beating their wives, women brawling outside public houses, gangs of pallid, destitute children marauding through squalid streets. These disquieting scenes remained with him when he returned to his father's farm in Rhodesia, and they grew in intensity as he surveyed the empty veldt. 'The waste of it all,' he wrote afterwards. 'Children's lives wasting while the Empire cried aloud for men.' The only way to save these underprivileged children, he decided, was to remove them from their deleterious home environment and resettle them in the British dominions overseas.[6]

Fairbridge determined that the best way to promote his scheme was to secure a Rhodes scholarship. At Oxford University he hoped to meet kindred spirits and influential patrons who would make his vision a reality. He set off on his quest in 1906, travelling by way of New Zealand and Canada in order to familiarise himself with other parts of the Empire. En route, he spent a few weeks in British Columbia. He noted afterwards that the province would be a good haven for underprivileged child emigrants.

Fairbridge eventually gained a Rhodes scholarship and a place at Exeter College, Oxford. He entered enthusiastically into 'Varsity life and became a noted boxer. He enjoyed a wide circle of friends, many of whom were members of the Oxford University Colonial Club. At a club meeting held in October 1909 Fairbridge formally outlined his scheme for 'the Emigration of Poor Children to the Colonies'.

Fairbridge proposed to emigrate destitute children between the ages of eight and ten – 'before they have acquired the vices of "professional pauperism" and before their physique has become lowered by adverse [environmental] conditions'. Eschewing the practice of Barnardo's, which apprenticed immigrant children with colonial farmers, Fairbridge proposed to establish a relatively self-contained children's village overseas. Residents would be grouped together in cottages or bungalows, under the care of a surrogate parent called a 'cottage mother'. The children would attend a day school where they would follow a curriculum prescribed by the local Education Department. But they would also receive practical training, so that on attaining the age of 16, boys would be hired as farm labourers and girls could find work as 'governesses, house-keepers, cooks and domestic servants'.[7]

Fairbridge never forgot that evening in October 1909 when he outlined his 'Vision Splendid' to members of the Colonial Club. His memory of the meeting, like his memory of that afternoon in company with the Colossus, reveals much about Fairbridge's personality and the character of this child welfare scheme. Gathered in a restaurant on the High Street of Oxford – amid tobacco smoke,

murmured conversations, clinking glasses and subdued laughter –
were men from all parts of the Empire. Gazing round the room,
Fairbridge noted the 'powerful, thoughtful face' of an Alberta
scholar. He registered the 'iron jaw' of a Prince Edward Island man;
the strong, sun-tanned face of a Queenslander; the 'ingenuous gaze'
of a South African; the 'bull-necked sturdiness' of a New Zealander;
and the 'wide open, untroubled eyes' of a Newfoundlander.[8] His
picture of these guileless, manly fellows is quite striking. He might
have been describing the executive of a rugby club, instead of a group
of child welfare activists.

According to Fairbridge, these men 'were animated by no
common shibboleth ... no single interest that would tend to make
them all think alike'. But of course they did have a great deal in
common. Most of them were beneficiaries of Cecil Rhodes and as
such they had to have met the criteria laid out by the Rhodes Trust.
Hence, they were unmarried and between 18 and 25 years of age.
Each of them had evinced a 'fondness of and success in manly sports';
each had demonstrated 'qualities of manhood' – notably 'truth, courage,
devotion to duty and sympathy for the protection of the weak'.[9]

This was all well and good, but what did these manly young
fellows, who hailed from relatively affluent colonial families, know
about underprivileged children and child care? What did they know
about chronic poverty and the underclass of Britain's industrial cities?
Possibly some of them had been involved with one of Oxford
University's Settlement houses, but none of them had any real
knowledge of child care or social work.[10] They were, to use a contemporary phrase, rank amateurs.

Still, they were earnest and well-intentioned men. Inspired by
Fairbridge's speech, they constituted themselves as the Society for
the Furtherance of Child Emigration to the Colonies. Later, their
organisation was formally chartered as the Child Emigration Society
(CES). When its charter members graduated from the university and
left England to pursue careers back home, the CES might easily have
folded. Fairbridge, however, was determined to carry out his scheme.
In 1912, after many setbacks, he established a farm school at
Pinjarra, near Perth, in Western Australia. Fairbridge devoted himself
completely to the enterprise, to such an extent that he jeopardised his
health. He died in 1924 at the age of 38. But the child resettlement
scheme he initiated survived. His work was carried on by a London-
based non-profit organisation known as Fairbridge Farms, Inc. and

later as the Fairbridge Society. The Fairbridge Society subsequently sponsored two other farm schools in Australia. To the chagrin of Canadian child-care workers, the Society also wanted to open a farm school in British Columbia.

As mentioned earlier, Kingsley Fairbridge had visited British Columbia en route to Oxford and in 1914 he was planning to establish a farm school there. He outlined his plans in a letter to Harry Logan, a friend and former Rhodes scholar who was teaching in the Classics department at the University of British Columbia (UBC) in Vancouver. 'A good farm school in British Columbia,' Fairbridge wrote, 'would not only train otherwise hopeless and homeless youngsters to be fine, upstanding, honourable men and women, it would also stand as a thanksgiving to God for the splendid unity of our far-flung Empire.'[11]

But the First World War intervened and any ideas Logan might have had about reactivating the farm school plan must have been dashed when Fairbridge died in 1924. Besides, the mid-1920s was a most inauspicious time to be contemplating a new child emigration scheme in Canada. A well-organised campaign against juvenile immigration was underway at the time and when it concluded Canada's doors were, supposedly, welded shut to dependent children from Britain.

The campaign against juvenile immigration was led by Charlotte Whitton, a formidable and complex woman whom contemporaries called the 'first lady of Canadian social work and child welfare'.[12] Whitton had entered the burgeoning field of social work in 1918 and by the mid-1920s was director of the Canadian Council on Child Welfare, an agency generally known as the Child Welfare Council (CWC).

These were exciting years for social workers in Canada and Whitton, more than anyone else, was responsible for advancing the status of the social work profession. She accomplished this by organising a series of systematic child welfare surveys in different parts of the country (the first of the surveys focused on British Columbia) and by articulating 'scientific and professional' child welfare policies. Crucial for her plans to implement new policies 'was the careful selection and placement of qualified protégées in key provincial and municipal child care agencies'.[13] Several of her protégées established the School of Social Work at the University of British Columbia in 1929.[14] In the years that followed, graduates of

UBC's Social Work programme filled key positions in the provincial government's Child Welfare Branch.[15]

As her biographers have said, Whitton never liked any of the British child migration schemes and 'although she suspected all the British societies, she despised the Barnardo Homes'.[16] In her opinion, Barnardo's was an archaic, unprofessional, and unprincipled organisation, more interested in self-promotion than developing realistic child welfare strategies. Her views, unfortunately, were coloured by contemporary ideas of eugenics and environmental determinism. She was convinced that British child welfare agencies such as Barnardo's were using Canada as a dumping ground for genetically sub-standard children. Not everyone shared her views on degeneracy, but most social service organisations agreed that Canada had insufficient resources to look after its own dependent children and so could not afford to care for home children from Britain. The campaign against juvenile immigration prompted the federal government to enact regulations in 1925 which banned dependent children who were less than 14 years of age from entering the country. The ban was intended as a temporary measure, but after further campaigning by Whitton and the Child Welfare Council it became a 'permanent policy' of the federal Immigration Department in 1928.[17]

Not surprisingly, Whitton was distressed when she heard in 1932 that the Fairbridge Society had reactivated plans for a farm school in Canada and that the federal government was going to allow the Society to bring children as young as five years of age into the country. Her colleagues and protégées in British Columbia were also alarmed to learn in 1934 that the Society had selected their province as the location for the new farm school. The province had no experience dealing with child migrants. (Most of the British home children sent to Canada prior to the First World War had been placed in the eastern provinces of Ontario and New Brunswick.) Moreover, their opposition to institutionalised children was well known.

The Canadian government's decision to allow Fairbridge to establish a farm school in British Columbia was shaped by a variety of factors.[18] Essentially, though, the Fairbridge Society was able to initiate its scheme because it seemed to be better organised and better funded than any of its predecessors. Children who trained at the farm school were not supposed to be at risk, while the farm school itself promised to inject a good deal of money into the local economy. The status, prestige and academic lustre of the Fairbridge

Society appealed to many Ottawa mandarins, especially those who had been to British universities. Affectionate ties to the Old Country and imperial sentiments were powerful factors, too, especially in Ottawa, which had been the host of the 1932 Imperial conference. So when the Fairbridge Society called upon the senior Dominion to assist 'an exceptional Empire in an exceptional time of difficulty', the call was warmly received.[19]

In British Columbia, the Society could call on friends who had been at Oxford with Kingsley Fairbridge. One friend, who had been present at the launch of the CES in 1909, helped the Fairbridge Society acquire a site for a farm school in the Cowichan Valley on southern Vancouver Island. Located near the hamlet of Cowichan Station, the property was ideally situated for this kind of enterprise. The land was cleared and was well suited for mixed farming and the neighbours were congenial. This part of the Cowichan Valley was renowned for its emigrant gentlefolk – a group of expatriate British sportsmen, retired Anglo-Indian Army officers, well-bred English-women, remittance men and sundry Oxbridge types who gave the district a distinctly genteel, 'county' ambience.[20] Always eager to employ youngsters from the Old Country, these settlers were among the Society's most ardent supporters.

The Society's supporters also included Dr George M. Weir, formerly Professor of Education at the University of British Columbia. Weir was not an Oxford man, but he held degrees from several prestigious universities in Canada and the United States and he represented a wealthy, cultured constituency (Vancouver-Point Grey) in the provincial legislature. More importantly, he was Minister of Education and Provincial Secretary, responsible for education, health and social welfare programmes in British Columbia. Despite objections from some of his cabinet colleagues, Weir persuaded the provincial premier to endorse the Fairbridge scheme and recommend it to immigration authorities in Ottawa. Weir also encouraged his neighbour and former colleague, Harry Logan, to take a leave of absence from UBC and become principal of the new Fairbridge Farm School.

All told, 329 children came to British Columbia under the auspices of the Fairbridge Society between 1935 and 1948. The children were selected from rescue homes and orphanages run by local authorities in Britain, and by churches and charitable founda-tions such as Middlemore Homes in Birmingham. A detailed profile of these children is beyond the scope of this study, but it should be noted that almost all of the children had been born into large, working-class families and an environment of acute poverty. Some were orphans, but most came from single-parent households. In a significant number of cases, the children's fathers were ex-servicemen who constituted Britain's 'burnt-out generation' after the First World War. When these broken-down men died or became physically incapacitated, as they did in large numbers during the late 1920s and early 1930s, precarious family units collapsed and children were taken into care. Geographically, most of the children sent to Canada came from Newcastle (where the Fairbridge Society maintained a branch office) and nearby towns in the distressed areas of Tyneside.[21]

The first party of children arrived in September 1935, with Geordie accents so thick that their Canadian teachers and cottage mothers could scarcely understand them. Predictably, and understandably in these Depression years, the newcomers were resented by left-wing organisations such as the Vancouver Mothers' Council who were concerned about chronic unemployment among local youths. But for the most part, the Fairbridge Farm School received a great deal of favourable publicity in Canada. Newspapers, newsreels and radio reports were lavish with heart-warming accounts of bonny lads and lasses from the slums of Tyneside. Next to the Dionne Quintuplets, the children of Fairbridge were probably the best-known children in Canada.[22]

The reputation of the enterprise was enhanced by the distinguished people who visited the site. The popular novelist John Buchan, who as Lord Tweedsmuir was governor-general of Canada from 1935 to 1940, was a frequent and much-publicised visitor. Other visitors included film stars, the Lord Mayor of London, the president of the Canadian Pacific Railway, officers of HMS *Hood* and, in a manner of speaking, the King and the Queen.[23] In the late 1930s and early 1940s, it was *de rigueur* for celebrities and dignitaries passing through British Columbia to pay a call to the farm school, to see erstwhile waifs from the Old Country flourishing in the New Land.

Despite the Depression, money was plentiful. In 1934, the Prince of Wales launched a fund-raising campaign for the new farm school by personally subscribing £1,000. (In appreciation, the facility in Canada was named the Prince of Wales Fairbridge Farm School.) The British government provided special funding to the Fairbridge Society through the Empire Settlement Act and through Special

(Distressed) Areas relief legislation. In 1936, Rudyard Kipling bequeathed £60,000 to Fairbridge, and large donations were received from many other benefactors, including the merchant banker Sir Charles Hambro who became chairman of the Society in 1934. Support also came from unexpected quarters, as in 1936 when a party of wealthy American tourists spontaneously opened their cheque-books during an Atlantic crossing. The tourists were returning from the Berlin Olympic games and were moved by the high-spirited, quaintly spoken youngsters on board who were en route to a new home in Western Canada.

These generous friends and visitors accounted for the sumptuous and substantial infrastructure at the farm school. A Canadian veterans' association donated ornamental gates and laid out the playing fields. A tourist from England provided funds for a chapel that was built to a design by the distinguished imperial architect, Sir Herbert Baker. The president of the Canadian Pacific Railway furnished the chapel. The Wills tobacco family built an infirmary, the Cadbury family endowed a library, and lumber magnate H. R. Macmillan provided a dining hall and gymnasium. The distinctive duplex cottages at the farm school village were provided by a consortium of provincial lumber exporters.

During these halcyon years, the Prince of Wales Fairbridge Farm School enjoyed a remarkable degree of sovereignty and freedom with respect to provincial government regulations. Just as the Fairbridge Society was allowed to circumvent federal immigration laws, so, too, was it excused from provincial health and welfare regulations. Fairbridge never deigned to register under the province's Child Protection Act, never bothered to apply for certification under the provincial Welfare Institutions Licensing Act, never made any attempt to have its infirmary approved under the provincial Hospitals Act. Whenever provincial social service workers requested compliance with these statutes, Principal Logan loftily referred them to his friend, Dr Weir, who explained to them that Fairbridge was a unique organisation and so was exempt from his ministry's otherwise rigorous regulatory policies.

Like the British Empire fifty years earlier, the Prince of Wales Fairbridge Farm School existed in a kind of splendid isolation and Logan certainly contributed to the mystique. Once he joined the Fairbridge organisation, he dropped his civilian title and instead used his military rank, Lieutenant-Colonel. He was always *Colonel* Logan to children, staff and visitors at the farm school. Logan was responsible to the executive of the Fairbridge Society in London, but the executive gave him great latitude. On local matters, Logan conferred with an advisory committee. During the first ten years of the farm school, the committee comprised retired military officers (including an army general), prominent lawyers and accountants, land surveyors and business leaders. Middle-aged and elderly, these men represented a post-colonial patriarchy. They had much in common with the imperial fraternity that had launched the CES many years before. Like the men who turned out for that memorable meeting of the Oxford Colonial Club in October 1909, these men were earnest, well-intentioned amateurs who had no formal training in child welfare practices. Moreover, like their predecessors at Oxford University, these men viewed their young charges from an exclusively male perspective. Despite the fact that nearly one hundred girls were sent to the farm school in British Columbia, no woman ever sat on the farm school's advisory committee.[24]

As long as the farm school was well connected, as long as it was financially independent and unfettered by local legislation, all was well. But the landscape changed dramatically with the advent of the Second World War. Funds were no longer available from the United Kingdom and so Logan had to appeal to the provincial government for funding. Dr Weir cheerfully obliged and in 1940 provided the farm school with a substantial operating grant.[25] Not long afterwards, Weir resigned his post as Provincial Secretary to join a federal government wartime agency in Ottawa.

Weir's successor as Provincial Secretary and Minister of Education was George Pearson, a collier's son and former wholesale grocer who represented Nanaimo, a gritty, working-class constituency in the provincial legislature. Pearson was not part of the sophisticated, urbane, imperial fraternity of Fairbridge friends. Since the farm school was now a recipient of provincial government grants, he insisted that it conform with provincial government health and welfare legislation. Reluctantly, Colonel Logan complied with the minister's demands. Soon after, the Prince of Wales Farm School came under serious attack.

The assault began in 1943 when Edith Pringle, Deputy Inspector of Provincial Welfare Institutions, carried out a preliminary assessment of the farm school's policies. She was distressed to find that the Fairbridge infirmary did not comply with the provincial Hospitals

Act and that its medical staff were not properly qualified. She also commented on the very 'narrow vision' of the Fairbridge system. Children were trained exclusively as farm hands or domestics. In Pringle's view, the children would be happier and would be 'more desirable citizens' if they received 'different training dependent upon their own capacity and adaptability'.[26]

The following year, the provincial government carried out a more searching enquiry, after complaints were received from a former cottage mother.[27] The enquiry was organised by Laura Holland, the provincial government's Chief Welfare Officer, and Charlotte Whitton's principal protégée in Western Canada. As head of the Vancouver Children's Aid Society, Holland had organised the first of Whitton's national child welfare surveys in British Columbia in 1927. She had helped to establish the School of Social Work at UBC a few years later.

Like most Canadian social workers, Holland opposed child migration and institutionalised child care. But Holland was particularly negative towards Fairbridge because of the sour relationship that existed between the women in her department and the men responsible for the farm school. Holland's deputy, Isobel Harvey, had clashed with Logan on several occasions over his refusal to conform to the Welfare Institutions Licensing Act. A graduate of the UBC's School of Social Work, Harvey had a low opinion of the colonel and his committee of gentlemen advisors. Likewise, Ruby McKay, a young graduate of the UBC programme, had been rebuffed when she had asked Logan to comply with other welfare legislation. These were the women assigned by Holland to undertake a thorough, first-hand report on the farm school in August 1944.

In their view, Fairbridge Farm School was 'reminiscent of an orphanage of the last century'. The English ambience that seemed so quaint and charming to some visitors was stifling and regressive to the two social workers. They were particularly struck by the 'astonishing degree of class consciousness' about the place. Isobel Harvey declared:

> A Child Welfare worker viewing Fairbridge is left with a feeling of helplessness. The basic idea – antagonistic to every concept of Canadian Child Welfare – that the children are poor English children and, therefore different from the ordinary child, is rooted so firmly in practically every staff member's mind that there is no use arguing against it. I was told over and over again by the Principal that I was incapable of understanding these children because they

were English children. Anything they do, any trait they develop, is laid to the [social] class from which they come.[28]

In the eyes of the social workers, the children's clothing confirmed the repressive and archaic character of the institution. Girls wore old-fashioned looking pinafores, boys wore heavy woollen shirts and short baggy trousers. Certainly these outfits set them apart from Canadian children of their age. Harvey and McKay were appalled by the fact that the children ate off metal dishes and drank from tin mugs – a practice which, the investigators said, was unknown in Canada outside prisons and penitentiaries. Most of the children, the investigators reported, were poorly fed, dirty and unkempt in appearance, and ignorant of personal hygiene.

Senior government officials in Victoria were distressed by the findings. 'I must say,' the deputy Provincial Secretary declared, 'that in spite of what I knew about the place I am appalled at what your survey has disclosed, and it is pitiful to think of those children having to live in such conditions.'[29] Worse was yet to come. During the investigation, the Child Welfare Branch unearthed information concerning sexual abuse at the farm school. The investigators discovered that a former Royal Navy officer, hired many years earlier as duties master and deputy principal, had repeatedly been accused of 'interfering' with Fairbridge boys. The man was eventually arrested, charged and imprisoned for gross indecency, yet incredibly was reinstated by Logan upon his release from jail. The man re-offended and was again imprisoned. Several other staff members were dismissed because of sexual improprieties involving children at the farm school.

The Child Welfare Branch was also disturbed by the high incidence of out-of-wedlock pregnancies among Fairbridge girls. Between 1938 and 1944, one-third of the girls (19 out of 57) who left for outside employment at the age of 16 became illegitimately pregnant. Their illegitimacy rate was three times higher than that among single girls of a similar age in the province.[30] Most of the girls had become pregnant within three years of leaving the farm school and going out to domestic service. The Child Welfare Branch regarded these statistics as evidence of Fairbridge's poor placement procedures and inadequate after-care programmes, and as testimony to the lack of sex education at the farm school. The figures were also a sad indictment of Colonel Logan's belief that 'domestic work is probably the safest work into which a woman of tender years may be placed'.[31]

The Provincial Secretary acted quickly on the social workers' report. He informed the Fairbridge executive that he would withdraw all provincial funding and launch a public enquiry, unless sweeping reforms were made at the farm school. Just a few years earlier, the executive might have dismissed the demands out of hand. But in 1944 most of the Society's champions in Ottawa and Westminster were preoccupied with the war effort; moreover, the farm school was almost totally dependent on the operating grant it received from the British Columbia government.[32] Grudgingly, the Fairbridge executive acceded to the Provincial Secretary's demands. Logan was relieved of his duties as principal and new local directors were appointed.

At first glance, it was business as usual. The new principal, William Garnett, was a former Rhodes scholar and had no training or experience in the field of social work or child welfare. However, he was accountable to a board that included Laura Holland and other professional child-care workers. Under their direction, several important changes were made. Unqualified and incompetent employees at the farm school were dismissed; attempts were made to steer Fairbridge trainees to employment opportunities beyond agricultural and domestic work. Better work placement procedures, sex education classes, and after-care programmes were established in the hope of reducing the number of teenage pregnancies.

The new board also thwarted a scheme that might have prolonged the farm school and taken it into uncharted territory. After the Second World War, the Canadian government expressed concern for the 'thousands of illegitimate children with Canadian fathers in Europe'. The government was especially concerned about the welfare of children born to Canadian soldiers during the liberation of Holland. On numerous occasions in 1947 and 1948, Canada's High Commissioner in London, Vincent Massey (an Oxford man) met with Fairbridge Society chairman Sir Charles Hambro (also an Oxford man) to discuss the possibility of accommodating these children in Canada. The plan was to bring the children over to England, care for them until they were old enough to travel, then send them to the Fairbridge Farm School in British Columbia, where they would be raised and educated at the expense of the Canadian government.

The Fairbridge Society was enthusiastic about the idea and amended its constitution in anticipation of the scheme going ahead. (Under the terms of its original articles of association, the Fairbridge Society was concerned solely with the welfare of 'poor British children'; under the terms of its amended constitution, the Society was able to provide assistance to 'children resident in Britain'.) Typically, the scheme devised by a couple of Oxford men in England was not discussed beforehand with child welfare professionals in British Columbia. The social workers who sat on the Fairbridge board in British Columbia opposed the plan on the grounds that it might reopen the door to large-scale child emigration and because it might legitimise and perpetuate institutionalised child care, a concept they fundamentally opposed. Faced with this strong opposition, the government of Canada abandoned the scheme and, lamentably, the children whom the scheme was intended to assist.[33]

By that time, the future of the farm school was very much in doubt. The financial outlook was grim, because of the unfavourable sterling–dollar rate and the British government's monetary restrictions, and the provincial government made it clear that it was not prepared to fund the farm school indefinitely. And the Children Act of 1948, which provided for a modern and comprehensive system of child care in Britain, meant that underprivileged children did not have to be sent to welfare institutions overseas. That, in any case, was the opinion held by the Canadian directors of the British Columbia farm school. Moreover, most of the directors were philosophically opposed to any kind of institutionalised child care. As they explained in a report to the London executive in September 1948: 'We may think we have substituted a family environment and *to a degree* in a cottage system of child care we have. But it is an impersonal relationship. Any security the child has is in the organisation itself, *and this cannot take the place of family relationships in the lives of most children.*'[34]

In May 1949 the British Columbia directors reiterated their concerns in a report urging the Fairbridge organisation to focus on rehabilitating families in England. Finally, in July 1949, the British Columbia directors resolved to disband their board and to close the facility. Since the provincial government effectively controlled the board, the London executive had little choice but to accept the decision. Children at the farm school were subsequently placed in foster homes in Victoria and Vancouver and in 1951 the gates of the farm school were closed. The Fairbridge Society continued to stand *in loco parentis* as guardian of the children until the early 1960s, when the last of the Canadian Fairbridgians attained the age of 21. But home supervision, job placement and after-care programmes for the young emigrants were carried out by social workers acting under the direction of the provincial Child Welfare Branch, rather than by representatives of the Fairbridge Society.

In British Columbia, the Fairbridge organisation collided with an ascendant profession, a profession made up in large part of Canadian-born, university-trained women. The impact of the collision was evident in 1944, following the investigation conducted by Laura Holland, Isobel Harvey and Ruby McKay. This is not to say that the investigation and reports that ensued were unbiased. The federal government's supervisor of juvenile immigration carried out a separate enquiry at the same time and found that children at the farm school were 'comfortably housed, well-fed, healthy and happy'. In his opinion, the report prepared by Harvey and McKay was 'an unfair presentation of conditions at Fairbridge'.[35] Without question, they painted an overly bleak picture of the facility.

Quite possibly, their report was coloured by personality clashes with the principal. Fairbridge alumni and former clerical staff at the farm school recall that meetings with the Child Welfare Branch investigators were usually fractious, that relations between Logan and the social workers were always strained. Contemporaries who are sympathetic to the principal recall that one of the social workers was short and pugnacious, that she was 'mannish' in her behaviour, that she chain-smoked unfiltered cigarettes. Logan, in contrast, is remembered as a patrician figure, 'tall and scholarly', aristocratic in manner; and he, of course, smoked a pipe![36] The situation may also have been exacerbated by the age of the protagonists. In 1944, Colonel Logan was 56 years of age, while Edith Pringle, Isobel Harvey, Ruby McKay and most of their colleagues were considerably younger. But at the end of the day, personality differences meant less than political strengths and in 1944 the social workers were simply more powerful than Colonel Logan and his committee of advisors.

The Prince of Wales Fairbridge Farm School represents the last chapter in the chronicle of trans-Atlantic child migration. The government enquiry into the operations of the farm school in 1944/45 and the decision to close the facility in 1949 marks the end of the Fairbridge Society's sojourn in Canada. But the struggle for control of the farm school also marked the start of a new era for social workers in British Columbia. The victory at Cowichan Station was exhilarating to members of the profession; it enhanced their public reputation and their status within the public service.

In 1946, a new government ministry, the Department of Health and Social Welfare, was created in British Columbia. The new ministry took over and greatly expanded work that had previously been done by a relatively small office within the Provincial Secretary's Department. In 1943, the Child Welfare Branch had employed fewer than a dozen professional social workers. By 1947, the Welfare Division within the new ministry employed five times that number and in 1951, when the Fairbridge Farm School closed, over 150 social workers were employed by the government.[37]

One of the new case workers was Bridget Moran. In her memoirs, she wrote: 'The welfare system which hired me in November 1951 showed no signs of the apathy which gripped [many other government departments] in Victoria. Far from a sense of lethargy, the Social Welfare Branch, [in] the Department of Health and Welfare, exuded an air of achievement and progress and growth.' The department's *élan* derived in part from the confidence and authority of veterans such as Ruby McKay, who was Superintendent of Child Welfare when Moran was hired. Moran recalled meeting her for the first time at an in-service training session in 1952. Although McKay was pleasant towards the new trainees, they soon learned that the superintendent's 'facade concealed a will of iron and that if there was ever a conflict between ourselves and a foster child, Ruby McKay would feed us to the lions'.[38] But as Colonel Logan might have remarked, in the arena of child welfare, it was not always the same pride of lions. In the province of British Columbia during the middle decades of the twentieth century, age, gender, and social status were significant in determining whether one was a lion or the lion's dinner.

Notes

1. British child migration has been the focus of several scholarly studies, notably Joy Parr, *Labouring Children: British Immigrant Apprentices to Canada, 1869–1924*, London, Croom Helm, 1981; Gillian Wagner, *Children of the Empire*, London, Weidenfeld and Nicolson, 1982; Neil Sutherland, *Children in English Canadian Society: Framing the Twentieth Century Consensus*, Toronto, University of Toronto Press, 1978; Patricia T. Rooke and R. L. Schnell, *Discarding the Asylum: From Child Rescue to the Welfare State in English Canada, 1800–1900*, Lanham, MD, University Press of America, 1983. British 'home children' in Canada have also been considered in 'popular' works such as Kenneth Bagnell, *The Little Immigrants. The Orphans Who Came to Canada*, Toronto, Macmillan, 1980, and Philip Bean and Joy Melville, *Lost Children of the Empire. The Untold Story of Britain's Child Migrants*, London, Unwin Hyman, 1989.

2. Fairbridge described his early years and the events leading to the launch of his child migration society in his posthumous autobiography entitled *The Story of Kingsley Fairbridge by Himself*, London, Oxford University Press and Humphrey Milford, 1927. The book was subsequently republished in 1933 under the title *The Autobiography of Kingsley Fairbridge*, With a preface by the Rt. Hon. L. S. Amery, PC and an Epilogue by the Hon. Sir Arthur Lawley, KCMG. All references in this essay are to the 1933 edition.

3. Kathryn Tidrick, *Empire and the English Character*, London, I.B. Tauris & Co., 1992, p. 52.

4. For a critical examination of Fairbridge and his child resettlement scheme see Geoffrey Sherington and Chris Jeffery, *Fairbridge: Empire and Child Migration*, London, Woburn Press, 1998.

5. Fairbridge, *Autobiography*, p. 18.

6. Fairbridge, *Autobiography*, p. 142.

7. Fairbridge, *Autobiography*, p. 234.

8. Fairbridge, *Autobiography*, pp. 172–73.

9. 'The Rhodes Scholarships', *Encyclopædia Britannica*, 11th edition, 1910–1911. The scholarships were established in 1902 by the Rhodes Trust. In the preamble to his will, Cecil Rhodes had provided guidance to his executors for awarding the scholarships. The preamble began: 'I consider that the education of young colonists at one of the universities in the United Kingdom is of great advantage to them for giving them breadth to their views, for the instruction in life and in manners, and for instilling into their minds the advantage to the colonies as well as to the United Kingdom of the retention of the unity of the Empire.'

10. The Fairbridge scheme was a pastiche of several different social welfare initiatives, including the Settlement House Movement which attracted many Oxbridge undergraduates. See Michael E. Rose, 'The Settlement House and Social Welfare: Britain and the United States, c. 1880–1940', *University of Manchester Working Papers in Economic and Social History* 6, January 1991, and Rose, '"Neighbourhood as Springboard": The Urban Community and the Settlement House Movement in Britain and the USA, c. 1890–1990', *University of Manchester Working Papers in Economic and Social History* 5, October 1993.

11. State Archives of Western Australia [SAWA], Fairbridge Society Records, ACC. 934A/2C: Kingsley Fairbridge letterbook, 5 November 1914, p. 63.

12. Patricia T. Rooke and R. L. Schnell, '"Making the Way More Comfortable": Charlotte Whitton's Child Welfare Career', *Journal of Canadian Studies* 17, Winter 1982/83, p. 33. See also James Struthers, 'A Profession in Crisis: Charlotte Whitton and Canadian Social Work in the 1930s', *Canadian Historical Review* 62(2), 1981, pp. 169–85.

13. P. T. Rooke and R. L. Schnell, 'Charlotte Whitton Meets "The Last Best West": The Politics of Child Welfare in Alberta, 1929–49', *Prairie Forum* 6(2), Fall 1981, p. 144.

14. Whitton and her contemporaries were determined that courses in social

service would be scholarly and academically rigorous. At UBC, the two-year social service diploma course, founded in 1929, was expanded to three years in 1935. In the early 1940s, it was elevated to a postgraduate course and in 1945 a permanent Department of Social Work was created. Lee Stewart, *'It's Up to You'. Women at UBC in the Early Years*, Vancouver, University of British Columbia Press, 1990, p. 100.

15. Rooke and Schnell, 'Making the Way More Comfortable', p. 36.

16. P. T. Rooke and R. L. Schnell, *No Bleeding Heart: Charlotte Whitton. A Feminist on the Right*, Vancouver, University of British Columbia Press, 1987, p. 52.

17. Child migration was also under attack in Britain, and local authorities there accused Canadian officials of being too lax in protecting British home children. In 1924, following a report by Margaret Bondfield, the British government withdrew funding from organisations which sent children under the age of 14 to Canada. Organisations such as Barnardo's subsequently redirected their programmes to Australia. Parr, *Labouring Children*, p. 151.

18. Patrick A. Dunae, 'Waifs: The Fairbridge Society in British Columbia, 1931–1951', *Histoire sociale–Social History* 21(42), November 1988, pp. 224–50.

19. Dunae, 'Waifs', p. 226.

20. Patrick A. Dunae, *Gentlemen Emigrants: From the British Public Schools to the Canadian Frontier*, Manchester, Manchester University Press, 1982, p. 110.

21. On the 'burnt-out generation', see J. M. Winter, *The Great War and the British People*, London, Macmillan, 1985, p. 273.

22. The Dionne quintuplets were born in May 1934 in Callendar, Ontario. The five girls were Canada's most newsworthy babies and attracted a great deal of attention from curiosity seekers, fortune hunters, and child development experts. See Pierre Berton, *The Dionne Years: A Thirties Melodrama*, Toronto, McClelland and Stewart, 1977, and Veronica Strong-Boag, 'Intruders in the Nursery: Childcare Professionals Reshape the Years One to Five, 1920–1940', in *Childhood and Family in Canadian History*, ed. Joy Parr, Toronto, McClelland and Stewart, 1993, pp. 160–78.

23. During the Royal Visit of 1939, the children of Fairbridge were taken by coach to Victoria, where they formed a special reception party for King George VI and Queen Elizabeth.

24. In the early 1940s, when Fairbridge was still independent of provincial government control, the British Columbia advisory committee consisted of twenty members, all of whom were men. Most of the members resided in Victoria or Vancouver, and so did not have much contact with the children at Cowichan Station.

25. The decision to fund the farm school was not discussed in the legislature, and Weir did not want to debate the matter with socialist members of the opposition party. Accordingly, he directed that the government grant to Fairbridge should be tucked away in the budget of the Department of Education, where the item appeared under the innocuous heading of 'Grants for patriotic purposes'. British Columbia, Public Accounts, 1940/41.

26. British Columbia Archives [hereinafter BCA], British Columbia. Provincial Secretary's Records, GR 496, Box 58, file 4, Edith Pringle, 'Fairbridge Farm School' [typescript, July 1943], p. 7.

27. Dunae, 'Waifs', p. 241.

28. BCA, Prince of Wales Fairbridge Farm School records, Add. MSS. 2045,

Vol. 1, file 14: Isobel Harvey, 'Report on a study made of Fairbridge Farm School during the month of August 1944' [typescript].

29. BCA, British Columbia, Provincial Secretary, GR 496, vol. 58, file 5: P. Walker to Isobel Harvey (24 August 1944).

30. BCA, British Columbia, Provincial Secretary, GR 496, vol. 58, file 5: P. Walker to Isobel Harvey (24 August 1944); British Columbia, Provincial Board of Health, *Vital Statistics Report*, 1944, pp. 63–64.

31. BCA, Add. MSS. 2045, vol. 1, file 14. Principal's Report, 17 November 1943, p. 7.

32. During the Second World War, the chairman of the Fairbridge Society, Sir Charles Hambro, was head of Britain's Special Operations Executive (SOE). He had been involved with the clandestine organisation (later known as MI6) for many years previously. See David Stafford, *Britain and European Resistance, 1940–1945*, London: Macmillan, 1980, pp. 36 and *passim*.

33. Dunae, 'Waifs', pp. 246–47. The scheme was devised by Sir Charles Hambro and Canada's High Commissioner, Vincent Massey, a long-time ally of the Fairbridge Society. The anglophile Massey had attended Oxford University just a few years after Kingsley Fairbridge had been there, and Massey keenly supported any cause that would promote imperial unity. He married the daughter of Sir George Parkin, who was the first secretary of the Rhodes Trust. See Claude Bissell, *The Young Vincent Massey*, Toronto, University of Toronto Press, 1981, esp. pp. 98–99, and Bissell, *The Imperial Canadian: Vincent Massey in Office*, Toronto, University of Toronto Press, 1986.

34. Dunae, 'Waifs', p. 246.

35. Dunae, 'Waifs', p. 243.

36. The colonel's courtly manners and aristocratic appearance are conveyed in Jasper H. Stembridge, *A Portrait of Canada*, London, Oxford University Press, 1943, p. 44.

37. BCA, Add. MSS. 708: Isobel Harvey, 'An Historic Review of the Social Services of the Government of British Columbia' [typescript].

38. Bridget Moran, *A Little Rebellion*, Vancouver, Arsenal Pulp Press, 1992, p. 59.

5

Child Rescue: The Emigration of an Idea

Shurlee Swain

Why did this happen to me? This sense of personal hurt lies at the base of a series of campaigns launched by adult survivors of child welfare systems of the past. While these are essentially political campaigns alleging a transgression of citizen rights, they have their origins in the search for an explanation for past pain and the need to integrate personal experiences of cruelty and loss into public representations of child welfare providers as essentially benevolent and kind. Once launched such campaigns can produce a second level of hurt as the now elderly carers are forced to re-examine their carefully constructed pasts in the face of angry accusations from the media, often retaliating with counter-accusations that the hurt arises from personal inadequacies or that campaigners are victims of a 'me-tooism' seeking to piggy-back on the success of others whose sense of hurt they do not dispute.

Over the last decade in Australia, British child migrants, the Aboriginal stolen generation, adult adoptees[1] and state wards from the 1950s have all sought compensation for removal from their families and their subsequent mistreatment in statutory and voluntary child welfare institutions. While there has been, in the media coverage, some sense that there is a historical context to contemporary debate this has seldom been pursued in any depth, with each new accusation greeted as a separate child welfare scandal. This paper examines this historical context, arguing that the policies which justified such removals had a common origin in the nineteenth-century child rescue movement which revolutionised child welfare by positing the parent as the enemy of the child, a shared legacy which provides the discursive context for many contemporary debates. It thus seeks to destabilise the comfortable assumption that such child welfare scandals can be confined to the past, arguing that contemporary practices, which are also ideologically driven, may be similarly fraught.

The Gospel of Child Rescue

The historiography of the child rescue movement has swung from the celebratory approach of writers such as Pinchbeck and Hewitt,[2] through to the condemnation of theorists who, following the work of Anthony Platt, deny that child saving had any altruistic intent,[3] positioning it instead as a subset of a range of new forms of social control designed to fit the working classes to the demands of monopoly capitalism.[4] In recent years there has been a move to replace such rigid binary judgements with dualities, allowing for the possibilities of multiple meanings, or multiple motivations in what previously had been seen as a unitary movement or event. Cunningham, for example, seeks to position the entire debate within what he describes as a story, a romance, which was itself a product of the industrial age.[5] By means of this romance childhood was simultaneously constructed and reified as separate from but constitutive of an adulthood whose nature determined the future of the nation.

The child rescue or child-saving movement had its origins in industrial Britain where a number of young men sharing deep religious convictions and a flair for publicity stepped aside from general rescue work to focus on children, whom they saw as innocent victims in a world permeated with sin. Common to all the founding stories which early child rescuers such as Thomas Barnardo (1845–1905), Edward Rudolf (1852–1933) and Thomas Bowman Stephenson (1838–1912) used to publicise their work was the notion of their being called, not directly by God, but by a child as the messenger of God, reflecting in its state all that was alien in the crowded areas of the inner city.[6] Child rescue, however, developed no critique of the social and economic changes which were responsible for creating such conditions. Rather it was a nostalgic philosophy which looked back to a rural England in which sin had not had so free a hand. Having failed to convert the inner city poor, child rescuers, positioning their work within the great evangelical story of redemption and salvation, turned their attention to the children who, they believed, could be saved if they were removed from this contaminating environment. The before and after photos were basic tools of the child rescuers' trade, darkness overtaken by light as filth or sin was washed away, the cleansing of the child emblematic of the baptism by which all were brought into life eternal.

> Is that not what God has done for me? He came to us who did not seek Him, and stripped us of our rags, and put on us the beautiful garments of Christ's righteousness, and adopted us into His own family.[7]

These British child rescuers founded child welfare empires whose propaganda ensured that the child rescue gospel spread throughout the English-speaking world. Their struggle was not against poverty but sin: a sin which attached not to little children but rather to their parents who, in failing to lead their offspring to a Godly life, had become the greatest barriers to their redemption. Yet, as Christine Stansell has argued in her study of child savers in the city of New York, the situation was far more complex than this simple solution would suggest.

> What reformers portrayed, then, as a stark tableau of virtue and vice was in actuality a complicated geography of family life, invisible to men and women who believed a child's place was in the home, under the moral tutelage of a woman.[8]

The child-saving gospel spread quickly in the Australian colonies. Growing rapidly, through both immigration and natural increase, colonial cities reproduced what child savers saw as the worst features of the cities of Britain, perhaps even more effectively than they did their best. While van Krieken argues for child saving as a response to economic and demographic changes, the growth in the population outstripping the ability of the economy to absorb child labour,[9] there was also a sense in which the need for child saving was taken as proof of a city's claim to great city status. The dismay with which the 'discovery' of a new social problem was greeted was always tinged with pride that here was another way in which the rough colonial city was mirroring its British models. The 'discovery' of a new social problem 'at home' often set off a search for its equivalent in Australia in order that the local cities not be left behind.

It is not surprising therefore that child saving found its most receptive audience in Melbourne, the greatest of Australia's nineteenth-century cities, where Scotswoman Selina Sutherland founded the Scots Church Neglected Children's Aid Society in 1881, following a shipwreck which she interpreted as God's message that her future work was to be found in Victoria.[10] Drawing on the writings of

Barnardo, Stephenson and Rudolf, many of which were reprinted in denominational journals, she was able to define a space for private child rescue in the colony. The pre-existing statutory child welfare system worked on a vagrancy model, providing for children who, if left unrestricted, would endanger public order. Sutherland, however, embraced the child rescuers' definition of neglect that positioned immoral or vicious parents as the enemies of the child and demanded active rescue.

> If the young are allowed to grow up in the midst of vice they must necessarily be vicious, and ... if they drink in depravity with their earliest years, they are not responsible for being depraved. If we suffer them to be corrupted while they are still unable to distinguish right from wrong, we are bound, of course, to thrust them sooner or later into prison, or otherwise inflict punishment on them in order to protect society. But there is horrid injustice in thus treating those who have only acted as they were taught to act.[11]

In this definition the child was identified primarily as a victim but as a victim who, if not immediately rescued, would grow up to threaten all that society held dear.

Local newspapers lauded the child rescuers' endeavours, reflecting uncritically their view of the problem, sentimentalising the children and criticising their parents, divorcing the individual family from its wider social context. Essentially these were narratives of darkness and light, evil and innocence, danger and rescue which placed colonial dramas within an international context. In an early example of investigative journalism, *Telemachus* wrote, in 1890, of discovering

> little children in a poisonous artery close set in the vitals of this city ... They were not starvelings of children, not hungry or thirsty or cold; but ragged and dirty, and surrounded by an atmosphere of moral and physical pollution. Drunkenness and grossest lasciviousness and theft and brutality, close about their pillows, as the guardian angels about the picture-book child's head ... I thought then that they were exceptions; it has since come to me that they are types, types of a class existent in all our great cities, and easy enough to be found by any who care to seek.

The solution advanced was a simple one: 'Take him out of the city; keep him out of the city. Train him for the country, and anchor him there. Is not such our duty to the waif?'[12]

Another journalist, Mary Gaunt, found her 'undergrown, stunted mites' at Miss Sutherland's receiving home surrounded by 'kindness, peace, and cleanliness such as they have probably never known before in their short troubled lives ... the only love and tenderness most of them have ever had has been from the kindly hands of the total strangers who have rescued them from poverty, dirt and depravity.' 'These little mites,' she concludes,

> might teach a lesson to their richer brothers and sisters in comfortable nurseries, they are so kind and gentle to each other ... the tiniest child there has learned through sorrow and suffering to make the best of the good things that come in the way, and to bear patiently and cheerfully the unavoidable troubles of this life.

For their parents there is no such sympathy, men and women united only in their desperation 'to get rid of the responsibilities they had taken on themselves of the unfortunate children they had brought into the world'. The widowed father who 'ought to have made a living for himself' but has not, deserted wives and single mothers all share in the common condemnation, 'very hopeless, very hopeless indeed ... idle, worthless, undeserving',

> but the children – some thought must be taken for the poor little sorrow-laden children who are learning the wickedness and woe of the world before they have reached their teens, suffering silently as only childhood can suffer ... To take the most mercenary view of the matter, they must be helped. The parents, even if they are willing, are incapable of training them into the good citizens the state needs.[13]

Within six years Miss Sutherland succeeded in having her views enshrined in legislation with the Victorian Neglected Children's Act of 1887, extending the authority to apprehend neglected and brothel children to 'any person authorised by the Governor-in-Council' and providing for the registration of private persons or institutions 'desirous of taking charge of neglected children'. Licensed child rescuers were thus empowered to have children committed to them by the courts or to accept transfers of guardianship signed by a child's parents in front of a justice of the peace, powers not available in Britain until the passage of the Custody of Children Act in 1891.[14] In the parliamentary debate on the legislation, only one member demurred, arguing that this was 'an entirely new departure in legislation ... not ... in accord with what had hitherto been recognised as the principle of English law ... Provision should be made for the protection of parents' rights.' However, his doubts were quickly cast aside by the Attorney-General, Alfred Deakin, who cited Miss Sutherland's work as evidence of the good which would flow from the legislation.[15] While the Neglected Children's Department continued to deal with the children apprehended by the police and committed through the courts, private child rescuers could now venture out to 'save' children they believed to be at risk. Rather than what they depicted as the harshness of state care, or the regimentation of the established orphanages, they promised to bring to their young charges the loving care of the home, ideally through boarding them out with rural families but maintaining as well small receiving homes where a pseudo-family model prevailed.[16]

Prominent child rescuers promoted their cause through both the secular and religious press, reproducing stories from their English models transposed into a colonial context. For her supporters Selina Sutherland produced a regular newsletter, its title *From Dark to Dawn*, an unacknowledged reference to Barnardo's *Night and Day*. On a trip to England in 1897 she argued that the colonies had surpassed the mother country in their child rescue endeavour.

> Nothing short of a consuming fire from heaven, which will wipe London off the face of the earth, will do any good ... I have walked through your streets and your slums and seen them swarming with children as thick as bees in a hive. I have visited the houses where these children and their parents live. I have asked myself what future can these children have to look forward to. There is nothing for them but the same miserable existence in which they have been born and bred. For the men I do not care, but it is terrible to think of the fate of the women and children.[17]

However, this was somewhat of a misrepresentation for after an initial burst of enthusiasm Sutherland and her colleagues had abandoned active rescue, their services overwhelmed by children voluntarily surrendered by parents as a result of poverty-induced despair. Although in order to find a safe placement for their child such parents had to constitute themselves as neglectful, there is little evidence to support such an appellation. Only 13 per cent of the children admitted to care through the agencies with which Selina Sutherland was involved during the Depression of the 1890s were removed from unfit parents while 64 per cent were voluntarily surrendered by parents unable to provide for their care.[18] As the colony recovered economically child rescuers found that they were toiling in a different philosophical environment. Mass poverty had shaken faith in the assumption that vice or sin lay at the base of child abuse and neglect, constituting some parents as the 'worthy poor' who needed to be supported in caring for their children. Boarding-out payments were extended to mothers considered fit to have care of their own children, a practice which was to expand, despite official opposition, long after the Depression came to an end.[19] Parents approaching child rescue agencies became more assertive, negotiating voluntary placements which allowed them to have continued access to their children.

Child rescuers who denigrated parents in order to solicit public support found themselves subject to criticism, their emotional appeals ridiculed as self-serving.

> Here is a picture showing a ragged, despairing little outcast applying for admission to 'the homes' ... Here is a second picture showing 'how we get them,' and a third shows half a dozen little lads devoutly praying beside their beds 'in the home' prior to luxuriating between snowy sheets perfumed with lavender. The photographer has apparently just popped in unawares, and, with an eye for the melodramatic effect, has taken a flashlight snapshot.[20]

Yet, at the level of practice, the child rescue ideology remained remarkably unchanged. In a feature article published in the *Argus* in 1911 the Matron of the Neglected Children's Aid Society Home was still advancing the same gospel:

> What can you expect from a child who has only the worst examples and environment and no sort of restraint or discipline. There is only one possible course for him. But supposing you take that child at three years, and train him carefully, then place him in the country beyond temptation, with good surroundings, the chances are that he will prove a man of use to the community.[21]

Whatever the circumstances surrounding a child's admission to care the victim/threat duality continued to provide the rationale for future treatment. Parents who were not assertive, or, more commonly, not able to make regular payments, continued to be characterised at the very least as failures, their children as victims whose placement could be understood as 'rescue' long after licensed child rescuers had disappeared from the scene.

The impact of this understanding of the nature of child care continues to the present day. In a series of articles published in a Melbourne newspaper in April 1997, state wards from the 1950s and 1960s recalled emotional, sexual and physical abuse, including lack of food, regular beatings, inadequate medical attention and public humiliation. Separated from their families with their origins often obscured they talked of being 'robbed ... of ... [their] culture and family roots', denied an education and forced into menial employment at an early age.[22] 'Being a state ward,' Leonie Hewitt wrote,

> I feel like a second-class member of the community. I feel different, I have no sense of belonging to a family. I have no past. I feel rootless ... I sometimes

feel like an alien; that I was dropped out of the sky at the age of three and a half and that my life only began then ... Why was I abandoned by my birth parents and extended relatives and left in the care of the state?[23]

Twenty years after the last of the large institutions had been dismantled, at a time when the major critique of existing child welfare systems is the failure of the state to protect children, the experiences of these wards were hard to understand. Arguments that this was the way it was in the 1950s, when resources were scarce and child psychology was little understood, were unsatisfactory responses to individual pain. It was easier to identify individual staff or organisations as aberrant, and deserving of punishment if the wrong was to be made right. Yet what was clear from the way in which these ex-wards formulated both their accusations and their claims for reparation was that they had some understanding that there was a systemic basis to their experiences, experiences which paralleled those of another group whose suffering had received recognition at much higher level, members of the Aboriginal Stolen Generation whose experiences were the subject of an official enquiry when these ex-wards raised their complaints.[24]

Aboriginal Child Removal Practices

The removal of Aboriginal children commenced with the arrival of Europeans, with individual 'orphans' being taken into the homes of white settlers well before the establishment of the first race-specific institution at Parramatta, outside Sydney, in 1814. Although some removals were built upon a curiosity factor, most were constructed as acts of charity, the opportunity to 'enjoy' the benefits of civilisation being compared favourably to the increasingly difficult lot of Aboriginal people both inside and outside the settlement.[25] The resistance of Aboriginal parents to parting with their children and a general hardening of racial attitudes in the colonies saw this language of charity increasingly specialised to become a language of rescue, in which the removal of Aboriginal children 'from their bad environments and parental influences' is posited as essential to the future of the nation.[26] The passage of Aboriginal Protection Acts in the various states in the early years of Federation transformed this widespread practice into official policy, with Protectors being given the power to act in place of parents for the Aboriginal children under their control.[27]

Officially the policy was applied to 'illegitimate children of not less than 50 per cent white blood' whose 'elevation' to the living standards 'of a white' was considered to be 'a matter of social and economic urgency',[28] but the decimation of the Aboriginal population in the course of European occupation, the prevalence of consensual and non-consensual cross-racial sexual relationships and the non-recognition of traditional marriage placed most Aboriginal children at risk. Although the love of Aboriginal mothers for their children was recognised, this was usually cast in animalistic terms, as something which dissipated as the child moved beyond infancy. A child removed at four or five, authorities believed, would quickly be forgotten.[29]

Although accurate statistics are hard to compile, the Stolen Generation Inquiry concluded that from 1910 to 1970 between one in three and one in ten Indigenous children were forcibly removed from their families. It concluded that no Indigenous family escaped the effects of forcible removal with most being affected in one or more generations.[30] Where states with small Aboriginal populations absorbed such children within the existing child welfare structures in New South Wales, Queensland, Western Australia, South Australia and the Northern Territory, separate institutions were established, some controlled by the Aboriginal Protection Boards and others by voluntary organisations.[31] Usually segregated by gender, they offered a minimal education designed to prepare the children to enter the workforce as farm workers or domestic servants. The move, in the 1950s, from institutional to substitute family care was also reflected within such separate child welfare systems with the various Boards advertising for foster and adoptive families for Aboriginal children, further promoting a policy of absorption into the white population where Aboriginality was denied and breaking up the residual sense of community which had been able to be maintained in the separatist institutions. Outside the Board's control large numbers of Aboriginal single mothers were coerced to part with their babies as new-baby adoption became common practice in the post-war years. Again the language was one of rescue, with benevolent white families lauded for their willingness to open their homes to children in need. Critical to the success of such placements was the breaking of all bonds between the child and its family of origin. Often, for the adoptive parents, this involved a denial of the child's Aboriginality as well.

The child removal policy, in its many guises, is increasingly being

positioned within an accusation of genocide as an essential con-
comitant of the European invasion.[32] Having eliminated most of the
Indigenous population through murder, poisoning, disease and starva-
tion in the process of taking possession of their lands, government
consistently under-resourced the reserves on which the survivors were
confined, creating the very conditions which were used to justify the
removal of the children, destined to be brought up in ignorance of
their Aboriginal culture. Buttressing such policies was the social
Darwinist belief that the 'real', that is 'full-blood', Aboriginal people
were destined to die out and that the interests of their mixed descent
children would be best served by maximising the white and therefore
superior side of their inheritance.[33] Yet the practice of removal was
seldom consistent with the promise, with too many children moving
from abusive institutional or family placement through to exploitative
employment, outsiders in a society intent on preserving its own
whiteness.[34] Ten per cent of children reported experiencing sexual
abuse in institutional care, a figure rising to 30 per cent for girls
placed in foster homes.[35] Genuine bonds of affection were discouraged,
children were deprived of any but the most basic levels of education
and were forced into menial employment.[36]

Historians of child welfare will recognise in such accounts much
that is common to other survivors of substitute care.[37] Where this
commonality is acknowledged in the Stolen Generation literature it
usually serves only as a base to argue for Aboriginal difference. The
'basic safeguards [which] protected the integrity of non-Indigenous
families and the well-being of non-Indigenous wards of the State',
the *Bringing them Home* report argues, 'were cast aside when it came
to Indigenous families'.[38] This distinction, Link-Up and Wilson
suggest, was the result of decision-making undertaken by 'untrained,
unqualified and unprofessional non-Aboriginal people' unlikely to
respect or inform Aboriginal mothers of their rights.[39] Such an argument
rests upon an imagined contrast with a qualified professional child
welfare service, which did not exist in Australia until the 1960s and
even then paid little regard to parents' rights.

A better explanation of the over-representation of Aboriginal
children among the victims of the child welfare system can be found
in an analysis of the way in which the criteria for entry into that
system were interpreted by professionals and non-professionals alike.
Here it was neglect or the likelihood of neglect which was central; yet
neglect does not exist in isolation but is always defined, by

practitioners if not by the law itself, in terms of its idealised imagined opposite. In a society which was unable to include slum dwellers within the category of mother, and later was to exclude almost all single mothers independent of their social class, racial difference, read as inferiority, combined with poverty to label all Aboriginal mothers as neglectful. Where, in the non-Aboriginal population, neglect had to be proved in terms of a series of material or moral standards, Aboriginal mothers were assumed to be neglectful unless they could prove otherwise.

> 'Neglect' was defined to include destitution and poverty was a constant feature of most Aboriginal people's lives. Aboriginal lifestyles, adopted from choice or necessity, such as frequent travelling for cultural activities or seeking employment, resistance to non-Indigenous control and child-rearing by extended family members were regarded by courts as indicative of neglect.[40]

Once within the system their children, similarly marked, were all too often predestined for failure, confined in under-resourced institutions,[41] or moved from placement to placement, with little expectation of change. The *Bringing them Home* report argues that the mass institutionalisation of Aboriginal children was evidence of a failure to provide care to contemporary standards, on the basis that the child welfare departments' acceptance of boarding out in the 1870s marked a decisive rejection of institutional care.[42] Such an argument ignores both the decline in boarding out in many states during the 1930s, and the survival of large-scale institutions, particularly for Catholic children, until well after the Second World War. The damaging experiences of Aboriginal children in care occurred independent of the location of care and related more to the way in which they were regarded by their carers.

> The consistent theme for post-removal memories is the lack of love, the strict, often cruel treatment by adults, the constantly disparaging remarks about Aboriginality – and the fact that the child should be showing more gratitude for having been taken from all that – and of course the terrible loneliness and longing to return to family and community.[43]

The survival of such attitudes beyond the demise of race-specific protective structures ensures that Aboriginal children continue to be over-represented among children in care and therefore disproportionately likely to incur the damage that such separation can entail.[44]

The Stolen Generation Inquiry gave this group of survivors a voice. Its recommendations, condemning Aboriginal child removal as a form of genocide and calling for apologies and reparation, have validated their experiences and recognised their pain. While the refusal of the government to issue a formal apology has prolonged the hurt, a widespread public sympathy as evinced in the rush to sign 'sorry books' in preparation for a national 'Sorry Day' suggests a substantial level of recognition of past policy as wrong. The legacy for those from whom children were removed is, however, still unresolved. The official explanation that children were removed for their own good or benefited from their removal reconfirms notions of the mother as the enemy of the child. This is a silence still to be addressed.[45]

Child Migration

A similar silence pervades debates around child migration where the concerns about the process by which children were separated from their families in Britain are conflated with allegations of physical and sexual abuse in the receiving institutions in Australia to construct a scenario in which child migrants become the descendants of the convicts, transported against their will.[46] In this scenario parents are reconstructed as victims who placed their children temporarily and were devastated to find them missing on their return. Trying to be sympathetic to the now elderly parents while also defending the practice of the child migration agencies, Barry Coldrey suggests that such accusations ignore the stigma surrounding illegitimacy in the immediate post-war years, arguing that the agencies tried hard to locate parents but most did not want to be found. 'Child migrants,' he argues, 'emanated from a chaotic lower class world where survival had to be the main objective.'[47] Yet child migration is really a late manifestation of the child rescue movement and needs to be under-stood within that historical context.

While child migration has a long history in Australia[48] most media attention has been focused on its final phase, the government-sponsored scheme that was an integral part of post-war reconstruc-tion. The enthusiasm of Australian child welfare authorities for the child migration scheme was in part a harking back to the child rescue ideal of the child who could be moulded in a new image without any threat of parental interference. This ideal remained as elusive as it had been in the past. From its very beginning this scheme was built upon a fundamental mismatch: Australia wanted young children to fill its empty spaces without threatening existing labour conditions, while the British sending institutions visualised a scheme in which young people, ready to go to work, could embrace the opportunities of Australia. It was a mismatch that was evident from the scheme's earliest days. Reporting back to the National Children's Home in London in 1951, Phyllis Dodman, secretary of Melbourne's Methodist Children's Home, noted, 'It does worry me that these young things, who seemed to expect to find our roads paved with gold, have found life here so different.'[49]

To the Australian government, child migration was an integral part of a plan to populate the country. Writing in June 1941 Federal Cabinet Minister F. M. Forde had argued,

> The war has shown us more vividly than ever that if we are to hold this country down the years we must increase our present population by several millions, at least, over the next thirty years … Of all immigrants, children are the most readily made into good Australians. They have no preconceived ideas. They will need careful nursing after the war. Australian food and sunshine will do the rest. In the demobilisation period, the child immigrants will not compete for jobs; they will not need family housing.[50]

Given the physical and social disruption which the war was bringing to Britain, it was generally assumed that there would be no problems with supply. The country had, after all, been exporting its excess children to the colonies for almost 300 years.[51]

It quickly became apparent, however, that the post-war child migration scheme was to be markedly different from these pre-war programmes. For the first time Australia was the petitioner, pleading with 'the Mother Country' to find children to send. Whereas, in the past, child migration agencies had concentrated on the 'opportunities' for the children, moving them quickly into employment and main-taining institutions only for reception and training, the new scheme had a wider net, including much younger children and allowing for an extended period of institutional care in order to introduce them to 'the Australian way of life'. Such children would fill beds left vacant as Australia recovered from war but participating organisations were also encouraged to add to their available accommodation, using federal government money to redevelop outdated facilities. The Commonwealth government was prepared to contribute one-third of the cost of any necessary capital improvement on condition that the state government and the participating organisation were prepared to fund the rest. Once the migrants had arrived, Commonwealth and state government contributions combined would provide seventeen shillings and three pence per child per week so long as they remained in school.

Such a promising offer, combining patriotism and profit, was difficult for voluntary agencies to resist. Add a dash of sectarianism and it became impossible.[52] As the Revd J. L. Watt argued at the Melbourne Anglican Synod in 1945, if '50,000 orphans were to come to Australia ... the clergy should see that the children of our Church were found Church of England homes'.[53] Drawing on sister organisations in the United Kingdom, 58 Australian child welfare organisations signed on to the scheme. The response in Britain, however, was not enthusiastic. The Australian government's sub-committee on child migration had been warned in early 1944 that Britain could no longer guarantee large numbers of child migrants. Most children in care had at least one surviving parent and the government was anxious to protect the few war orphans that did exist from being forced to make a decision that they might later regret.[54] The Australians, however, were not daunted by this news and planning continued apace, the 50,000 target unchanged.

Most participating organisations received a much smaller number of children than they had been hoping for, saw them to adulthood and assumed that any controversy surrounding the scheme had passed away. Over thirty years later, however, it burst again into the public arena with some of those brought to Australia under the child migration scheme accusing the British and Australian governments and the participating child welfare institutions of deception and neglect and seeking redress for the exploitation and ill-treatment they had experienced.[55] Many former child migrants believe that the process itself was unjust, denying them knowledge of their origins and depriving them of continuing contact with their families, too readily judged to be dispensable by institutional authorities. The documentation that accompanied the children was minimal and those who wanted to locate lost family had few clues to follow. Even in schemes which encouraged parents to follow their children, the transfer of guardianship, however short-term, meant that they had to prove their fitness on arrival in order to regain custody of their child.[56] It was one of many aspects of the scheme that tended not to be discussed by its enthusiastic promoters.

A second set of concerns about child migration centres around the treatment which the children received in their new homes. Those who had come from English cottage homes and children's villages felt lost in the large congregate care institutions of Australia, where staff continued to be employed on the basis of call or mission rather than any child-care expertise. Within such institutions migrant children were particularly harshly treated, Gill suggests, as a result of a reverse racism, abused as the 'scum' of the British working class.[57] To Coldrey, the explanation lies more in the personalities of the children themselves, an emotional vulnerability which resulted from the multiple deprivations of their past.[58] While the allegations of abuse tend to focus on a small number of Roman Catholic institutions there would be no institution which could comfortably assert that it did not have similar skeletons in its past. Located outside the supportive networks which formed among residents, differentiated from them on the basis of accent and, most importantly, with no regular visitors from outside the home likely to be interested in their fate, child migrants were highly vulnerable to such institutionalised abuse.

Conclusion

This chapter has argued that the two sets of concerns that activated child migrants are common to all the self-identified victims of child welfare practices of the past because they share a common origin in a child rescue ideology which identified the parent as a danger to the child. This belief justified both the original removal and the disregard of any need for further contact. While increasing levels of affluence and social assistance in the non-Indigenous population reduced the numbers on whom such policies impinged, and opened space for negotiated, temporary placements, they further stigmatised parents who 'failed', leaving them ill-equipped to maintain or negotiate contact, and providing no motivation for those who provided care to sustain such links. Children thus absorbed into the child welfare system were left with no one to speak in their defence.

At its best, institutional care provided the equivalent of a boarding school experience for an otherwise destitute child. At its worst, it was a mismatch of disturbed and disturbing children and staff that created a hell on earth. For most, the experience was somewhere in between, but a system that positioned the staff as benevolent left no space for the child to be anything but grateful. The child rescue philosophy constituted children not as citizens but as recipients of charity, objects of mission to have good works done to them, to be traded or given away or employed for the good of the nation/parent.

In the debate consequent upon the accusations of abuse which have formed the basis of this chapter, history has played a dual role, engaged both to uncover and to explain the practices of the past. As such it has sometimes served as a barrier to claims for compensation with the argument that treatment which was standard for its time should not be condemned with the wisdom of hindsight, just as it has been used very effectively to argue for compensation by demonstrating that the treatment was aberrant even for its time. Both of these arguments, however, assume that the practices being condemned can be safely confined to the past. This comfortable assumption needs to be questioned. The institutions may be gone but the factors that allowed mistreatment survive in the smaller residential structures which replaced them. Any institution that places adults in charge of vulnerable children has the potential to become abusive.

At the same time the retreat of the state from a duty of care, in the face of a discourse of individual rights, sees the number of homeless children rising to unprecedented levels. Arguments for the benefits of deinstitutionalisation, individual contracts and self-determination do not disguise the fact that the future for such young people, in a climate of high unemployment and increasing drug use, is grim. While the demand for inter-country adoption makes it clear that the appeal of child rescue is far from dead, the street children of today do not have the sentimental appeal of their nineteenth-century forebears. The original goals of the child welfare movement were both idealistic and disciplinary, based on a desire to 'rescue' the children of the 'dangerous' classes and to prepare them for active citizenship in the democratic nation. The movement attracted first the moral and later the financial support of government because these goals were shared – the nation could see the value of maximising its productive workforce. Economic change has eroded much of this shared value base, reducing the need for the future labour of young people and returning them again to the category of a 'dangerous class' needing to be contained. Voluntary agencies used to designing programmes to 're-establish' 'disoriented' young people into an essentially benevolent society now aim to give alienated youth the skills to survive in a community which accords them little value.[59]

Such developments do not bode well for services to children and youth in Australia. The individualistic ideologies which underlie current government policy do not encourage or endorse a discourse of shared responsibility for community well-being. Yet unless a community is ever-vigilant, listening and watching for signs of distress, children will remain at risk. We need to analyse current as well as past child welfare systems with a critical rather than a self-congratulatory eye, recognising that good works can simultaneously countenance evil and arguing against attempts to use history to condemn the past in order to endorse a complacency about the present.

Notes

1. Although their experiences intersect with those of the other survivor groups, adult adoptees are not included in this paper. For a discussion of the scope and impact of adoption in Australia see S. Swain with R. Howe, *Single Mothers and their Children: Disposal, Punishment and Survival in Australia*, Cambridge, Cambridge University Press, 1995, ch. 8.

2. I. Pinchbeck and M. Hewitt, *Children in English Society*, vol. II, London, Routledge and Kegan Paul, 1973.

3. A. Platt, *The Child Savers*, Chicago, University of Chicago Press, 1969.

4. R. van Krieken, *Children and the State*, Sydney, Allen and Unwin, 1991, p. 17.

5. H. Cunningham, *The Children of the Poor: Representations of Childhood since the Seventeenth Century*, Oxford, Blackwell, 1991, p. 9.

6. These founding stories are widely used in celebratory accounts of child rescuers and their work. See, for example, M. Weddell, *Child Care Pioneers*, London, The Epworth Press, 1958; G. Wagner, *Barnardo*, London, 1979.

7. Wesley Church, Melbourne, Home Mission Society, Annual Report, 1890, p. 66.

8. C. Stansell, *City of Women: Sex and Class in New York, 1789–1860*, New York, Knopf, 1986, p. 208.

9. Van Krieken, *Children and the State*, p. 80.

10. For a short biography of Selina Sutherland see S. Swain, 'Selina Sutherland: Child Rescuer', in *Double Time: Women in Victoria – 150 Years*, ed. M. Lake and F. Kelly, Melbourne, Penguin, 1985, pp. 109–16.

11. *From Dark to Dawn* 1(14), 1 March 1898. *From Dark to Dawn* was issued by Selina Sutherland's Victorian Neglected Children's Aid Society.

12. *Argus*, 15 November 1890.

13. *Argus*, 13 March 1897.

14. D. Jaggs, *Neglected and Criminal*, Melbourne, Centre for Youth and Community Studies, Phillip Institute of Technology, pp. 53–55. In the neighbouring colonies of

New South Wales and South Australia, child savers were incorporated into the statutory child welfare system at a policy level with legislation in the 1880s establishing advisory boards which included both prominent child rescuers and government officials. These boards had authority over child welfare departments but did not argue for voluntary child rescuers to be given powers of intervention. B. Dickey, 'The Evolution of Care for Destitute Children in New South Wales, 1875–1901', *Journal of Australian Studies* 4, June 1979, p. 43.

15. *Victorian Parliamentary Debates* (VPD), Vol. 55, Melbourne, Parliamentary Printer, 1887, pp. 974–75.

16. R. Howe and S. Swain, *All God's Children*, Canberra, Acorn Press, 1990, ch. 2.

17. *Age*, 1 August 1897.

18. S. Swain, 'The Victorian Charity Network in the 1890s', PhD thesis, University of Melbourne, 1977, p. 391.

19. Widows and deserted wives, supporting at least two children by their own efforts, were allowed to apply to have subsequent children boarded out to them through the Neglected Children's Department. By the 1920s this practice had become so widespread that the requirement of having children made wards in order to qualify was removed. In the 1930s eligible women were granted an additional payment in recognition of their own needs, the forerunner of the widows' pension introduced by the Commonwealth government during the Second World War.

20. *Age*, 7 August 1905.

21. *Argus*, 17 June 1911.

22. *Age*, 16 April 1997.

23. *Age*, 18 April 1997.

24. The National Inquiry into the separation of Aboriginal and Torres Strait Islander children from their families was undertaken by the Human Rights and Equal Opportunities Commission at the request of the Australian Government. It held hearings around Australia, beginning in 1995, and reported in 1997.

25. *Bringing them Home: National Inquiry into the Separation of Aboriginal and Torres Strait Islander Children from their Families*, Canberra, Commonwealth of Australia, 1997, pp. 27–28.

26. New South Wales (NSW) Board for the Protection of Aborigines, 1883, quoted in Link-Up (NSW) and Tikka Jan Wilson, *In the Best Interest of the Child? Stolen Children: Aboriginal Pain/White Shame*, Aboriginal History Monograph 4, Sydney, 1997, p. 50.

27. Aboriginal people were designated as a state responsibility in the federal constitution (as was child welfare). However, despite differences as to timing and practical details, child removal policies were remarkably consistent across the country. For NSW the transition from practice to policy takes place with the Aborigines Protection Act of 1909, although this still required the Aborigines Protection Board to seek a magistrate's order under the Neglected Children and Juvenile Offenders Act, 1905 before removing a child. For details of co-operation between the two bureaucracies see Link-Up and Wilson, *In the Best Interest of the Child*, pp. 52–53. The Act was amended in 1915 to free the Board of the need to take the child before the court.

28. Northern Territory policy derived from 1931–32 report of the Chief Protector of Aborigines, quoted in Link-Up and Wilson, *In the Best Interest of the Child*, p. 17.

29. Link-Up and Wilson, *In the Best Interest of the Child*, p. 18.

30. *Bringing them Home*, p. 37.

31. In all of these states Aboriginal children were also removed via the child welfare system, particularly those of lighter skin colour deemed to be more assimilable.

32. This has been the most controversial finding of the stolen children inquiry. *Bringing them Home*, pp. 270–75.

33. Link-Up and Wilson, *In the Best Interest of the Child*, pp. 33–35.

34. Only 25.1 per cent of witnesses before the inquiry had experienced one institutional placement, and 14.3 per cent a single family placement, the rest moving through several different placements during their time in care. *Bringing them Home*, p. 153.

35. *Bringing them Home*, p. 163.

36. *Bringing them Home*, pp. 169–72.

37. See for example the account of the isolation of bed-wetters in *Bringing them Home*, p. 84, which parallels closely the accounts of Victorian state wards from the 1950s. *Age*, 16–18 April 1997.

38. *Bringing them Home*, p. 252.

39. Link-Up and Wilson, *In the Best Interest of the Child*, p. 37.

40. *Bringing them Home*, p. 47.

41. Aboriginal-specific institutions were funded at a much lower level than government institutions for non-Aboriginal children, but even within the general child welfare system Aboriginal children tended to be placed in remote or under-resourced institutions. Well-resourced institutions were rare and tended to be used for children assumed to be best positioned to benefit from their 'advantages'. *Bringing them Home*, p. 159.

42. *Bringing them Home*, p. 262.

43. *Bringing them Home*, p. 159.

44. Link-Up and Wilson, *In the Best Interest of the Child*, ch. 5.; *Bringing them Home*, part 6.

45. Link-Up and Wilson, *In the Best Interest of the Child*, pp. 26–27.

46. A. Gill, *Orphans of the Empire: The Shocking Story of Child Migration to Australia*, Sydney, Millennium Books, 1997, pp. 6–7.

47. B. Coldrey, *Child Migration: Consent of Parents to their Children's Emigration: The Legal and Moral Dimension*, Manning, Tamanaraik Press, 1996, p. 2.

48. Gill traces schemes dating back to the 1830s designed to remove poor children from Britain and relocate them in the Australian colonies (*Orphans of the Empire*, pp. 36–50).

49. Miss Dodman to Miss Coleman, National Children's Home, 5 April 1951, National Children's Home Archive.

50. Quoted in B. Coldrey, 'Child Migration: Governments and Churches, Politics and Practice, 1920s to the 1960s', unpublished conference paper, September 1992, p. 7.

51. The greater distance involved in the trip to Australia served as a major deterrent in the early years but the decision of the Canadian government in the late 1920s to restrict entry swung the balance in Australia's favour. The story of Britain's long history of child emigration is told in G. Wagner, *Children of the Empire*, London, Weidenfeld and Nicolson, 1982.

52. Coldrey argues that sectarian rivalry provided the primary motivation for Catholic agencies to become involved in the scheme ('Child Migration', p. 4). The Methodists, Howe and Swain argue, were more moved by the promise of financial aid and long-stay children which the scheme promised (*All God's Children*, pp. 63–65).

53. *Church of England Messenger*, 19 October 1945.

54. Coldrey, 'Child Migration', pp. 11–12.

55. These accusations are best summarised in P. Bean and J. Melville, *Lost Children of the Empire: The Untold Story of Britain's Child Migrants*, London, Unwin Hyman, 1989, ch. 10.

56. These schemes have been little discussed in the existing child migration literature but were an integral part of the Commonwealth government's post-war migration scheme. The Anglican Council for Empire (later Commonwealth) Settlement which operated from the 1940s through to the 1960s, for example, offered assisted passages to supporting mothers and their children with the children offered institutional placements while their mothers established themselves in Australia.

57. Gill, *Orphans of the Empire*, p. 72.

58. B. Coldrey, *The Scheme: The Christian Brothers and Childcare in Western Australia*, O'Connor, Argyle-Pacific Publishing, 1993, p. 393.

59. Compare for example the views outlined in the report of the Church of England Boys' Society–St John's Hostel Committee of September 1977 with those of the St John's Home, Annual Report, 1989. St John's Home Archives.

6

Changing Childhoods:
Child Emigration since 1945

Kathleen Paul

In 1967, a small party of children accompanied by an escort departed Southampton docks. Their destination was Australia, although in the past they could just as easily have been travelling to Canada, New Zealand, South Africa, or Southern Rhodesia. Although the children could not understand the importance of this moment, their departure constituted the last gasp of a vast historical process, a process in which children had played a leading role. For over three hundred years, both British and Dominion governments and voluntary societies had assigned child emigrants – children sent abroad without family members to be boarded out or placed in orphanages upon arrival – a particular space within the practice of imperial migration. To the British government the children represented links in an imperial chain, sent to the 'outposts of Empire' in order to help bind the whole ever tighter; to the Australian government the children were demographic assets, imported to help populate the 'vast country'; and the British charities, in whose care the children travelled, saw in their departure the transformation of 'problem' children into worthy imperial citizens.

In recent years, the policy of child emigration has come under attack in the United Kingdom and Australia, with the greatest condemnation being reserved for the dispatches of the post-war period. Sensationalist newspaper headlines portraying 'the bitter legacy of child trafficking' and the story of 'exiled orphans seek[ing] lost families' have focused on the consequences of emigration for the children involved while suggesting that the number of children sent reached into the tens or even hundreds of thousands.[1] This chapter takes a different starting point, exploring not the consequences of child emigration but rather the reasons behind the policy's origin and decline. It also proposes that the suggested figures of tens of thousands of child emigrants are seriously misleading and that a more realistic assessment suggests that, in the twenty years after 1945, just under 3,000 of Britain's youngest citizens emigrated to other parts of the Commonwealth.

The practice of sending children from Britain to parts of the Empire/Commonwealth can be traced back to the early decades of the seventeenth century, but the numbers really began to rise in the latter part of the nineteenth century.[2] At that time, as sea travel became less expensive, and as the Dominions of Canada, Australia, South Africa and Rhodesia began to assume independent national identities within the Empire, so voluntary societies began to look afresh at the possibilities of child emigration. In some cases, such as Barnardo's, the voluntary society already existed to serve deprived children in Britain; in other cases, such as Fairbridge, the society was created solely in order to send children abroad. Whatever the origins of the particular society, however, the impulse and expectations were broadly similar.

By 'transplanting' children from Britain to the Dominions, societies hoped to cut them off from 'the entail of frustration and hopelessness which had brought low so many of their parents' and thereby offer them 'a new start in a new land'.[3] Assumed to be beneficial to the child, this removal also benefited the sending and receiving countries. For removed from Britain were children who would likely have become paupers and whose 'presence would inevitably have added to the serious complications with which the country was wrestling'.[4] Received by the Dominions, however, were children who would constitute 'a body of healthy, alert young people taught to respect lawful authority'.[5] This shift from potential paupers to worthy citizens was not a paradox but rather represented the very essence of the voluntary societies' programme. Relocating vulnerable children before they had succumbed to the inexorable criminal temptations wrought by poverty and family circumstances, emigration was the first and necessary step in the re-formation of the child's identity. Integral to the voluntary societies' practice was their collective belief in the transformative properties of the rural ideal. Where the cities of Britain were dirty, overcrowded and unhealthy so the farmland of the Dominions was clean, under-populated and regenerative. Thus, physical transplantation was to effect a spiritual transformation as actual and potential juvenile delinquents metamorphosed initially into deserving child emigrants and ultimately into worthy adult citizens. Essential for the future of the individual, beneficial to both the sending and receiving countries, child emigration was also critical for the future of the Empire, since there was 'general agreement as to the necessity for sending fit and able citizens of the Motherland to the sparsely-occupied spaces of our great Dominions overseas'.[6]

Such conviction on the part of the voluntary societies, and the assistance of British and Dominion authorities, resulted in a steady flow of emigrant children from the late nineteenth century through to the outbreak of the Second World War. A number of organisations managed this flow, with some, such as Barnardo's and the Roman Catholic Church, emigrating children already in care, while others, such as the Fairbridge Society and the Northcote Fund, emigrated children directly from their families. Until 1924, the vast majority of these children, and indeed those in the care of other societies, travelled to Canada, but with the Canadian government's decision in that year to forbid the immigration of children under the age of 14 without an accompanying relative, voluntary societies shifted their focus towards Australia.[7] At the same time, the British government, determined to build up the British populations overseas as a source of strength for the Empire, introduced legislation providing for financial assistance for adult and child emigration to the Dominions. As a result, by 1940, eight different voluntary societies operating 38 separate institutions were involved in the emigration of children to Australia and all, under the auspices of the Empire Settlement Act, received both capital and maintenance grants from the British government to help defray costs.[8]

With the outbreak of the Second World War, all child emigrant societies suspended their operations for fear that the emigrant ships might fall victim to German torpedoes. Just as the actual practice of emigration ceased, however, so Australian authorities, particularly at the national level, took a renewed interest in the idea. As a result, in December 1944, the Australian government announced its intention of accepting 50,000 child emigrants over the first three post-war years, of whom it hoped that the greater part would be British.[9] Australian authorities saw the post-war period with its 'greater number of orphans, stray children, "war babies", etcetera' as 'a time of unparalleled opportunity for Australia to build up her population with child migrants who, on account of their easier assimilation, adaptability, long working-life ahead and easier housing, constitute a particularly attractive category of migrant'.[10] New Zealand soon followed suit, offering a home to any British child orphaned by the war.[11] Several months later the Australian government again made clear that child immigrants – 'the best immigrants of all' – constituted an essential element in Australia's long-term demographic planning by contributing capital grants to voluntary societies to help finance the provision or remodelling of buildings designed to house additional child migrants in Australia.[12]

In the light of this official Australian encouragement of child emigration, the voluntary societies in the United Kingdom planned, with varying motivation, for the resumption of their pre-war schemes.[13] The Catholic Church, both in the UK and Australia, appeared bent on ensuring both that the 'thinly populated land' of Australia received its fair share of Catholics, and that children of unsuitable parents were placed at such a distance from them that the parents could not interfere in the child's life.[14] Barnardo's claimed that emigration was 'in the best interests not only of the State, but of the suitable child' and offered 'excellent openings to boys and girls of intelligence', while the National Children's Home and Orphanage, a newcomer to child emigration, emphasised the wide range of employment opportunities available.[15] This range differed markedly from pre-war schemes which, whether through established practice in Canada or by order of the government in Australia, had restricted child emigrants to employment as farmhands or domestic service workers.[16] Before re-opening their schemes after 1945, however, voluntary societies obtained an assurance from the Australian government that all child emigrants would be free to choose any occupation for which their talents and intelligence suited them.[17] While this reassurance might have helped the voluntary societies 'sell' their schemes to prospective emigrants or parents, more important to the schemes' revival was the commitment on the part of the British and Australian Federal and Commonwealth governments to contribute towards the cost both of each child emigrant's passage and individual maintenance through the age of 16.[18] Even with this agreement, however, a lack of available shipping delayed the first departures until 1947, but in that year the voluntary societies collectively sent 415 children under the age of 16 to Australia. 1,060 additional children followed over the next four years.[19]

The re-opening of the child emigration schemes did not win universal approval. Indeed, the influential 1946 Care of Children

Committee (the Curtis committee) even went so far as to question whether the sponsored departure of children 'of fine physique and good mental equipment' (the type most preferred by host nations) was to Britain's advantage and recommended instead that emigration should be restricted to children 'with an unfortunate background' in greater need of a fresh start.[20] While it did not go so far as this, the 1948 Children Act, which drew much of its content from the Curtis committee, did contain provision for the possible regulation of child emigration by the Home Office. The voluntary societies responded to the government's threat of control by forming what was to prove one of the most significant developments in post-war child emigration – the Council of Voluntary Organisations for Child Emigration. Established in early 1951, the Council enabled the 15 child emigrant societies to speak 'with one voice' for the promotion of child emigration, to pool resources between societies, to facilitate relations with government departments, and to counteract those who objected to child emigration.[21] More succinctly, voluntary societies formed the Council in an attempt to control the process by which regulations might be made, and to work towards increasing the number of children emigrated each year. Once formed, the Council instituted what amounted to a public relations campaign in favour of child emigration.

The Council began by meeting with representatives of both the British Home Office, the department responsible for children prior to emigration, and Australia House, the body responsible for accepting children as emigrants. In both cases, the Council urged that the voluntary societies should retain maximum flexibility in their operations, being allowed effectively to draw up their own policies and practices while limiting governmental influence to the provision of financial assistance. Specifically, the Council tried to win the approval of Australia House for the emigration of children whose parents planned to follow them, claiming that if parents believed themselves to be giving up their children permanently, recruitment would decline significantly.[22] During their discussions with the Home Office, Council members also sought to influence the character of the regulations likely to be brought in by the government. The Council argued against the need for a statutory period of pre-emigration training, for example, on the grounds that while the Home Office might think such a period necessary in order 'to give the child some idea of the conditions and life overseas', the resultant delay between selection and departure would only be 'unsettling' besides imposing a financial burden upon the smaller societies. The Council also argued for elasticity in terms of age and placement, claiming that emigrant children of all ages could be housed in a variety of settings, ranging from homes in private families, to small cottage homes and larger residential centres. Council members also emphasised the care with which they already approached the selection process: children were chosen only after a thorough review of their case histories, no child was emigrated against its will, and, where possible, the emigration was arranged with the 'fullest co-operation of the parents or ... guardians'. Council members were equally eager to assure the Home Office that the resettlement process was already operating efficiently and for the good of all children. Thus, Council members outlined the importance of employing staff suited by 'experience and temperament' for child-care work, the central role of religion in the Australian homes, and the importance of ensuring that emigrant children received the same opportunities as local children, and became 'acclimatized to the life of the community'. And finally, the Council collectively reassured the Home Office that it accepted the need for a detailed scheme of after-care, carried out by 'experienced officers' who could ascertain a child's individual 'capabilities and desires'.[23]

In addition to trying to control arrangements within the *process* of child migration, the Council attempted to control *perceptions* of child migration. Within months of its formation, the Council agreed to produce 'an attractive pamphlet' about child emigration, helped create a display on child emigration for the windows of Australia House, discussed making a film of child migrants, and arranged for emigrant children to enjoy a 'farewell tea-party' immediately prior to departure. These tea-parties were attended by the societies' top officials, high-ranking representatives of both governments, and perhaps most significantly, members of the press. As a result of this last initiative, post-war newspapers regularly included features and photographs of child emigrants, invariably presenting the children as fortunate youngsters offered the wonderful opportunity of a fresh start in a new land.

The cumulative effect of the Council's representations was to present an image of child emigration as an extremely well-ordered, efficient process which existed only for the benefit of the child. The reality was not quite so clear-cut. In many cases, although the original inspiration for child emigration appeared to stem from the conviction that it offered children a fresh start, once the schemes were in place, the voluntary societies sometimes appeared to focus more on getting enough children to fill the vacancies in Australian homes rather than upon ensuring that emigration was the best possible option for each child sent. One official at Australia House even suggested that organisations sometimes 'deliberately' withheld information about children in order to get them accepted for emigration, or at the very least frequently did not investigate each child's circumstances thoroughly enough.[24] In another case, Home Office officials suspected that one child had been put forward for emigration by his local authority Children's Officer in part because he was 'difficult', making the officer 'uncertain how to plan for his future'.[25] Likewise, although the voluntary societies liked to suggest that only the best children were chosen for emigration, one Home Office visit to a group of children awaiting emigration produced the conclusion that the children represented 'a definite scraping ... of the bottom of the barrel'.[26] Finally, while the voluntary societies emphasised the care given to the children while en route to Australia, the Home Office questioned the use of apparently unskilled escorts for the six- to eight-week sea crossing.[27]

Despite this inconsistency between appearance and reality, two factors ensured that child emigration continued to receive the blessing of successive Australian and British governments. First, the Australian government persisted in its belief that with regard to migrants, it was a case of 'the younger, the better'.[28] To this end, Australia House advertised child emigration possibilities in the British press, and complained repeatedly that not enough children were being sent, even to the point of asking Prime Minister Macmillan in 1958 to do his best to send more child migrants.[29] Second, the British government remained firmly committed to the practice of sponsored adult emigration. From 1946 to 1962 an average of 125,000 people annually left the United Kingdom for destinations elsewhere in the Empire/Commonwealth. Many of them did so in receipt of free or assisted passages paid for by the British and Australian governments. All of them did so under the umbrella of official encouragement. For throughout the post-war period, successive British administrations made clear the importance of helping the Dominions 'remain British in blood and tradition' through the sending of 'British stock' to refresh, replenish and fortify the 'life-blood of the "old" Commonwealth countries'.[30]

Such official enthusiasm for adult departures facilitated those who believed that if adults were good migrants, children were better, especially since some in government circles believed that this class of children was the most likely, if left in the United Kingdom, to become a burden on the state, and that a child emigrant constituted less of a financial loss to the UK than an adult.[31] In opposition to this view were those, primarily based within the Home Office, who expressed particular concern about the institutional nature of care in Australia, and suggested that adoption in the UK or resettlement with some family member offered a better life for most 'deprived' children.[32] These doubts remained confined to a minority of policy-makers, however, and in light of a favourable report from a semi-official visit to the Australian homes in 1951, even the threatened regulations of 1948 failed to materialise.[33] As a result, the voluntary societies remained free to emigrate as many children as were available throughout the 1950s.

If the Council had succeeded in one of its primary objectives, however – heading off the threat of government regulations – it had not yet succeeded in the second – increasing the number of child emigrants. Although 193 children emigrated in 1955, the voluntary societies believed that this was too small a number and remained convinced that there existed huge numbers of children who would emigrate if only they were given the chance.[34] In reality, the flow of children was limited by the insistence of Australia House that not-withstanding its stated desire for child emigrants, it would not accept as suitable for emigration physically or mentally deficient children, or even those suffering from minor ailments such as squints. Nor, in accordance with its White Australia policy, would it accept 'coloured children' who by the mid-1950s comprised an increasingly significant element of children in care.[35] Although chafed by these restrictions, however, the voluntary societies remained convinced that it was the fault of the local authorities and county councils that so few children were available for emigration.

This suspicion about local authorities' reluctance to emigrate children was shared by Australia House, which, as a result, urged the Home Office to try to persuade local authorities to adopt a more favourable attitude towards emigration.[36] This the Home Office refused to do but it did agree to arrange a meeting between the child emigrant societies, Australia House, and the County Councils Associ-ation, if only so that officials in Australia House could hear for themselves why the local authorities refused to promote emigration.[37] As might have been expected, the meeting revealed three quite different perspectives. Australia House emphasised the vacancies existing in Australian institutions built or expanded with Australian government funds on the promise of future child emigrants who had not materialised, and explained the government's desire now to look to local authority children as a means of filling empty spaces. In response the local authority representatives explained that of the 50,000 children in their care, at least 40 per cent were already boarded out, 'surely the best way of dealing with the so-called deprived child', and 30 per cent were in care only temporarily or because of a need for special treatment as 'sub-normal' children. Of the remainder, the local authorities suggested that to send abroad 'those acceptable as physically and mentally fit would be denuding Britain', and was in any case unnecessary at a time of full employment.

In their belief that boarding out offered better opportunities than institutional care, and their suspicions concerning emigration as a solution for troubled children, the local authorities were echoing arguments which had been put forward almost a decade earlier in Canada. There, as Patrick Dunae recounts elsewhere in this volume, the Fairbridge Farm School ceased emigrant operations largely because its standards of child welfare clashed sharply with the newly rising class of university-educated social workers who deemed institutional child care a strategy of the past and resented the involvement of amateurs in what was becoming their professional field.[38] The appointment of Children's Officers in many British local authorities after the Second World War marked a similar trend within the UK with the result that many of the child welfare practices utilised by voluntary societies for decades past came under new and frequently critical scrutiny, and in the case of child emigration, attack.

Faced with this almost implacable hostility to the idea of emigration, the voluntary societies emphasised that the objects of their schemes were not children happily settled in the UK but children who 'because of broken homes, or other circumstances, would be better off in the Commonwealth'. For such children emigration had the added advantage of removing them from the unwanted attentions of undesirable relatives likely to place a claim upon earnings once the children started work. Council members also sought to reassure the local authority representatives that their organisations in Australia already practised many of the recommendations regarding child care made by both the Curtis committee and the 1948 Children Act. Despite their best efforts, however, Council representatives failed to win the local authorities over to the idea of child emigration. They were successful, however, in obtaining the County Councils Association's agreement to consider the question again, and in more detail, if provided with additional information regarding the children already settled in Australia and the arrangements available for those who might follow.[39] To this end, the voluntary societies agreed to complete a questionnaire drawn up by the local authorities and to participate in a 'Fact Finding Mission' to Australia. The idea of a 'Mission' to report on conditions for British emigrant children in Australia sprang partly from within the Home Office and partly from the Oversea Migration Board – a body appointed by the government to review general migration. It was the voluntary societies who most hoped to benefit by it, however, sure that it would produce a resounding endorsement of child emigration.[40] In the event, the Mission marked the first failure of the Council's public relations campaign.

Consisting of a former Home Office Under-Secretary, a former Deputy British High Commissioner to Australia, a local authority Children's Officer and a representative from the Commonwealth Relations Office (CRO), the Mission visited 26 of 39 Australian institutions for emigrant children. Taking as its starting point the conviction that for child emigration to be approved, standards and methods of care in Australia must at least be equal to those prevailing in the United Kingdom, the Mission also examined the process by which children had been sent abroad. Under this dual spotlight, both the work of the voluntary societies in the UK and their counterparts and branches in Australia fell far short of expectations.

The Mission found children ill-suited for emigration who had nevertheless been sent, and children whose behavioural difficulties, 'backwardness' and even 'physical defects' had been concealed by the sponsoring society. The Mission also told of brothers and sisters who though emigrated together had been sent to different institutions, of children disturbed by the separation from their parents still in the UK, and of children who did not understand why they had been sent abroad. Furthermore, many children were cared for by untrained staff incapable of helping the children to adjust to life in a new setting. In addition to these failings of personnel on both sides of the Pacific, the report found that the material conditions in which the children lived were of a generally poor standard. The majority of children resided in large institutions and even those resident in cottage-type accommodation spent much of their day in an institutional atmosphere lacking both amenities and privacy. Only one institution manifested a high standard of furnishings and decoration, with the majority demonstrating 'little or no evidence of any attempt to make the most of institutional premises', and two institutions falling 'far below a tolerable level'. Commenting on the assumption that children's alleged adaptability made them the best emigrants, the Mission found that the majority of the homes were situated in isolated rural areas, and doubted that the resultant segregation would do much to help children assimilate to Australian life and culture. And finally, the report questioned the very heart of child emigration policy. Hearing 'the widely held view that many children whom life had treated badly would benefit by transfer to a new country where they could be given a fresh start, away from old scenes and unhappy associations', the Mission countered with the opinion that 'it was precisely such children, already rejected and insecure, who might often be ill-equipped to cope with the added strain of migration'.[41]

Despite these negative findings, the Mission did not call for an end to child emigration but rather called for greater controls upon the process of selection and resettlement. Institutional care was to be replaced where possible with foster care, and where institutions remained they were to maintain adequate standards of comfort and amenities while employing more staff, particularly women, better trained in child care. In order to enable children to assimilate into Australian society, they were to be encouraged to be self-reliant and to mix with the local community and were not to remain in institutions beyond their childhood years. And finally, voluntary societies were to seek the approval of the British Home Secretary for each child suggested for emigration.

In spite of its acceptance of the continuation of child emigration, this published report was clearly damning of the work of the voluntary societies. Yet more damning were the confidential notes taken by the members of the Mission. On the whole the Mission found the homes to be rarely better than satisfactory and many were unacceptable. Children at Fairbridge Farm School in Molong, NSW, had 'to work hard and have no luxuries', girls at St Joseph's

RC home in Sydney 'appeared to lack spontaneity and initiative', and for boys at St Vincent's RC home in Perth, it was doubtful 'whether provision for even their physical welfare ... [could] ... be regarded as adequate'. The situation was even worse at Dhurringile Training Farm, Victoria, where showers and lavatories were 'inadequate in number and in poor condition', the sickroom was 'dark and cheerless', and the 'place bare, and comfortless'. Of St Joseph's in Bindoon, the Mission reported that it was 'hard to find anything good to say about accommodation, care or the appearance and demeanour of boys'.

Such criticism of the institutions to which child emigrants were sent, in addition to the questions raised about the mental and physical welfare of the children, could not but be a criticism of the practice of child emigration itself. As a result the CRO hoped not to publish such a 'hasty' report, believing that to do so would only 'put the cat amongst the pigeons' and might 'lead to such an outcry in this country against organized child migration, as to end or limit the activities of the voluntary societies'.[42] In general, the CRO was angry because they perceived the Mission as having 'exceeded its purpose' since rather than 'confining itself to finding facts ... [it had] ... taken upon itself the task of recommending government policy'.[43] After some debate, however, the CRO decided that the very publicity which had been generated in expectation of a favourable report made it difficult not to publish. To avoid as much publicity as possible, however, the CRO opted to publish the report in August, during the Parliamentary recess, rather than in April as originally intended.[44] This delay meant that voluntary societies remained unaware of the report's contents until they were handed copies in late July.[45]

In the intervening period, the CRO and the Home Office faced the question of whether to continue child emigration. The Home Office leaned towards a complete cessation but the CRO favoured stalling, not sending any children but not acknowledging that any ban was in place. The most obvious option – allowing selective emigration but avoiding the black-listed homes – was not taken for to have done so would have revealed the identity of homes deemed particularly unsuitable, and by association have brought the whole practice of child emigration into disrepute.[46] In the event, however, this stalling tactic was tested almost immediately since Fairbridge was in the process of sending 16 children overseas that summer. In order to avoid a 'rumpus' with Fairbridge, and more specifically with their president, HRH Duke of Gloucester, who might have raised questions in the House of Lords, the government opted to allow the children to sail, internally rationalising its decision because it was an 'exception to the current standstill policy'.[47]

In addition to the Fact Finding Mission, 1956 saw the publication of two other major reports on emigration. Each of these dealt primarily with adult emigration – the main focus of both the British and Australian governments – but each also contained a section dealing with child emigration. The internal Interdepartmental Committee on Migration Policy, consisting of senior civil servants, was the least accepting of child emigration, concluding that had it been 'untrammelled by precedent' it might not have recommended either child migration or the existing methods of operating it. As it was, however, the practice was well established, had had the support of both governments over the past 30 years, could count on 'influential support from churches and prominent laymen' and had probably benefited those children who had made use of it. The committee qualified its decision, however, by acknowledging that a 'strong public reaction' to the Fact Finding Mission demanding that child migration be ended might be enough to force the government to close down the schemes.[48]

The second report, presented by the Oversea Migration Board (OMB), was far more receptive to the prospect of continued child emigration and far more forgiving of the voluntary societies. This attitude showed most clearly in the Board's conclusion that requiring the Home Secretary's permission for each potential child emigrant, as recommended by the Fact Finding Mission, would only cause delay and might reduce the numbers available for emigration yet further. The Board also rejected the Mission's condemnation of the isolation of Australian homes, arguing that children could just as easily be assimilated into a rural community as an urban society, and that for young farmers, a rural setting was preferable. In general, the OMB accused the Mission of holding the voluntary societies in Australia to too high a standard, a standard not met in every children's home in the UK. The Board did accept, however, that in light of the Mission's findings, the conditions prevailing in existing Australian homes should be reviewed, but stipulated that in the interim government financial support for child emigration should continue, and in the long term be increased.[49]

For their part, the voluntary societies expressed disappointment in the Fact Finding Mission's report, rejecting the majority of its conclusions. Boarding out, for example, was deemed to be neither practical nor in the child's best interests, life in the countryside was healthy and full of opportunity, while the Mission's failure to take the success of former child migrants into account when assessing the conditions of current migrants undermined the value of the conclusions. Most importantly, however, the Council rejected the proposal that they should seek the Home Secretary's permission for each potential child emigrant, claiming that such a restriction would 'make it almost impossible to operate ... child migration schemes'.[50]

Faced with these quite different perceptions of child emigration, the CRO, and in turn the government, opted for a middle course. Accepting the major recommendations of the Mission with regard to selection and resettlement, the CRO refrained from introducing legislation to limit child emigration and opted instead to implement a non-legislative two-pronged strategy of damage control. First, the CRO relied upon the Australian government, which had undertaken its own far more forgiving inspection of the black-listed homes, to ensure that essential changes were carried out at the homes.[51] Second, the CRO adopted a carrot and stick approach toward the voluntary societies, attempting to bring them into line with the major recommendations of the Fact Finding Mission without actually mandating that they do so. Thus, reminding the Council that the Empire Settlement Act was due to expire in May 1957, the CRO made clear that, as had happened in 1948, it expected the debate surrounding the Act's renewal to include calls for the regulation of child emigration. The CRO assured the voluntary societies, however, that their position would be 'safeguarded' if Parliament could be told that the voluntary societies were co-operating with the government.

With this threat of control in the background, the CRO then laid out a new framework for the continuation of child emigration. First, voluntary societies were to show collective evidence of a general move towards placing future child emigrants in foster care with private families rather than in institutions. Second, where existing institutions remained, children were to be encouraged to assimilate into the local community. Third, each society was to submit details of its operations in Australia, including information on staffing, educational facilities, and job opportunities. Finally, a government representative was to be allowed to sit in on interviews with prospective child emigrants. In response to the voluntary societies' claim that they could not be responsible for Australian methods of child care, the CRO somewhat bluntly suggested that 'if Australia felt unable to accept the standards of child care which the UK Government now believed to be the minimum allowed here, then that would mean that they would not get children. The Organisations would not be able to send them.' In the face of such apparent determination, Council members accepted the new framework, including the commitment to move towards foster care. In return, the Empire Settlement Acts were to be renewed, no formal regulations were to be issued and voluntary societies retained some freedom of action by not having to seek the approval of the Home Secretary for each child emigrant.[52]

In spite of this new code of practice, however, the damage to the image of child migration had already been done. At a meeting in late December 1956, the County Councils Association voted against the implementation of child emigrant schemes for children in local authority care.[53] Explaining its decision to the Council, the Association identified the report of the Fact Finding Mission as having been an influential factor in its deliberations. Thus, the very group whom the voluntary societies had hoped to win over had turned resolutely against child migration as a direct result of what had looked like being the high point of the Council's public relations campaign.

From this point on, although small parties of children continued to emigrate to Australia, the practice of child emigration was clearly in decline. By 1959, only Barnardo's remained active in the field, hoping still to send up to 30 children a year to Australia. By contrast, the National Children's Home and the Catholic Church had withdrawn from the field entirely, the Church of England and Fairbridge had turned their attention to family migration, and the Salvation Army to youth migration, while Northcote was receiving 'practically no children at all' and expected to have to admit Australian children into the homes in the near future. In short, as the Fairbridge Society acknowledged in 1959, 'obviously child emigration was a thing of the past'.[54]

Much the same views were echoed in a government report two years later. Reporting that just under 3,000 children had been sent abroad since 1945, the CRO concluded that the voluntary societies had 'virtually outlived their usefulness' and that the institutional care for which the societies were famous 'should be the last resort for the child who cannot live with his own parents'. As proof of its assertions, the CRO noted that child emigration had declined significantly since the publication of the 1956 Fact Finding Mission's report, and that only 64 children had emigrated in 1960. Furthermore, only 20 per cent of the places available in Australian homes for British migrant children were occupied in 1960. Despite these findings, however, the report did not recommend the formal abolition of child migration schemes on the grounds that the societies' ability to count on the support of influential members of Parliament and the existence of published tributes to their work from successive Secretaries of State for Commonwealth Relations would make such a course difficult. It was better, according to the report, to continue the assistance, an ever-declining sum in any case, and allow the societies 'to die a natural death before long for lack of child migrants'.[55]

In the light of this prediction, and the voluntary societies' own observations in 1959, it is perhaps not surprising that this is precisely what happened. Perhaps fittingly, Barnardo's, long the most prolific child emigration society, remained committed to the practice the longest, sending out small parties of children throughout the early 1960s.[56] Even within Barnardo's, however, there was a split between Regional Officers, who had the most direct access to children, arguing against emigration, and members of the Board, far removed from direct child care, still advocating child emigration as general policy.[57] This policy changed only in the light of a 1967 internal report which, though in favour of continued emigration, revealed many short-comings in the existing system. Of a sample of 45 child emigrants, for example, the report estimated that only half could be seen as successful emigrations, while fewer than half the children could be seen as having been suitable for emigration in the first place. Emphasising the Australian homes' desire for more rigorous selection, the report stressed that all child emigrants should be stable, able to form new relationships, and capable of adjusting to a new country. Somewhat gloomily, the report noted that not all previous child emigrants had been so equipped. In addition, many former and current child migrants complained that they had been 'deceived' in their preparation for life in Australia and had emigrated expecting to 'ride to school on horses' and see kangaroos at every turn. The report made clear the need for more accurate pre-emigration training, and the importance of arranging emigration over a long period, both to avoid rushing a child, and to allow Australia to find the most suitable placement for each child. Finally, the report suggested that Barnardo's should be prepared to contribute to the cost of one visit 'home' to the UK by each child up to the age of 21.[58]

In spite of the fact that the report called for the continuation of child emigration so long as the recommended safeguards were put in place, Barnardo's officials concluded that while the supply of children was likely to be ever-decreasing, the suggested new selection pro-cedures would both be too time-consuming and too costly. More important than procedure, however, was the information that 'approximately fifty per cent of 45 cases of recent migrations ... could not be considered as reasonably successful'. In the light of this statistic, and bearing in mind the difficulties involved in attempting to continue child emigration, Barnardo's resolved 'that the organiza-tion of parties of children for migration should no longer be under-taken'.[59] Although Barnardo's remained willing to assist individual children to emigrate to live with relatives or friends, and to continue to offer the possibility of emigration to young adults, this decision effectively ended the practice of post-war child emigration. In the twenty years since it began approximately 3,000 children had emigrated, primarily to Australia, but also to New Zealand, South Africa and Southern Rhodesia.[60]

The importance of this last gasp of child emigration lies neither in its longevity nor the number of children sent but rather in the changed context surrounding its origin and demise as the meaning and consequences of child emigration changed dramatically from one century to the next. In the nineteenth century, facilities for rehabilitation, adoption or removal from a poor home environment were few. Under those circumstances, it is perhaps reasonable to suggest that emigration under the guidance of a voluntary society did offer some hope to some children, who, if left to their own devices, might well have succumbed to the 'entail of frustration and hopeless-ness which had brought low so many of their parents'. Likewise, the placing of children onto isolated farms for work as labourers or domestic servants must be understood in the nineteenth-century context where, becoming adult at 14, the majority of working-class children could expect to become labourers or domestics in Britain. In the same vein, successive British governments' sanctioning of the shipping off of thousands of its youngest citizens is not so shocking when one accepts that a relationship between state and citizen, with attendant rights and responsibilities, was only barely developed by the late nineteenth century. One hundred years later, however, with the institution of the welfare state, and the effective implementation of universal national citizenship, the societal framework of Britain was very different, and the object of the voluntary societies' attention had changed almost beyond recognition.

In the period after 1945, children were no longer merely little adults but rather young citizens worthy of special attention and care simply because of their youth. As a result, the concept of 'childhood' assumed a new importance as a stage in life to be defined, protected, and if possible elongated. The changing societal framework of twentieth-century Britain meant that responsibility for this care and protection had moved beyond the immediate family to the nation at large. Thus, whereas potential paupers of the nineteenth century were 'rescued' from the streets by voluntary societies, or given into their care by desperate relatives, in the years after 1945, the Home Office and ultimately local authorities assumed primary responsibility for deprived children. And whereas voluntary societies of the past were largely free to do with their children as they would, including the apparently radical option of pursuing emigration, local authorities tended to interpret their obligation to children in their care as being to minister to the child in Britain rather than to export him or her to another country. Indeed, in the light of the bountiful future promised by the new welfare state, those with direct responsibility for deprived children came to believe that a material transformation at home would replace the need for a spiritual transformation thousands of miles away. Thus, the post-war welfare state established elaborate child welfare services, including possibilities for family re-unification, fostering and adoption, improved medical and educational opportunities, and in general increased the range of possible solutions to the problem of deprived children. In short, the potential pauper of the nineteenth century had become a twentieth-century 'child in need'.

Paradoxically, at the same time as the protection of the country's children came to be perceived as a national obligation, and children to be seen as a population unto themselves, so those responsible for children came to see the relationship between a child and its immediate family as an essential element in the child's well-being. As a result, many children in care, including those in the care of voluntary societies, retained contact with family members, who, in the light of the increasingly broad array of options for deprived children, were increasingly unwilling to sanction such an apparently radical solution as emigration. In a similar vein, whereas in the nineteenth century children who came into the care of voluntary societies were seen as individuals, for whom a variety of options, including emigration, could be explored, by the mid-twentieth century even children who lived apart from all family members and were to all intents and purposes the responsibility of voluntary societies were increasingly perceived to be members of a larger family group and the focus of care began to shift from individual opportunity to family rehabilitation.[61]

If the changed position accorded to children in the post-war period limited the freedom of movement of the voluntary societies, it also constrained the activities of the British government. Whereas in the nineteenth and early twentieth centuries, the children had been used as 'mules' of culture sent to maintain the Empire as a British institution, and as demographic assets imported to build a Dominion, in the period after 1945 such treatment appeared outmoded and even improper. Interestingly, Australian officials were not so constrained and continued to believe both in the practice of child emigration and institutional child care long after both had lost favour in Britain. They were perhaps inspired to do so partly by a continuing belief in the rhetoric of rescue, if not from the nineteenth-century vice of poverty then from the twentieth-century terror of warfare, partly because child migration worked to Australia's advantage, and partly because the Australian welfare state and accompanying concept of social citizenship were only just developing. Whatever the reasons behind the disparity, however, the result was a clash of interests, so that although the Australian government continued to seek child emigrants, it became increasingly difficult for the British government first to promote and then defend the practice. And since it was Britain to whom the children initially 'belonged', it was Britain's prerogative not to give them up. Hence, unlike the Canadian schemes where it was changes in the receiving country which brought about the end of child emigration, the Australian schemes closed owing to changes in British child-care practice and outlook. As a result, over the course of the post-war era British government policymakers opposed to child emigration gradually won out over those in favour, and although legislation to abolish the policy was never introduced, successive governments did make significant inroads upon the practice. Equally influential in arresting the emigrant flow was the changed voice of the child. When child emigrant schemes first began, much of their trade relied upon volunteers; by the 1950s, voluntary societies were finding it increasingly difficult to muster sufficient enthusiasm among their charges to make up a feasible party. In effect, although not asked their opinion of emigration per se, by not volunteering to leave and therefore preferring to stay, children in care were voting with their feet to accept a changed understanding of childhood within Britain rather than a changed circumstance of childhood abroad. In the light of this fundamental shift in the perceived place of the child in British society, where children had moved from being seen and not heard within the family, to acquiring independent voices protected by the state, it is perhaps less surprising that post-war child emigration ceased in 1967 and more surprising that it survived for twenty years.

Notes

1. *The Times*, 23 July, 1997; *The Guardian Weekly*, 28 July, 1997. The most recent book condemning child emigration and suggesting a figure in the tens of thousands is M. Humphreys, *Empty Cradles*, London, Doubleday, 1995.

2. A. McVeigh, 'A History of Child and Juvenile Migration Schemes to Australia', unpublished PhD dissertation, Queens University, Belfast, 1995. See also J. Parr, *Labouring Children*, London, Croom Helm, 1980; G. Wagner, *Children of the Empire*, London, Weidenfeld and Nicolson, 1985; P. Bean and J. Melville, *Lost Children of the Empire*, London, Unwin Hyman, 1989; E. Hadley, 'Natives in a Strange Land: The Philanthropic Discourse of Juvenile Emigration in Mid-Nineteenth Century England', *Victorian Studies* 33(3), 1990, pp. 411–39.

3. D239/C2/6/3 Migration Policy 1945–65, 'Notes on Migration to Canada', A.E. Williams, 1951. University of Liverpool Special Collections and Archives (hereafter ULSCA).

4. D239/C2/6/3 Migration Policy 1945–65, 'Notes on Migration to Canada', A.E. Williams, 1951. ULSCA.

5. D239/C2/6/3 Migration Policy 1945–65, 'Notes on Migration to Canada', A.E. Williams, 1951. ULSCA.

6. D239/A3/1 Dr Barnardo's 62nd Annual Report, 1927, ULSCA.

7. D239/A3/1 Dr Barnardo's 60th Annual Report, 1925, ULSCA.

8. Public Record Office (hereafter PRO) DO35/4881 Report of the Inter-Departmental Committee on Migration Policy, 1956.

9. *The Times*, 12 December, 1944.

10. Select Committee into Child Migration, Western Australia Legislative Assembly, 1996, ULSCA.

11. *The Times*, 3 February, 1945.

12. LAB 13/96 Statement to the House of Representatives by the Minister for Immigration, A. A. Calwell, 2 August, 1945, PRO. Calwell identified the Pacific War as the single event which most convinced the government that Australia needed a larger population if it was to hold its territory in the face of future threats. D541/L3/1/3 Minutes of the Council of Voluntary Organizations for Child Emigration (CVOCE), Report of the Fact Finding Mission to Australia, March 1956, ULSCA.

13. The Big Brother movement, catering for the emigration of youths aged 16 to 19, also restarted its operations in the post-war period. Given the age range, however, and the boys' immediate placement into an independent work setting under the guidance of an Australian 'Big Brother', its rationale and clientele are not included in this chapter.

14. 12 July, 1945, Archbishop of Perth to Griffin, Archives of the Catholic Child Welfare Council, London; MH102/1884 Extract from report of visit to St Edward's (Boys) Home, Fr Hudson's Homes, Coleshill, 23 January 1953, PRO.

15. MH102/1894 8 February, 1949, Migration of Children of Dr Barnardo's Homes – A History, PRO. 15 D541/L3/3/11 Migration Overseas, Draft Copy of Reverend Litten's Address to the NCH Convention, 1954, ULSCA.

16. The failure of the Fairbridge Farm School in Vancouver to provide a wider range of employment opportunities ultimately played a part in the provincial government's decision to cease funding for the school. See Patrick Dunae's chapter in this volume.

17. D239/B1/13 Dr Barnardo's Council Minutes, 21 November 1945, ULSCA.

18. D541/L3/1/3 Minutes of the CVOCE, Report of the Fact Finding Mission to Australia. March, 1956, ULSCA.

19. D541/L3/1/3 Minutes of the CVOCE, Extract from the Moss Report, 1953, ULSCA.

20. LAB 13/835 Extract from Report of the Care of Children Committee (the Curtis Committee), Cmd. 6922. London, HMSO, 1946, PRO.

21. D541/L3/1/3 Minutes of the CVOCE 6 March, 1951, ULSCA. It was through discussion with a Home Office official that Sir Charles Hambro of the Fairbridge Society first conceived of the utility of a council. MH102/2037 Prestige minute, 14 November, 1950, PRO. The Council consisted of the following societies: Australian Catholic Immigration Committee, Dr Barnardo's Homes, Big Brother Youth Migration Movement, Catholic Child Welfare Council, Church of England Advisory Council of Empire Settlement, Church of Scotland Committee of Social Services, the Fairbridge Society, Middlemore Emigration Homes, National Children's Home, New Zealand Sheep Owners' Acknowledgement of Debt to British Seamen Fund, Northcote Children's Emigration Fund, Over-Seas League, Rhodesia Fairbridge Memorial College, the Salvation Army, YMCA Community Services. The vast majority of children emigrated to Australian institutions with a small proportion travelling to New Zealand foster homes, courtesy of the Over-Seas League.

22. D541/L3/1/3 Minutes of the CVOCE, Brief Notes of Informal Discussion at Australia House, 12 December, 1951, ULSCA.

23. D541/L3/1/3 Minutes of the CVOCE, Draft Letter to the Home Office, September, 1951; Delegation to the Home Office, 11 July, 1951, ULSCA.

24. MH102/2042 Note of a Conversation with Mrs Hunt (Australia House), 20 January, 1954, PRO.

25. MH102/2042 M. Glyn-Jones to Chief Inspector, 25 August, 1951, PRO.

26. MH102/2042 Extract from Mr Croft's Visit to John Howard Mitchell Home, 20 September, 1955, PRO.

27. MH102/2042 Minutes, J. M. Northover, 22 July, 1955, PRO.

28. D541/L3/1/3 Minutes of the CVOCE, Brief Notes of Informal Discussion at Australia House, 12 December, 1951, ULSCA.

29. D541/L311/3 Minutes of the CVOCE, Meeting with Noel Lamidey, 20 October, 1953; Lamidey to Hall, 19 February 1954, ULSCA; PREM 11/2419 Migration 1951–58, Macmillan Meeting with Australian Cabinet, 11 February 1958, PRO.

30. Kathleen Paul, *Whitewashing Britain: Race and Citizenship in the Post-War Era*, Ithaca, NY, Cornell University Press, 1997, p. 41.

31. DO35/6379 Annual Report of the Oversea Migration Board, 1954, PRO. Assuming an annual rate of 200 children per year, the Home Office estimated that emigration saved the state between £12,000 and £17,000 per year. DO35/4881 Report of the Interdepartmental Committee on Migration Policy, 1956, Annex: Savings to Public Funds Due to Child Migration, PRO.

32. LAB13/836 Inter-departmental Committee on Migration Expenditure, Emigration of 'Deprived' Children, Note by the Home Office, 1954, PRO.

33. MH102/2047 Minutes, 17 March, 1954; 29 June, 1954, PRO.

34. Second Report of the Oversea Migration Board, 1956.

35. D541/L3/1/3 Minutes of the CVOCE, 9 December, 1954, ULSCA.

36. MH102/2051 N. Lamidey to Sir F. Newsome, 18 January, 1954, PRO.

37. MH102/2051 A. F. Morley to C. P. Hill, 5 January, 1955, PRO.

38. See Patrick Dunae's chapter in this volume.

39. MH102/2051 Memorandum for Secretary of Immigration, 20 June, 1955, PRO. D541/L3/1/3 Minutes of the CVOCE, Notes of Meeting Between the County Councils Association Representatives and Members of the CVOCE, 9 June, 1955, ULSCA.

40. MH102/2051 Minutes, H. L. Oates, 8 August, 1955, PRO; Second Report of the Oversea Migration Board, 1956.

41. D541/L3/1/3 Minutes of the CVOCE, Report of the Fact Finding Mission to Australia, March 1956, ULSCA.

42. D035/6380 R. H. Johnson to G. B. Shannon, 28 June 1956; DO35/6382 Shannon to Sir S. Garner, 29 June, 1956; D035/6381 Fact Finding Mission to Australia, Departmental Note, no date, PRO.

43. DO35/6381 C. Costley-White to I.M.R. Maclennan, 7 April 1956, PRO.

44. DO35/6381 Shannon to C. Costley-White, 12 June, 1956, PRO.

45. D541/L3/1/3 Minutes of the CVOCE, 14 August, 1956, ULSCA.

46. D035/6382 C. G. Costley-White to Shannon, 18 June, 1956; C. G. Costley-White to Shannon, 5 June, 1956; Shannon to Garner, 29 June, 1956; DO35/6381 Shannon to Garner, 29 May 1956, PRO.

47. D035/6382 C. Costley-White to Shannon, 3 July, 1956; C. Costley-White to Shannon, 5 July, 1956, PRO.

48. DO35/4881 Report of the Interdepartmental Committee on Migration Policy, 1956, PRO.

49. Second Report of the Oversea Migration Board, 1956.

50. D541/L3/1/3 Minutes of the CVOCE, 14 August, 1956; Copy of a Letter sent by the CVOCE to the Permanent Under-Secretary of State, Commonwealth Relations Office, 13 September, 1956, ULSCA.

51. W35/6382 E. J. Bunting (Prime Minister's Department, Australia) to G. W. Tory (High Commissioner's Office, Australia), 10 September 1956, PRO. The accompanying British observer, however, agreed with the Fact Finding Mission, reporting, for example, that ablution facilities at Dhurringile were 'generally dirty' and 'inadequate' and that the Principal of St Josephs, Bindoon, appeared 'utterly callous and lacking in all understanding of child welfare'. DO35/6382 Report of R. H. Wheeler, Assistant Secretary, Department of Immigration, Canberra and J. V. Nelson, Children's Welfare Department, Victoria, Annexure C – Mr Rouse's Report (Rouse was the official from the British Embassy sent to accompany the Australians as an observer), September 1956, PRO; Illegible to Shannon, 22 January 1957, PRO.

52. D541/L3/1/3 Minutes of the CVOCE, Notes of Meeting at CRO, December 14, 1956; Minutes of meeting 31 January, 1957; D239/C2/6/49 Response to Fact Finding Mission, E. R. Sudbury to E. H. Lucette, 27 December, 1956, ULSCA.

53. D541/L3/1/3 Minutes of the CVOCE, W. L. Dacey to D. R. Hall, 31 January 1957, ULSCA.

54. D541/L3/1/3 Minutes of the CVOCE, 28 April, 1959, ULSCA. Only the Big Brother movement reported an increase in activities.

55. CAB129/107 C(61)201 1 December, 1961, British Emigration Policy: Memorandum by the Secretary of State for Commonwealth Relations, PRO.

56. D239/A3/1 Annual Reports, Dr Barnardo's, ULSCA.

57. D239/C2/6/49 L. Roundell to V. L. Cornish, 9 May 1967, ULSCA.

58. D239/B4/13 Three Weeks With Barnardo's in Australia, September 6 to September 27, 1967, ULSCA.

59. D239/B4/13 Minutes of the Meeting of the Standing Committee of Executive Officers, 22 May, 1968; 24 October, 1968 General Superintendent to Chairman, General Purposes Committee, ULSCA.

60. CAB129/107 C(61)201 1 December, 1961, British Emigration Policy: Memorandum by the Secretary of State for Commonwealth Relations, PRO.

61. D541/L3/1/3 Minutes of the CVOCE, Notes of Meeting with the Chief Migration Officer, Australia House, 20 October, 1953, ULSCA. LAB13/836 Inter-departmental Committee on Migration Expenditure, Emigration of 'Deprived' Children, Note by the Home Office, 1954, PRO.

III
Rethinking Philanthropy

7

From Barrack Schools to Family Cottages: Creating Domestic Space for Late Victorian Poor Children[1]

Lydia D. Murdoch

'The family system is the foundation of everything that is valued in our institutions. Our whole structure of society rests on it. Any attempt to rear children artificially on a wholesale principle, is necessarily defective, will prove abortive, and be attended, one way or another, with bad effects.'[2] So declared the journalist William Chambers (1800–1883) in his opening article for the 9 June 1877 issue of *Chambers's Journal*. His comments heralded a great change in public opinion about how government and philanthropic organisations should treat the children in their care. Chambers condemned the grouping of orphaned, deserted and pauper children in large residential institutions as artificial, and urged England to follow Scotland's more family-based programme of boarding out, or placing children with foster parents. Boarding out gained support in England during the 1870s and 1880s, but it nonetheless remained a limited solution, eventually used more by philanthropic societies than the state.[3] In England, the emphasis on family in state and philanthropic programmes for children took a different form. Institutions organised into 'family cottages' – each containing approximately 20 to 40 children who were cared for by foster 'mothers' and sometimes 'fathers' – became popular options instead. The cottages were arranged in model villages, such as the Girls' Village Home in Ilford, founded in 1876 by the child philanthropist Dr Thomas Barnardo (1845–1905), and the Kensington and Chelsea Poor Law District School at Banstead, opened in 1880. These family-based institutions quickly became the prevailing ideal for state Poor Law and philanthropic children's institutions in England, replacing in public favour the workhouse and large block-style residential schools, labelled 'barrack' schools by many for their militaristic structure. As Chambers hoped, the family system had become a model for teaching children social and political values. What was often overlooked, however, was that the cottage homes were not necessarily less artificially constructed than the barrack schools; the version of the family that they promoted was indeed a peculiar one.

This chapter examines the transformation from barrack schools to family cottages by focusing on the role that middle-class conceptions of the family, domesticity and domestic space played in late Victorian debates concerning institutions for poor children. It is an analysis of dominant discourses among Poor Law administrators, philanthropists and middle- and upper-class reformers regarding proper environments for poor children, rather than an examination 'from below' of how the working-class inhabitants of various environments associated these spaces with their own, often conflicting, meanings.[4] My study of poor children's institutional environments stems from inter-disciplinary work on the significance of space that has been developing since the 1970s. Integrating anthropological, architectural, geographical, historical, literary and psychological approaches, scholars have focused on the role of space as a mirror and a constituent of culture and society.[5] The examination of spatial arrangements is one means to approach not only cultural and social relations in a specific period, including class, race, and gender, but also past conceptions of the individual, the family and society as a whole.[6] The organisation of space also has direct political meanings. During the nineteenth century, as historians such as Leonore Davidoff, Catherine Hall and F. M. L. Thompson have demonstrated, notions of domestic space became associated with middle-class values and political ideologies.[7] Meanwhile, certain areas of the urban landscape were causally linked with anti-social behaviour: drunkenness, vagrancy, sexual immorality and political instability.[8]

I argue that reformers who supported model villages and family cottages for children used middle-class ideals of domesticity and domestic space as means to incorporate pauper children into the social hierarchy as labourers. Specifically, reformers asserted that poor children could develop individualism, perhaps the key component of liberalism, only within a recognised, disciplinary domestic space, such as the model village homes. At the same time, reformers described the urban dwellings of the poor as intrinsically undomestic and therefore unsuitable for nurturing individual subjectivity and civic identity in children. Thus, by the 1870s, social class had become a key factor in defining legitimate domestic spaces, family relations, and, in turn, citizenship. By citizen, the reformers meant an individual who accepted his or her role as a productive member of the social order, who was neither a threat to the state nor to established social relations. The first section of this essay briefly places the debates about poor children's institutions within the broad context of mid-to-late-Victorian public debates on working-class housing. I then examine the specific criticisms of barrack schools. The final section explores how reformers envisioned institutional model village homes and family cottages as a means of promoting a distinct form of liberal individualism based not on free agency but on maintaining one's ties to the community. Such institutions presented an organic view of English identity, meaning that the health or well-being of each part was dependent on all others, situated within a stable class and social order. Through the analysis of these topics, I hope to trace how notions of environment and domestic space were used to promote certain ideals of family, individualism and citizenship in late Victorian society.

The Undomestic Poor

Numerous scholars have examined how popular representations of the urban poor contributed to the idea that their very environment precluded all domestic life. The working-class home lacked the high degree of spatial segregation and the number of specialised rooms that were becoming so important to middle-class concepts of domesticity and individualism.[9] Children and adults, males and females, and even lodgers and family members mixed freely in the homes of the poor. As Felix Driver has noted, 'The poor were repeatedly said to be housed *en masse* in countless courts and back-alleys, without regard for distinctions of age or sex, and with little differentiation between rooms according to their function.'[10]

In addition to raising fears about the lack of specialisation within working-class houses, critics argued that these homes failed to provide a private haven distinct from urban industrial disorder.[11] Working-class homes seemed to contradict the late nineteenth-century distinction of public and private space as separate spheres with definite boundaries.[12] For example, the working-class home often served as a place for paid labour, or even living quarters for the family pig and other urban livestock, thereby blurring the boundaries between productive and reproductive space, as well as the separations between humans and animals.[13] Furthermore, as Anna Davin has thoroughly chronicled, working-class children ventured unchecked into streets and courtyards for recreation.[14] The homes of the urban poor were also conceptualised as being open to external influences – both 'the literal refuse from the streets' and the growing number of religious, sanitary and philanthropic district visitors.[15]

The supposed lack of private space in working-class neighbourhoods led some middle- and upper-class reformers to argue that it was impossible for poor families to develop any domestic life. The philanthropist Ellen Barlee wrote: 'Alas! in many of the abodes of the poor of our city, there is not space to raise the household hearth – no gathering the members of one family together under the sanctity of a common roof exclusively their own.' According to Barlee, these '*brutal*' physical living conditions prevented families from developing affection. 'Children are reared,' she claimed, 'hardly knowing, among the numbers that surround them, who are their kindred.'[16] Barlee argued that like animals, poor families 'herd together night and day, eating, drinking, sleeping in common' in unsegregated, unspecialised one-room dwellings that 'cannot pass under the name of home – it would be but desecration so to term it'.[17]

Many child reformers interpreted the alleged undermining of the domestic order in urban areas as a direct political threat to the state. Some suggested that poorly furnished, impoverished surroundings encouraged socialism and atheism, claiming that the worst of London's communal lodging houses were 'well laden with copies of the *British Workman*'.[18] Writing to *The Times* as part of the renewed attack on lodging houses resulting from the 1888 Whitechapel murders, Revd Lord Sydney Godolphin Osborne (1808–1889) used particularly strong language to draw a connection between housing conditions and political subversion. He declared that a growing proportion of the population lived under conditions leading to the 'utter subversion of the very commonest principles of civilisation'. Osborne contrasted the 'luxury and ease within homes ... surrounded with all that can promote civilised life' with the chaos and degeneration of the slums. In these areas dwelled 'tens of thousands of our fellow creatures begotten and reared in an atmosphere of godless brutality – a species of human sewage, the very drainage of the vilest production of ordinary vice'. '[S]uch sewage,' wrote Osborne, is 'ever on the increase, and in its increase for ever developing fresh depths of degradation.'[19] To Osborne and others, the enclosed, clearly demarcated space of the single-family home had become the essential foundation of English civilisation. Without such homes, the aggregate poor lacked all bodily and spatial boundaries associated with classical, bourgeois individualism. Viewed as non-subjects, the urban poor represented 'human sewage', 'drainage' whose uncontrollable communal flow threatened to erode all notions of a stable society.[20]

Barnardo and other child advocates argued that in order to protect the interests of the nation, poor children had to be removed from their urban environments and 'disciplined into orderly citizens and useful servants'.[21] He proclaimed: *The children must be saved.* To do so they must be rescued from the lodging-houses; from their awful homes, utterly unworthy of the name. ... They must be transplanted, so to speak, from the wilderness where their existence is every moment in danger, to the fair garden of a Christian Home.'[22] This 'fair garden of a Christian Home' represented the predominance of middle-class domestic ideals, as well as a strong English faith in the environment's ability to shape the individual. In order to be saved, children had to be transplanted to a new kind of domestic space.

The Female Critique of Barrack Schools

Until the 1870s, most support for poor children's institutions was not founded on Barnardo's vision of a 'Christian Home', but rather on the barrack model of large district schools, which combined children from several poor law unions so that over 1,000 children could be contained within a single building.[23] The older generation of Poor Law authorities generally supported district schools as an affordable means to remove children from the workhouses in urban areas. In the 1870s, however, there was significant official as well as unofficial criticism not only of the workhouse schools, which allowed for interaction among workhouse children and adults as well as temporary and long-term inmates, but also of the larger barrack-style separate (single-union) and district schools.[24] The leading opponents of the mass, barrack schools were upper- and middle-class women who argued for an increase in female government and philanthropic positions based on women's knowledge of the domestic sphere.

Figure 1: A washroom in the North Surrey District School.

These women used domesticity as an important rhetorical tool as they superimposed the domestic sphere onto children's institutions – a notably public realm – as a way to legitimise their involvement in public issues.

Louisa Twining (1820–1912) represented the first generation of women who worked to increase the involvement of upper- and middle-class women in Poor Law administration. Louisa was the daughter of the tea merchant Richard Twining (1772–1857), whose own father Richard (1749–1824) had been a director of the East India Company. Twining concentrated her activities on workhouse reform and the establishment of the Workhouse Visiting Society in 1857.[25] She called on women to become involved in the management of Poor Law institutions, often in the face of direct opposition from local Boards of Guardians, whom Twining characterised as men of little perception from a generally lower social class.[26] Typically drawing sharp distinctions between male and female approaches, she asserted that

> a great part of the evils which had grown up around the [Poor Law] system were owing to the fact that it was carried out entirely by men – that the

'female element' ... had been entirely ignored, and that the fate and control of
the thousands of women and children who came under the Poor Law was in
the hands of guardians, who could hardly be supposed to know all that was
needful on this subject.[27]

According to Twining, women like herself were in a unique position
to shape Poor Law policies, since male officials systematically mis-
understood or ignored the concerns of women and children.

The appointment of Jane Elizabeth Nassau Senior (1828–1877),
daughter-in-law of Nassau Senior (1790–1864) and sister of the
novelist Thomas Hughes (1822–1896), as Inspector of Workhouses
and Pauper Schools in February of 1874 was a major victory for
female advocates of workhouse and school reform. Senior was the
first female Poor Law inspector and a great believer in the powers of
women's influence to reform poor children.[28] In 1874, Senior established her reputation as an authority on Poor Law administration
with the publication of her influential *Report on the Education of Girls
in Pauper Schools*. Commissioned in 1873 by the president of the
Local Government Board, James Stansfeld (1820–1898), the report
examined the 'physical, moral and domestic training' of girls in the
17 London metropolitan Poor Law schools (the girls' scholastic work
was notably exempt from study), in addition to the conditions of girls
from Poor Law schools after they were placed in service.[29] Senior's
report was significant because it was an official condemnation of the
district and separate schools. It gave voice and authority to the growing
philanthropic literature against large schools in favour of family
models for poor children, such as foster homes and institutions
comprised of separate cottage homes. Among her criticisms, Senior
argued that barrack schools were overcrowded to the point that they
were unhealthy, causing the spread of contagious diseases such as
opthalmia, the eye disease that became synonymous with district
schools.[30] She condemned the insufficient separation of temporary
and long-term child inmates in metropolitan Poor Law schools, and
identified such intermixing as a major cause of moral corruption and
the children's subsequent failures later in life.[31] Like Twining, Senior
claimed that women had a unique, domestic perspective as both
potential maternal figures and employers of servants that it was
essential to include for the proper training of pauper girls.[32]

Senior met with harsh resistance from the well-respected Senior
Inspector of Poor Law Schools, Edward Carleton Tufnell (1806–
1886), who resigned after a long career in the same year as Senior's

1874 report. Tufnell was an early supporter of district schools, along with James Kay (1804–1877), who advocated the large schools as a cost-effective means for urban unions to segregate children from adult paupers in workhouses. The Tufnell–Senior debate exemplified the conflict between district schools and family-based models for children, a conflict that often boiled down to a dispute about gender and professional authority. Tufnell and his supporters, including Edwin Chadwick (1800–1890), portrayed female reformers not as professionals, but as dilettantes limited by the narrow prejudices of their own class and gender. Tufnell quipped that Senior and her fellow lady inspectors would readily condemn a girl as making unsatisfactory progress after leaving the schools simply because she had been spied 'sitting on a door step' or 'in the streets with long curls down her back, and not looking respectable'.[33] Most importantly, Tufnell believed that poor boys and girls required similar treatment and that this was well provided by the district schools.[34] He rejected the idea that women were by nature more qualified to administer the care of pauper girls and that institutions built along domestic lines were better able than the district schools to reform children into artisans, servants and citizens.

In spite of Tufnell's resistance, the large barrack schools fell out of favour. Poor Law authorities began to look more and more to smaller philanthropic institutions as reformatory models. The colony of cottage homes for French juvenile delinquents founded in 1840 at Mettray near Tours became an important prototype for British reformers.[35] Barnardo's Girls' Village Home, established outside London in 1876, was also hailed as an innovative example that should guide the direction of state institutions. In addition to Senior's report, other influential publications and government reports called for the application of the family system to institutions for pauper children, such as Florence Davenport Hill's *Children of the State* (1868), a favourable 1873 Poor Law report on Mettray, and the 1878 parliamentary *Report on Cottage Homes*.[36] During the 1890s, Henrietta Barnett (1851–1936) and others renewed the assault on the barrack schools. Barnett was active in several movements that focused on housing design and urban planning as solutions to class conflict. She was the co-director of the settlement community Toynbee Hall in East London with her husband Revd Samuel Barnett (1844–1913) and later a leader of the garden suburb movement in the early 1900s.[37] From 1875 to 1897, Henrietta Barnett served on the board of managers of Forest Gate district school. It was here that two major disasters – a fire in 1889 killing 26 children and an outbreak of ptomaine poisoning in 1893 resulting from the use of rotten meat – incited widespread criticism of the barrack system, resulting in the formation of a departmental committee to examine metropolitan Poor Law schools.[38] The committee was chaired by A. J. Mundella (1825–1897) and included Barnett as a prominent member. Their report helped establish a strong movement against the aggregation of children in the large schools by recommending that the large barrack schools be 'broken up', that 'no more large schools be built', and further accommodation of children be handled by the expansion of boarding-out programmes and institutional cottage homes.[39]

This change in opinion began to have limited effects. Private charities made the most widespread use of cottage homes. During the year 1877–1878, Barnardo housed just over half of all in-care children in cottage homes; 260 girls (51 per cent of all children) had been provided for at the Girls' Village Home, while 253 boys (49 per cent of all children) had been maintained at Stepney Causeway, a facility built according to the barrack model with large dormitories. During the 1880s, the proportion of children in Barnardo's family-based institutions increased slightly. Although Barnardo founded additional barrack-style institutions during the late 1870s and 1880s for boys, the Girls' Village Home had more than doubled in size by the early 1880s. By 1885–1886, 53 per cent of Barnardo's in-care children were maintained in cottages at the Girls' Village Home or in institutions that housed fewer than 40 children in one building.[40] Barnardo increased the proportion of children in family surroundings by placing younger children in village foster homes, beginning in 1886. In 1895, Barnardo testified that slightly less than one-fifth of the children in his care (including boarded-out children) were in barrack institutions, while two-fifths were in cottage homes, and two-fifths were boarded out.[41]

Compared to Barnardo, Poor Law authorities were slower to approve the initial costs involved in constructing cottage homes. In 1878, only eight parishes, unions or school districts in England and Wales had built or planned to build cottage homes for children.[42] The number of Poor Law institutions structured according to the cottage home system increased to 19 by 1895 and to 24 by 1901–1902.[43] Changes within London metropolitan Poor Law schools best illustrate the growing preference for cottage homes by the turn of the century. In 1894, there were 11,539 in-care children in London Poor Law schools (as opposed to workhouses, infirmaries, Roman Catholic or other certified schools, the training ship Exmouth, or foster homes).[44] Of these, 90 per cent were in large, aggregated institutions and only 10 per cent were in London's two groups of cottage homes for Poor Law children: the Kensington and Chelsea district school at Banstead and the Shoreditch separate school at Hornchurch.[45] By 1909, however, there were nine metropolitan Poor Law schools with cottage home facilities. Fifty-seven per cent of the children in metropolitan Poor Law schools were in barrack-style institutions, 39 per cent were in cottage homes, and 4 per cent were at St Marylebone's separate school, which was a mixture of both systems.[46] By the turn of the century, a substantial number of children were being cared for in cottage homes largely as a result of women's growing professional acceptance as Poor Law authorities.[47]

'Unfeminine' Masses

Closer analysis of the critiques of large children's institutions reveals the centrality of the concept of domesticity to these debates. Senior and her supporters asserted that the militaristic barrack schools were doomed to fail in reforming poor children because they were not structured according to the domestic model. The underlying assumption in the condemnations of mass institutions for girls was that the 'normal condition of woman's life is domestic; and that which most closely follows the dictates of nature is almost invariably the most healthy course to pursue'.[48] Many reformers – women, but also men, such as Barnardo – considered large institutions to be completely inappropriate for girls. The discussion of barrack schools focused overwhelmingly on the condition of girls, often presenting the female child as the model inmate for whom future policies and institutions should be structured. Critics of barrack schools characterised them as masculinised spaces that hampered the social development and reformation of pauper girls and ultimately all children. The debates over barrack schools versus cottage homes demonstrate how thoroughly gender ideals had become a key gauge of a child's rise from the pauper class and his or her ultimate development of individual subjectivity.

The most common criticism of large children's institutions was that they failed to provide girls with the training that they needed to become domestic servants.[49] Girls from workhouses and mass institutions were completely unprepared for domestic duties on the single-family scale. The co-ordinator of training for workhouse girls through the Girls' Friendly Society wrote:

> The girl may have seen the matron's dinner-table in the Workhouse laid with the ordinary articles, but their names and uses she has not had explained to her. She has seen a large dinner cooked, or perhaps a single chop for an officer, but never a dinner *réchauffé* from yesterday's repast. She has scrubbed a floor, but has had no carpet to shake and put straight; made her bed, but never polished mahogany furniture; washed strong crockery at the Workhouse, but will have many a bitter tear over the unexpected brittleness of the delicate stem of her mistress's best wine-glasses.[50]

In sum, girls from workhouses and mass institutions were portrayed as ill-prepared to take on the duties of the single-family home. On the most basic level, reform efforts to improve girls' domestic instruction were an attempt to increase the supply of better-trained servants and to help the girls' prospects. A lady from Kent claimed that 'No person would come to the Union for servants unless very much in want of them, and then only for servants-of-all-work, at very low wages, not sufficient to buy clothing.'[51] Without proper training, reformers forewarned, girls would most likely lose their positions and return to the workhouse as adults, after having first attempted to gain an alternative livelihood through prostitution.[52]

Girls trained in large institutions were portrayed as hard, uncontrollable, violent, apathetic, sullen and unnurturing – traits that contrasted sharply with middle-class visions of working-class respectability, particularly for female servants. Described as 'a class proverbial for audacity and shamelessness', pauper girls seemed to contradict all idealised bourgeois feminine qualities.[53] The typical girl from Poor Law schools was described as

> Below average height and development. Well taught in elements of religion, in reading, in writing, and arithmetic. Sullen, violent, and unmanageable in temper. Apathetic when not out of temper. Ignorant of all practical matters, and deficient in aptitude for learning. Self-possessed. Hard. Untruthful. A good-tempered variety is occasionally to be found, but it is very rare.[54]

The girls' violence was a dramatised symbol of their resistance to authority – notably to the female authority of fellow servants or mistresses. Female servants trained in large schools were 'reported to be sullen and ill-tempered'.[55] Reform literature chronicled representative acts of rebellious violence. One 'rather violent' girl broke 'a plate on the head of her fellow servant. Another tried to stab the nurse. A third threw herself on the ground when it was attempted to teach her anything.' This particular list continues, ending with the generalisation that the 'girls were constantly described as seeming like people possessed'.[56] Senior recounted how a girl from a London district school had such a 'perverse' temper that 'the mistress has sometimes tried the experiment of telling her *not* to do the thing she wants to have done, and always with success'.[57] In another, more extreme case, the female servant, 'violent and obstinate beyond belief, offered to stab her own mother when she came to remonstrate'.[58] These were the commonly accepted representations of girls trained in mass institutions. Such portrayals of the girls' violence reinforced the view that they were 'possessed' by the spirit or will of another, rather than distinct individuals conscious of their actions.

Another frequent criticism of girls from barrack schools was that they were completely lacking in maternal skills and interest. A female workhouse observer noted that girls raised in the union's large separate school displayed a 'strange want of natural affection'. When asked why they quit their positions as servants, the girls typically responded, 'Oh, there were too many children', or 'Oh, I can't suit myself with children.'[59] According to female reformers, women trained in mass institutions were even unwilling to care for their own children. They 'let their babies fall out of bed, and often take a dislike to them'.[60] Critics of barrack schools blamed the girls' lack of nurturing skills on the aggregate structure and routine of the institutions, which made it impossible for officials 'to individualise and influence the girls under their care' with affection and personal example.[61] The alleged lack of domestic bonds among the poor in general were also a common target. Florence Hill (1829–1919) reported that adult workhouse inmates raised in barrack schools described their own mothers in only the harshest terms: 'My mother left me in a ditch'; 'Mine ran off when I was three'; 'Mine was always drunk, and I don't know anything about her.'[62] Such cases led one lady workhouse worker to conclude that there was 'a grave and shocking want among the future mothers of the poor; and how, but by placing these poor things in families, are they ever to develop that God-implanted instinct, which, in these girls, I find totally absent?'[63]

On the whole, reformers blamed the girls' hardness, violence and lack of mothering on the male-dominated, masculine model of the barrack schools, which, instead of replacing the domestic life that the children allegedly lacked in their natural families, worked to undermine the association between subjectivity and domesticity. The 'monster' schools, as Senior's colleague Menella Smedley (1820–1877) termed them, came to represent boundless, out of control disorder – the direct opposite of what Tufnell and his colleagues claimed was an efficient military model for creating good citizens, be they male or female.[64] Critics argued that girls in the barrack schools lacked all signs of subjectivity. They were either possessed by violent rages or dulled into a state of apathetic slumber, but not functioning as conscious individuals. As Joan Scott and Sally Alexander have suggested, gendered constructions of class and personal subjectivity defined female identity within the confines of the home and thus excluded women from full participation in group identities, such as class-based activity.[65] The gendered character of group and individual identity helps to explain some of the more sweeping condemnations of barrack schools. For example, a writer for the *Westminster Review* stated: 'Females never mass well, either in schools, orphanages, homes, or institutions of any kind, whether as girls or as adults.'[66] Barnardo expressed the sentiment best of all. 'I do not know why it is,' he testified, 'but when a number of females are massed together, girls or women – it is the same in large factories – they seem to re-act upon each other in a degrading way.' While the massing of boys could develop their sense of 'public spirit', the massing of girls produced public disorder and personal degradation.[67] As one Poor Law official claimed, 'very large assemblages of girls are unfeminine'.[68]

Some critics generalised the connection between domesticity and subjectivity so that it applied to all pauper children, not just girls. As in the case of the impoverished inhabitants of urban slums, reformers described the children in mass institutions as lacking classical bodily distinctions. Many of the practices in large institutions did tend to blur the common divisions of gender, age and humanity. Workhouse authorities dressed inmates in uniforms and gave males and females similarly styled cropped haircuts upon entering.[69] Within large institutions, there was often no special treatment or cultivation of individual tastes and needs. Unable to remember hundreds of children's names, authorities often simply referred to each as 'child'.[70] Children were fed the regulation portion of food, regardless of the 'size, appetite, taste, or physical condition' of the individual.[71] The typical girl 'takes no interest in anything, she cares for nothing, she is like an old person'.[72] Endless routine, a 'hideous uniform and cropped hair', and heavy shoes 'change[d] the natural lightness of the step of youth to the shuffle of old age'.[73] Reformers frequently wrote that while the family encouraged the development of individuals,[74] the 'herding together of children' like 'dogs' or 'horses' in overcrowded schools promoted nothing but their identification with the aggregate pauper class.[75] By focusing on issues of individuality and applying expectations of idealised childhood to working-class children as early as the 1870s, these reformers were quite radical. They condemned the necessary discipline of the large schools as stultifying, and instead called for the cultivation of youthful identity and experience at a time when few thought that working-class children should be distinguished from adults.

At the same time, the critics of barrack schools demonstrated a heightened fear of class disorder. The barrack or 'monster' schools seemed to take on a life of their own as reproducers of social ills. The spread of disease was a primary concern, and large segments of the reports on these schools concentrated on issues of hygiene, ventilation and cubic space. Communal washing practices were particularly circumspect. The 'jet systems' (Figure 1) used in some large schools were praised as models of efficiency by some directors, while critics viewed them as 'rather a barbarous system'. Children bathed at troughs and sometimes 'share[d] the towels promiscuously', thus spreading eye and skin diseases.[76] Reformers also frequently compared the large schools to machines made up of children as the unthinking parts. The 'unnaturally' uniform and dull routine of mass institutions created 'half-formed creatures', who were 'dull, sullen, and mechanical'.[77] 'One feels,' wrote Florence Hill, 'as though these children should be little automata instead of human beings, to obey all these clockwork arrangements.'[78] Children raised in the 'artificial' surroundings of large schools were frequently described as 'human machines'; 'a mere cog in an engine of many wheels'; 'parts of a machine'; and 'automatons'.[79] According to one writer for *Cornhill Magazine*, the final result of mass institutions was to produce children who were 'not individuals, but children of the State, machine-made paupers growing up for the market'.[80] The mass, unspecialised, factory-like architectural spaces of the barrack schools failed to encourage recognised forms of domesticity and individuality, the main qualities which, in the eyes of new generations of reformers, disassociated children from the mass of paupers and prepared them for inclusion in the social body.

By making the issue of individuality one of the key points of the debate, critics of barrack schools demonstrated how age, gender and class identity are intertwined. Implicit in these discussions of individuality was the notion that the environment, not heredity or free will, creates the individual. The process of individuation does not come from within; it is imposed from without, as the reformers' common usage of the transitive verb 'to individualise' suggests.[81] In many ways, however, the cottage homes were just as factory-like as the barrack schools. They had similarly strict daily schedules and their primary goal was to produce good citizens and qualified, deferential labourers. The main difference was that the recreated 'family' in the cottage homes served to naturalise and legitimise this process, while at the same time further delegitimising the children's biological family structures.

Family Cottages and Model Village Homes

The assumption underlying the architectural arrangements of model villages and cottage homes was that spatial designs could shape the individual's subjectivity and regulate his or her role in the larger society. In England, proposals for internal colonies such as William Booth's Salvation Army scheme became increasingly popular as means to contain and incorporate the poor into the social body. Model villages for poor children stemmed from a more general European trend to build juvenile reformatories along domestic lines, such as Rauhe Hause in Germany and Mettray in France, which, as Felix Driver has demonstrated, were important models for mid-to-late-nineteenth-century British child advocates.[82] The children's villages represented miniature societies, seemingly self-sufficient gated communities that generally included school rooms, a chapel, carpentry, shoemaking, ironsmith and other workshops for boys and laundry and cooking facilities for girls, a village green often surrounded by the children's cottages, and a larger superintendent's or director's house. Reformers argued that cottage homes in open, green spaces away from central London and other cities were the ideal environment in which to 'depauperise the children' and reform them into artisans and servants.[83] Cottage homes were the cradle of the citizen; they evoked a pastoral, village ideal in sharp contrast to the uncontrollable, undifferentiated urban slums and the factory-like, monstrous barrack schools.

Figure 2: Barnardo's Girls' Village Home, 1876.

The family cottages simultaneously reinforced a specific version of domesticity and unwittingly undermined the concept of natural domesticity. In spite of repeated demands for institutions based on natural domestic models, there remained the irony that the domestic arrangements in model villages were clearly artificial.[84] For example, describing the case of a girl brought to the Girls' Village Home, Barnardo wrote that she was 'removed from a lodging-house and from the care of a tramp whom she called "mother," and brought into a cottage home ...' Within this home, he continued, 'She becomes at once a member of a *family*' surrounded by a 'dozen and a half' other girls all under the control of the cottage 'mother'.[85] There is no mention of the unusual fact that this new family comprised 18 girls, or that their new 'mother' was of a distinctly higher class than the children. It is unclear how reformers distinguished the communal sleeping arrangements in family-based institutions from the over-crowded sleeping areas in urban slums or barrack schools that they had so thoroughly condemned. Although Poor Law relief officers would often not allow children to return to homes deemed overcrowded and unsanitary,[86] the children at the Girls' Village Home slept four to six in a room (each in a single bed).[87] In one of Barnardo's fund-raising appeals, the rhetorical dichotomy between overcrowded, promiscuous, undomestic slums and ordered model villages completely dissolved. Requesting donations to build a new school at the Girls' Village Home, Barnardo described how the current school buildings were in converted stables and coach houses. '[T]he physical and nervous health of the children has already suffered seriously from overcrowding in the ill-lit and ill-ventilated structure now being used as a schoolroom', which, according to Barnardo, by 1891 was needed to accommodate 1,200 children instead of the 500 for which it was built.[88]

The recreated domestic order for poor children in cottage homes highlighted the fluid definitions of the home and the family in Victorian society, definitions that were often more dependent on class than on blood relations. The class and social positions of the cottage parents supported their privileged domestic status. At Banstead, the first house 'fathers' were drawn from the 'respectable' poor – a baker, plumber and glazier, carpenter, tailor, smith, shoemaker, gardener and drillmaster. These men were artisans who provided role models and industrial training for the boys.[89] Some institutions also recruited cottage 'mothers' from the working class, generally unmarried women or widows of respectable artisans. Barnardo, however, preferred evangelical abstainers, 'educated women, *ladies*', to be the 'heads of our families', believing that 'the advantages of culture and of fine feeling are inestimable in influencing the girls we rescue'.[90]

To accentuate these class and cultural differences spatially, each cottage at Barnardo's Girls' Village Home contained a separate bedroom for the 'mother', in addition to 'a separate sitting-room of her own, a private *sanctum* suitably furnished, whither she can retreat for those moments of quietude so necessary for one fulfilling her important duties'.[91] (There is no mention of such a distinct space for house 'fathers'.) This need for private, domestic, specifically female space reflected contemporary trends in middle-class housing.[92] Perhaps more importantly, it accustomed the girls to the living conditions that they could anticipate in their expected role as servants. Girls became familiar with the layout of the types of homes in which they might serve, and accustomed to the female authority of the mothers/mistresses who 'ruled' each cottage by demanding 'loving obedience'.[93]

Cut off from the external world, the model villages used the domestic arrangement of space and persons to teach children their social roles. A visitor to the Girls' Village Home noted, 'The furniture of their rooms, the arrangement of their cottages, are all such as they are likely to meet with in domestic service.'[94] Each cottage contained in addition to the bedrooms and mother's sitting room, a living room, playroom, kitchen and scullery, 'such as a girl would meet in service of a medium character'.[95] Supporters of the family system praised cottage homes for dispensing with the worst signs of institutional life characterised by mechanical routine: cropped hair for girls, uniforms and identification numbers assigned to each child.[96] Yet clearly the cottages had a routine of their own which was reinforced by the architectural design. A visitor to the Girls' Village Home remarked how 'Each small domestic duty is performed over and over again, till each child learns to be quite an adept at cooking potatoes, or cleaning out a room, or washing and dressing a younger one; and takes pride in her work, so as to be able to do it *as well as Mother*.'[97] According to a former mother at the Girls' Village Home, 'The control of the "Mother" over her household and its internal arrangement is undisputed, and her aim is to train the girls in ways of goodness and practical usefulness, more especially for domestic service.'[98] This sort of industrial training was generally highly valued by the children and their natural parents. It is important to ask, however, why much-needed industrial training and material aid were overlaid and intertwined with the rhetoric of domesticity. By presenting model village homes as idealised visions of domesticity, in spite of key glaring artificialities, reformers naturalised the children's social role as labourers. The contained, clearly divided spaces of model villages presented an organic model for society, in which poor children were safely incorporated as mediators between the 'private sanctum' of their superiors, the house 'mothers', and the controlled public areas of the community – the village green, the church and the school.

These naturalised domestic and social orders were necessary in order for poor children to be recognised as individuals and potential citizens separate from the mass of paupers. Whereas the aggregation of large groups of children in the barrack schools allegedly prevented the children from 'being completely individualized', the family model provided 'individualization, and mutual affection and responsibility';

it was thus widely recognised as the 'primary group of the body politic'.[99] Drawing a relationship between individuation and demonstrations of idealised femininity for servants, a visitor to the Girls' Village Home unfavourably compared a girl raised in a workhouse school with the girls at Barnardo's. Although the girl from the workhouse was more intelligent in academic matters, she was ignorant in all matters of housework and completely lacking in deference to her mistress. '[S]he knew a smattering of geography, a jumble of history and poetry, but such an amount of bad language and viciousness that we were horrified at her knowledge.' The visitor lamented that the 'stolid', 'indifferent', 'insolent' child 'stared absently' and 'merely acted like a machine' when providing services. The visitor concluded that if the girl 'had been subjected to the refining and humanising effects of Home surroundings, [she] might have developed into a thoroughly useful maid'.[100] To be human, for the female child, was to be a good maid, and it was through the regulated structure of the recreated 'home' that she might have acquired these attributes. The visitor further explained that Barnardo's village mothers carefully trained the children's 'individuality of character' into 'usefulness for the benefit of the whole community'.[101] In the end, this was a limited definition of individuality, a definition that rested not on ideas of free agency, but on the children's perceived usefulness to the greater community as workers.

Conclusion

The increased popularity of family-based institutions over barrack schools among reformers corresponded with the growing criticism of family relations among the poor during the 1860s and 1870s. By the 1870s, the homes of the poor were highly contested. The confusion over the status of poor dwellings as legitimate *homes* exemplifies the vexed position of the poor within mid-to-late-nineteenth-century conceptions of the nation or social body, as well as the essential role of the idealised home and family as fundamental units of the nation. Despite Victorian exaltations of the family and the home, early welfare and charity programmes were designed in a manner that attempted (often unsuccessfully) to undermine the validity and bonds of poor families. The promotion of model villages and family cottages for children went hand in hand with the cutting of outdoor relief during the 1870s, which had previously made it easier for families to remain intact without resort to philanthropic or Poor Law institutions for children. By the 1870s, social welfare programmes that promoted poor children's integration into the body politic often called for the public erasure of their natural families and the creation of new institutional domestic models. Allegedly without domestic havens of their own, the poor required family-based institutions to teach them key social values: maternalism, affection, deference, individualism and citizenship.

The preference for family cottages and model villages over barrack schools also demonstrates the growing importance of gender to reform.[102] Idealised, recreated domestic models became the primary means of separating poor children from their impoverished surroundings and naturalising their incorporation as newly defined individuals into the political body. The popularity of children's institutions based on domestic models was the result of middle-class women's growing role as philanthropists and Poor Law authorities, in addition to the general nineteenth-century importance of the home for middle-class men and women. Female reformers validated their expanding public duties by referring to their special domestic knowledge, bringing the language of gender to debates about social reform. Although earlier children's institutions were clearly gendered in their own ways, it took the involvement of female reformers to structure the debates about children's institutions according to gender differences: the militaristic barrack schools versus the domestic family cottages. One of the effects of emphasising gender in these debates was that gender ideals became increasingly important means to measure pauper children's reform and, moreover, their individual subjectivity.

Lastly, the reformers' association of domesticity with citizenship suggests the importance of interpreting changes in social welfare within the context of political history. The preference for family cottages over barrack schools first became strong in the 1870s – perhaps in reaction to public anxiety caused by the 1867 Reform Act and the 1871 Paris Commune. Pastoral ideals of deferential communities (as defined in contrast to the undifferentiated mob) implied a desire for political stability in the face of major challenges to and modifications of the liberal system. The children's model villages and institutional homes represented an ideal for all of society. Within the cottage homes class conflict was resolved or at least regulated through domestic affection. At the same time, many of the poor – the urban dwellers and the casual poor or 'ins and outs' who blatantly contradicted and complicated these ideal social visions – were represented as inhuman, unindividuated threats to the liberal political body, beyond the pale of reform.

Notes

1. I am grateful to Andy Evans, Jon Lawrence, and Jeanne Peterson for their generous comments and advice on earlier drafts of this essay. I also thank John Kirkham of the Barnardo Photographic Archive, the London Metropolitan Archives, University College London, and the University of Liverpool for access to their collections.

2. William Chambers, 'The Boarding-Out System', *Chambers's Journal of Popular Literature, Science, and Art*, ser. 4 Vol. 14, 9 June 1877, p. 353.

3. On boarding out in England see Henry Aveling, *The Boarding-Out System and Legislation Relating to the Protection of Children and Infant Life: A Manual for Poor-Law Guardians, Boarding-Out Committees, and Practical Workers*, London, Swan Sonnenschein and Co., 1890; George Behlmer, *Friends of the Family: The English Home and its Guardians, 1850–1940*, Stanford, Stanford University Press, 1998, pp. 285–89, 293–94; Danby Palmer Fry, *The Boarding Out of Pauper Children: Containing the General Order of the Poor Law Board, and the Accompanying Circular, with Notes & Introduction*, London, Knight & Co., 1870; Wilhelmina L. Hall, *Boarding-Out, As a Method of Pauper Education and Check on Hereditary Pauperism*, London, Hatchards, 1887; Florence Davenport-Hill, *Children of the State*, London, Macmillan & Co., 1889 (first edn 1868).

4. For a collection of case studies that explore the meanings of space from the inhabitants' perspectives, see *The Cultural Meaning of Urban Space*, ed. Robert Rotenberg and Gary McDonogh, Westport, CT, and London, Bergin & Garvey, 1993. M. J. Daunton discusses working-class conceptions of domesticity in *House and Home in the Victorian City: Working-Class Housing, 1850–1914*, London, Edward Arnold, 1983, pp. 263–85, as does Martin Hewitt, 'District Visiting and the Constitution of Domestic Space in the Mid-Nineteenth Century', in *Domestic Space: Reading the Nineteenth-Century Interior*, ed. Inga Bryden and Janet Floyd, Manchester, Manchester University Press, 1999, pp. 121–41.

5. See Elizabeth Grosz, 'Bodies–Cities', in *Sexuality and Space*, ed. Beatriz Colomina, New York, Princeton Architectural Press, 1992, pp. 244–49, and Setha M. Low, 'Cultural Meaning of the Plaza: The History of the Spanish-American Gridplan-Plaza Urban Design', in Rotenberg and McDonogh, eds, *The Cultural Meaning of Urban Space*, p. 75.

6. There is an immense literature on space. For examples of historical studies of space see Annmarie Adams, *Architecture in the Family Way: Doctors, Houses, and Women*, Montreal, McGill-Queen's University Press, 1996; Clifford E. Clark, Jr, 'Domestic Architecture as an Index to Social History: The Romantic Revival and the Cult of

Domesticity in America, 1840–1870', *Journal of Interdisciplinary History* 7(1), Summer 1976, pp. 33–56; Colomina, ed., *Sexuality and Space*; Felix Driver, 'Moral Geographies: Social Science and the Urban Environment in Mid-Nineteenth Century England', *Transactions of the Institute of British Geographers* 13, 1988, pp. 275–87; Henri Lefebvre, *The Production of Space*, trans. Donald Nicholson-Smith, Oxford, Basil Blackwell, 1991; Teresita Martínez-Vergne, *Shaping the Discourse on Space: Charity and its Wards in Nineteenth-Century San Juan, Puerto Rico*, Austin, TX, University of Texas Press, 1999; Mary Poovey, *Making a Social Body: British Cultural Formation, 1830–1864*, Chicago, University of Chicago Press, 1995; Rotenberg and McDonogh, eds, *The Cultural Meaning of Urban Space*; Dell Upton, 'Lancasterian Schools, Republican Citizenship, and the Spatial Imagination in Early Nineteenth-Century America', *Journal of the Society of Architectural Historians* 55(3), Sept. 1996, pp. 238–53.

7. Leonore Davidoff and Catherine Hall, *Family Fortunes: Men and Women of the English Middle Class, 1780–1850*, Chicago, University of Chicago Press, 1987, pp. 357–64 and passim; F. M. L. Thompson, *The Rise of Respectable Society: A Social History of Victorian Britain, 1830–1900*, London, Fontana Press, 1988, pp. 152–96.

8. Felix Driver, 'Discipline Without Frontiers? Representations of the Mettray Reformatory Colony in Britain, 1840–1880', *Journal of Historical Sociology* 3(3), 1990, p. 273; Driver, 'Moral Geographies', p. 277 and passim.

9. Adams, *Architecture in the Family Way*, pp. 136–42; Clark, 'Domestic Architecture', pp. 49–53; Davidoff and Hall, *Family Fortunes*, pp. 364–70, 375–80; Hewitt, 'District Visiting', pp. 127–28.

10. Driver, 'Moral Geographies', p. 281.

11. On the resilience of working-class domesticity and privacy, see Hewitt, 'District Visiting', pp. 121–23, 129–34, 137–38.

12. Daunton, *House and Home*, pp. 12–15, 35.

13. Peter Stallybrass and Allon White, *The Politics and Poetics of Transgression*, Ithaca, NY, Cornell University Press, 1986, pp. 48–50, 132, 147.

14. Anna Davin, *Growing Up Poor: Home, School, and Street in London, 1870–1914*, London, Rivers Oram Press, 1996, pp. 57, 63–68, and passim.

15. Poovey, *Making a Social Body*, p. 144; Martin Hewitt, 'The Travails of Domestic Visiting: Manchester, 1830–70', *Historical Research* 71, June 1998, pp. 196–227, and 'District Visiting', p. 126 and passim.

16. Ellen Barlee, *Our Homeless Poor; and What We Can Do to Help Them*, London, James Nisbet and Co., 1860, p. 217. Emphasis in original.

17. Barlee, *Our Homeless Poor*, p. 218.

18. Annie Macpherson, *The Little London Arabs*, London, Morgan and Chase, 1870, p. 8. See 'Bare Walls, Little Furniture, and Other Scenes', *Our Log Book: A Monthly Record of the National Refuges for Homeless and Destitute Children and Training Ships 'Arethusa' and 'Chichester'*, 15 April 1899, p. 315, and Howard Goldsmith, *Dottings of a Dosser: Being Revelations of the Inner Life of Low London Lodging-Houses*, London, T. Fisher Unwin, 1886, p. 50.

19. Revd Lord Sydney Godolphin Osborne, quoted in *'Something Attempted Something Done, Being the Annual Report of Dr Barnardo's Homes, East End Juvenile Mission'*, London, John F. Shaw & Co., 1888, p. 12, University of Liverpool Special Collections and Archives (hereafter ULSCA).

20. Stallybrass and White, *The Politics and Poetics of Transgression*, pp. 125–48, skilfully summarise Victorian reformers' association of the poor with dirt, sewage, disease and moral depravity. For discussions of the aggregate, embodied rhetoric used to describe the poor, see Poovey, *Making a Social Body*, p. 37, and Moira Gatens, 'Corporeal Representation in/and the Body Politic', in *Writing on the Body: Female Embodiment and Feminist Theory*, ed. Kate Conboy, Nadia Medina, and Sarah Stanbury, New York, Columbia University Press, 1997, p. 83. Mikhail Bakhtin's distinction between the 'grotesque body' and the 'classical body' is also useful. See Bakhtin, *Rabelais and his World*, trans. Helene Iswolsky, Cambridge, MA, MIT Press, 1968, pp. 25–27, 303–22, and passim.

21. Barnardo, 'London Lodging Houses, I. As They Were', *Night and Day*, January 1877, p. 11.

22. *Annual Reports*, Barnardo's, 1883–84, p. 9, ULSCA. Emphasis in original.

23. Legislation in 1844 (7 & 8 Vict. c. 101) and 1848 (11 & 12 Vict. cap. 82) empowered unions to build communal district schools, yet most Boards of Guardians continued to use schools connected with the workhouse or single-union schools known as separate schools. Still, district schools were used by many large cities, and they were upheld as the preferred institutions for Poor Law children until the 1870s. See Felix Driver, *Power and Pauperism: The Workhouse System, 1834–1884*, Cambridge, Cambridge University Press, 1993, p. 97; Derek Fraser, 'The English Poor Law and the Origins of the British Welfare State', in *The Emergence of the Welfare State in Britain and Germany, 1850–1950*, ed. W. J. Mommsen, London, Croom Helm, 1981, p. 15; Frederic J. Mouat, 'On the Education and Training of Children of the Poor', *Journal of the Statistical Society* 43, 1880, pp. 206–07; Edward Carleton Tufnell, *Training of Pauper Children*, London, Eyre and Spottiswoode, 1880, p. 2.

24. Driver, *Power and Pauperism*, pp. 96–101.

25. Louisa Twining, 'Recollections of Workhouse Visiting and Management', reprinted from *Quarterly Magazine* in *Recollections of Workhouse Visiting and Management During Twenty-Five Years*, London, C. Kegan Paul & Co., 1880, pp. 22–25. On Louisa Twining, see F. K. Prochaska, *Women and Philanthropy in Nineteenth-Century England*, Oxford, Clarendon Press, 1980, pp. 175–81.

26. Twining, 'Recollections of Workhouse Visiting', pp. ix, xi, 10, 31, 33, 64, 152, 171–72, 181–82.

27. Twining, 'Recollections of Workhouse Visiting', pp. 64–65.

28. 'The Late Mrs Nassau Senior', *The Times*, 29 March 1877, pp. 5f.

29. Jane Elizabeth Nassau Senior, *Report on the Education of Girls in Pauper Schools* (January 1, 1874) reprinted in Menella B. Smedley, *Boarding-Out and Pauper Schools Especially for Girls: Being a Reprint of the Principal Reports on Pauper Education in the Blue Book for 1873–4*, London, Henry S. King & Co., 1875, pp. 52, 53–54.

30. Senior, *Report on the Education of Girls in Pauper Schools*, pp. 82–83.

31. Senior, *Report on the Education of Girls in Pauper Schools*, pp. 63–64.

32. Senior, *Report on the Education of Girls in Pauper Schools*, pp. 52, 70–76, 117–19.

33. Evidence from Senior's 1874 report quoted in E. C. Tufnell, *Observations on the Report of Mrs Senior to the Local Government Board as to the Effect on Girls of the System of Education at Pauper Schools*, London, George E. Eyre and William Spottiswoode (Queen's printers), 1875, p. 1. Also see Tufnell, *Observations on the*

Report of Mrs Senior, pp. 7, 13; Edwin Chadwick quoted in Tufnell, *Training of Pauper Children*, p. 7; Chadwick, manuscript in file, 'Sickness and Death Rates in District Schools, Questionnaire for 1883', papers on sanitation and health in schools, including details of illnesses in District Schools, c. 1875–1888, the Papers of Sir Edwin Chadwick (1800–1890), 97, University College London.

34. Tufnell, *Observations on the Report of Mrs Senior*, p. 6.

35. Driver, 'Discipline without Frontiers?', p. 278 and passim.

36. Driver, 'Discipline without Frontiers?', pp. 286–87, and *Power and Pauperism*, p. 101.

37. Seth Koven, 'Henrietta Barnett, 1851–1936: The (auto)Biography of a Late Victorian Marriage', pp. 31–53, and Standish Meacham, 'Raymond Unwin, 1863–1940: Designing for Democracy in Edwardian England', pp. 97–100, in *After the Victorians: Private Conscience and Public Duty in Modern Britain*, ed. Susan Pedersen and Peter Mandler, London and New York, Routledge, 1994.

38. Henrietta Barnett, *Canon Barnett: His Life, Work, and Friends*, II, Boston and New York, Houghton Mifflin Co., 1919, pp. 288–300; Forest Gate District School, *Annual Reports of Managers*, 1890, pp. 6–10, 1894, pp. 5–7, FGSD 19, London Metropolitan Archives (formerly Greater London Record Office, hereafter LMA).

39. *Departmental Committee on Existing Systems for the Maintenance and Education of Children under the Charge of Managers of District Schools and Boards of Guardians in the Metropolis* PP 1896 xliii, p. 15.

40. See Barnardo's *Annual Reports*, 1877–1886 (back covers), ULSCA. It is particularly difficult to categorise Barnardo's institutions into barrack and family-based systems. The populations of Barnardo's barrack-style institutions were relatively small compared with the massive Poor Law schools. Moreover, Barnardo's philan-thropic literature describes even his barrack-style institutions with a rhetoric of domesticity that belies their actual spatial organisation. For Barnardo's distinction between his barrack schools and cottage homes, see PP 1896 xliii, para. 9146–9153.

41. PP 1896 xliii, para. 9112–9114.

42. *Report on the Home and Cottage System* PP 1878 lx.

43. PP 1896 xliii, para. 16,180 and *Return on Cottage Homes* PP 1903 lix.

44. The children in London Poor Law schools comprised 65% of all in-care children above two years old chargeable to the Metropolitan Boards of Guardians. See PP 1896 xliii, para. 27.

45. PP 1896 xliii, para. 5–8.

46. List of Metropolitan Poor Law Schools, A Return of the Particulars of Salaries and Emoluments, etc., received by Superintendents and Matrons in Metropolitan Poor Law Schools, directed to be prepared by the Managers, 8th Jan., 1909, Kensington and Chelsea School District, KCSD 171, LMA. The average number of children in the schools during 1909 was 9,562.

47. On the expanding number of female Poor Law authorities, see M. A. Crowther, *The Workhouse System, 1834–1929*, Athens, GA, The University of Georgia Press, 1982, pp. 77–78, and Prochaska, *Women and Philanthropy*, pp. 180–81.

48. 'Pauper Girls', *Westminster Review* 93, 1870, p. 472.

49. Driver, 'Discipline without Frontiers?', pp. 285–86.

50. Joanna Hill, *Practical Suggestions for the Use of Associates for the Department for G.F.S. Candidates from Workhouses and Orphanages*, London, Hatchards, 1884, p. 3.

51. A Lady from Kent quoted in Ellen Barlee, *Friendless and Helpless*, London, Emily Faithfull, 1863, p. 216.

52. See for example, Barnardo, 'Preventive Homes; A Paper Read Before the Social Science Congress at Liverpool, October, 1876', reprinted in *Night and Day*, 15 January, 1877, p. 4; Frances Power Cobbe, 'Workhouse Sketches', *Macmillan's Magazine* 3, 1861, p. 454; Cobbe, 'The Philosophy of the Poor-Laws', *Fraser's Magazine* 66, 1862, p. 383; Florence Hill, 'The Family System for Workhouse Children', *Contemporary Review* 15, 1870, pp. 248–49, 373–74; Senior, *Report on the Education of Girls in Pauper Schools*, pp. 121, 141; Smedley, *Boarding-Out and Pauper Schools*, p. 19; Twining, 'Workhouses and Woman's Work', reprinted in *Recollections of Workhouse Visiting and Management During Twenty-Five Years*, pp. 150–52.

53. Florence Hill quoted in Henrietta Barnett, 'The Home or the Barrack for the Children of the State?', *Contemporary Review* 66, 1894, p. 243.

54. Menella Smedley, 'Workhouse Schools for Girls', *MacMillan's Magazine* 31, 1874, p. 28.

55. Henrietta Synnot, 'Little Paupers', *Contemporary Review* 24, 1874, p. 958.

56. Synnot, 'Little Paupers', p. 958.

57. Senior, *Report on the Education of Girls in Pauper Schools*, p. 144.

58. Smedley, *Boarding-Out and Pauper Schools*, p. vi.

59. Letter from a lady worker in a metropolitan female adult ward quoted in Florence Hill, 'The Family System', p. 247.

60. Letter from a lady worker in a metropolitan female adult ward quoted in Florence Hill, 'The Family System', p. 248.

61. Senior, *Report on the Education of Girls in Pauper Schools*, p. 73.

62. Letter from a lady worker in a metropolitan female adult ward quoted in Florence Hill, 'The Family System', p. 247.

63. Letter from a lady worker in a metropolitan female adult ward quoted in Florence Hill, 'The Family System', p. 247.

64. Smedley, *Boarding-Out and Pauper Schools*, pp. viii, xviii, 15, 44, 49.

65. Sally Alexander, 'Women, Class, and Sexual Differences in the 1830s and 1840s: Some Reflections on the Writing of Feminist History', *History Workshop* 17, Spring 1984, pp. 125–49; Joan Wallach Scott, *Gender and the Politics of History*, New York, Columbia University Press, 1988, pp. 53–67.

66. 'Pauper Girls', p. 472.

67. PP 1896 xliii, para. 9250.

68. T. B. Browne quoted in 'Pauper Girls', p. 472. Also see Browne quoted in Smedley, *Boarding-Out and Pauper Schools*, p. xviii.

69. Crowther, *Workhouse System*, pp. 195–96; Anne Digby, *Pauper Palaces*, London, Routledge & Kegan Paul, 1978, p. 157.

70. Barnett, 'The Home or the Barrack?', p. 245.

71. Barnett, 'The Home or the Barrack?', p. 245.

72. Smedley, *Boarding-Out and Pauper Schools*, p. 48.

73. Barnardo, *'Rescuing the Perishing'*, 1874–75, p. xiv, ULSCA.

74. See Florence Hill, 'The Family System', p. 241; Mouat, 'Education and Training', p. 220.

75. Mouat, 'Education and Training', p. 221.

76. PP 1896 xliii, para. 612–614.

77. Smedley, 'Pauper Homes', *Good Words* 17, 1876, p. 51; Henrietta Barnett, 'The Verdict on the Barrack Schools', *Nineteenth Century* 41, 1897, p. 57.

78. Florence Hill, *Children of the State*, p. 27.

79. Smedley, 'Pauper Homes', p. 48; idem, 'Pauper Girls', p. 471; idem, 'Workhouse Schools for Girls', p. 30; M. B. Edwards, 'English Orphans in Paris', *Good Words* 19, 1878, p. 598.

80. 'Little Paupers', *Cornhill Magazine* 22, 1870, p. 373.

81. Joanna Hill, *Practical Suggestions*, p. 6; Senior, *Report on the Education of Girls in Pauper Schools*, pp. 73, 84.

82. Driver, 'Discipline without Frontiers?'.

83. Forest Gate School District, *Annual Reports of Managers*, 1893, p. 8, FGSD 19, LMA.

84. For criticisms of the artificial nature of cottage homes, which could become 'large pauper colonies', see PP 1896 xliii, para. 416–423.

85. Barnardo, 'Preventive Homes; A Paper Read Before the Social Science Congress at Liverpool, October, 1876', *Night and Day*, 15 January 1877, p. 4. Emphasis in original.

86. See for example Bermondsey Board of Guardians (St Olave's Union), Reference to and Enquiry by General Relieving Officer, 10 February 1896–3 April 1897, BBG.539/1, LMA: cases No. 17, Edith Simmonds (22 April 1896); No. 23, Denis McCarthy (14 May 1896); No. 25 and 32, William Currier (21 May 1896, 30 June 1896); No. 50, William Codling (9 Sept. 1896); No. 66, George and Maud Pugh (14 Jan. 1897); No. 68, James Driscoll (27 Jan. 1897).

87. Barnardo, *'Something Attempted, Something Done': Dr Barnardo's Homes*, London, John F. Shaw & Co., 1889, p. 86; 'The Village Home, Ilford', *Night and Day*, 1 September 1877, p. 117.

88. 'Wanted: A Village School', *Night and Day*, April 1891, p. 61.

89. *The First Annual Report of the Managers of the Kensington and Chelsea School District in Respect of the School at Banstead, Together with an Account of their Proceedings from the Formation of the District in 1876*, London: J. W. Wakeham, 1881, p. 21, KCSD 201, LMA. For a similar description of cottage 'fathers' see Barnett, 'The Home or the Barrack?', p. 256.

90. Barnardo, 'Our Village Home at Ilford', *Night and Day*, 15 March 1877, p. 28. Emphasis in original. Also see the advertisement for 'mothers' at the Girls' Village Home, 'To Ladies Seeking Work for Christ', *Night and Day*, 2 June 1879, p. 68.

91. Barnardo, 'Our Village Home at Ilford', p. 28. Emphasis in original.

92. Adams, *Architecture in the Family Way*, p. 139 and Clark, 'Domestic Architecture', p. 50.

93. Barnardo, *'Something Attempted, Something Done': Dr Barnardo's Homes*, p. 86.

94. Cheyne Brady, 'A Visit to the Village Homes for Girls at Ilford', *Night and Day*, 1 August 1877, p. 91.

95. Barnardo, 'Our Village Home at Ilford', *Night and Day*, p. 28. By 1889, the layout was slightly changed: '*Each cottage now contains* on the ground-floor a Mother's Sitting-room, a Sitting-room and Play-room for the girls, a large Dining-room for the family meals, and a Kitchen, Scullery, Pantry, and Store-room.

Upstairs there are either five or six Bedrooms, four of which in the older cottages, and five in the new, contain each from four to six single beds, the remaining one being the "Mother's" room. There is further, of course, a Bath-room and necessary offices in each building.' Barnardo, *'Something Attempted, Something Done': Dr Barnardo's Homes*, p. 86.

96. 'A "Village Home"', *Chambers's Journal* 14, 14 July 1877, reprinted in *Night and Day*, 1 August 1877, pp. 101–102; Barnardo, 'Preventive Homes', *Night and Day*, 15 January 1877, p. 4.

97. 'A "Village Home"', *Night and Day*, 1 August 1877, p. 102. Emphasis in original.

98. Anon [A Late 'Holiday Mother'], *My Cottage: A Story of Dr Barnardo's Village Home for Orphan and Destitute Girls*, London: J. F. Shaw & Co., c. 1885, p. 4.

99. Florence Hill, 'The Family System', pp. 240–41.

100. 'A "Village Home"', p. 103.

101. 'A "Village Home"', p. 102.

102. See Seth Koven and Sonya Michel, eds, *Mothers of a New World: Maternalist Politics and the Origins of the Welfare State*, New York, Routledge, 1993.

8

The Campaign for School Meals in Edwardian Scotland

John Stewart

In February 1888 the renowned Medical Officer of Health for Glasgow, James Russell, gave a speech entitled *Life in One Room, or Some Serious Considerations for the Citizens of Glasgow*. Russell described in detail the nature and consequences of overcrowding in Glasgow tenements – housing conditions in urban-industrial Scotland were widely acknowledged to be the worst in Britain – and urged his middle-class audience urgently to address these issues. Not to do so, he argued, would be not only a failure of Christian charity, but would also result in the physical degeneration of the population and the advance of socialist ideas. Russell put in a 'special word for the children because of their essential helplessness, and because they are the men and women of the future'. To this end he urged his listeners to contribute to philanthropic organisations such as the 'Poor Children's Dinner Tables', one among a number of societies specifically concerned with feeding impoverished children.[1]

Twenty years later the wide-ranging Education (Scotland) Act 1908 allowed School Boards[2] to provide school meals and clothing, as well as introducing school medical inspection. One important characteristic of the 1908 Act in respect of school meals was that it was more comprehensive in scope than its English equivalent, the 1906 Education (Provision of Meals) Act – for example in not setting an upper limit on expenditure and in requiring Boards to investigate all cases of 'neglected' children. Superficially this is rather surprising, as Scotland had been excluded from the 1906 Bill by the House of Lords during its parliamentary passage. Nonetheless the 1906 and 1908 Acts, along with the Education (Administrative Provisions) Act, which introduced medical inspection to England and Wales, were extremely important. They addressed the growing concern with child welfare throughout early twentieth-century Britain by creating the school meals and school medical services. These services were, furthermore, without any associated Poor Law stigma; and an important element in the welfare reforms passed by the Liberal administrations in the wake of the party's landslide election victory in 1906.[3]

There was not, however, a simple, straightforward progression from the arguments of social critics such as Russell to the school meals clauses of the 1908 Act, as Scotland's exclusion from the 1906 Bill might already suggest. Indeed by the Edwardian era the nature, purpose, and method of delivery of child welfare were matters of considerable controversy, and Russell's comments alert us to some of the principal reasons for this. Fears of degeneration and the rise of socialism were having a profound impact on the British ruling classes, and appeared to some to suggest the need for ameliorative, state-sponsored social policy. On the other hand, there was considerable opposition to such proposals from the powerful and influential voluntary sector. This included the actual providers of the vast majority of existing school meal services – including that specifically commended by Russell, the Poor Children's Dinner Table Society – and these were in the forefront of the opposition to school meals legislation.

Russell's speech had also dealt with the especially poor environmental circumstances of the Glasgow working class and their socio-economic and medical consequences. Scottish reformers in the early 1900s sought to expand on such insights, although different conclusions were drawn from the findings of the social investigations of the period, again invariably revolving around individual versus collective responsibility. Finally, although not an issue directly addressed by Russell, Scotland's particular political circumstances played a significant part in shaping the timing and content of the 1908 Act. These themes form the substance of this chapter.[4] As will become apparent, the debate over school meals in Edwardian Scotland highlights the highly contested relationship between the child, the family, and the nation-state, the very subject matter of child welfare policy.

Anxieties

The condition of the 'children of the nation', as they were increasingly called, became of concern to the middle and upper classes around the turn of the nineteenth century, for two reasons.

First, the labour and socialist movements were adopting increasingly high profiles, and in both propaganda and action paid considerable attention to child welfare matters, and especially school meals. An amendment to the education resolution at the Scottish Trades Union Congress in 1898, for instance, demanded that free meals be supplied to all children. This was both a matter of social justice and, as one delegate suggested, an insurance against employers trying to starve strikers and their families back to work, as had happened during the recent engineering dispute. The labour movement throughout Britain played a prominent role in the debates over state-provided school meals. The 1906 School Meal Bills for Scotland and for England and Wales, although later consolidated and taken up by the government, were both originally introduced by Labour MPs.[5]

However, working-class organisations, particularly in Scotland, were weak, and it is unlikely that on their own account they would have been able to exert any serious political pressure on the school meals issue. Nonetheless, the socialist 'threat' was taken seriously, and had an important impact on both supporters and opponents of state intervention in child welfare. On the one hand, socialism was a factor in the emergence of the ideology of 'new' Liberalism. This was much more inclined to state intervention than 'traditional' Liberalism, and saw a key role for some form of collectivist social welfare in both improving the quality of the population and resisting any political challenges from the left. On the other hand, opponents of state-sponsored school meals argued that such a proposal was inherently socialistic. Were it to be enacted, among the unwelcome consequences would be the decline of voluntarism and the subversion of the family. This was central to the claim that one of socialism's aims was the 'state maintenance' of all children. Socialism therefore influenced the Edwardian debates over child welfare in a complex range of ways.[6]

The second cause of Edwardian anxiety over children was that concern over population quality was not confined to 'new' Liberals. The Boer War, and especially the poor quality of potential recruits to the Army, had helped crystallise the belief that the British race was 'deteriorating' or 'degenerating'. Consequently a number of official and unofficial investigations into working-class health took place in the early twentieth century. In these the condition of children, including Scottish children, figured prominently. The young were thought to have a crucial role in arresting racial decline since they were both the future of the nation – adults in poor shape were in any case felt to be beyond saving – and relatively accessible through their institutionalisation in schools. Before discussing these investigations, however, it is necessary to examine in more detail the voluntary provision of school meals in Edwardian Scotland.

Voluntarism

Philanthropy was a major component of social welfare in the early twentieth century. Ideologically, it comprised a number of related principles. Of particular relevance to child welfare were the centrality of the family; the need to combat moral and spiritual dangers such as alcohol, and hence an emphasis on individual characteristics and responsibility rather than socio-economic circumstances; and the ability of charitable organisations, supported by voluntary donations, to provide a personal form of care and attention, enlightened by an intimate knowledge of local conditions. This was the 'traditional' approach to social welfare. As elsewhere, voluntarism in Scotland drew heavily on nineteenth-century evangelicalism, with the influence of one of its most famous clergymen, Thomas Chalmers, being particularly notable. Indeed the Scottish churches had historically played a central role in social policy, partly through the participation of their members and clergy on statutory bodies, partly through evangelical zeal. Both voluntarism and evangelicalism were, in general, resolutely hostile to any state intervention in matters such as feeding needy children.[7] These attitudes were shared by all the main philanthropic bodies actually supplying school meals in Scotland; by the principal anti-cruelty organisation, the Scottish Society for the Prevention of Cruelty to Children; and by the influential Charity Organisation Society (COS) which, aside from its attempted coordinating function in voluntary welfare, had strong views on the need to ensure that parental responsibility was fully carried out.

In the major cities at least, voluntary organisations were providing meals to needy children, and had done so for some time. The Flora C. Stevenson Committee for Feeding and Clothing Destitute Children was founded in 1878, and by 1907 was Edinburgh's largest single provider of school meals. Displaying typically voluntarist attitudes, a representative told Poor Law investigators in 1908 that if parental duties could be enforced then only in 'rare instances' would there be any call on provision from outside the family. Child misery and degradation were, from this standpoint, overwhelmingly attributable to parental alcohol abuse. Flora Stevenson herself had been an active member of the Edinburgh School Board since its foundation and a prominent supporter of the Unionist Party. As she put it in a memorandum to the 1906 Commons Select Committee on School Meals, it would be an 'evil day' for Scotland should School Boards be obliged to provide school meals. What was required, Stevenson argued, was an 'awakening of public conscience', not a weakening of parental responsibility.[8] Here was a further expression of the need for a voluntarist, moralistic, and individual – as opposed to a statist – approach to welfare.

The Select Committee also heard evidence on the situation in Glasgow. George Newlands, Secretary and Treasurer of the Poor Children's Dinner Table Society, explained that his organisation had been founded in 1869; was financed primarily by voluntary contributions; and in 1904–05 had supplied over one quarter of a million dinners at nearly 20 locations. This made it the city's most important provider of meals, with needy children being selected by its three lady visitors. Like Stevenson, Newlands was a strong advocate of the virtues of philanthropy which he believed more efficient and more sensitive to individual needs than any statutory body. He was thus hostile to the state provision of school meals which would, he further argued, have an unwelcome impact on family life.[9] The approach of Stevenson and Newlands was shared by the leaders of the School Boards in their respective cities, William Henry Mill and R.S. Allan, both of whom noted with alarm socialist agitation for school meals. Allan, for example, remarked that at a recent labour demonstration in Glasgow the 1906 School Meals Bill had been explicitly seen as 'an instalment towards the complete maintenance of children by the State'. 'That,' he continued, 'is how it is interpreted by a certain class of the community'. Allan foresaw a time when, if the Bill passed, a socialist School Board could 'feed every child and charge nothing'.[10]

Charitable effort was not, however, without its problems. Almost by definition, it was incapable of providing uniform, regular, and systematic coverage. Olive Checkland notes that by the late nineteenth century philanthropy was characterised by 'wasteful overlap in provision, together with its opposite, serious gaps'; and that this proved incapable of resolution by voluntarism itself. In respect of school meals, both contemporary observation and subsequent interpretation bear this out.[11] Furthermore School Boards, even had they desired to do so, were statutorily disbarred from directly providing meals, although they were allowed to cooperate with existing voluntary agencies. There is some evidence that legal constraints were either circumvented or ignored. In 1887 the Dundee School Board provided over 8,000 free meals, and another 24,000 at a halfpenny each. At around the same time the education inspectorate noted the wide-spread habit of making available 'warm dinners' in many rural schools in northern Scotland for the benefit of children in poverty or who had to travel some distance to attend. The practice here was to recover costs while incurring small expenses to do with apparatus and supervision, and was to be explicitly recognised and legitimised by the 1908 Act.[12] Such practices notwithstanding, existing law and the limitations of charitable effort worked against any comprehensive attempt to address the health and condition of the 'children of the nation'.

Investigations

Fears over 'physical deterioration' prompted a number of investi-gations which addressed, inter alia, the feeding of schoolchildren, and evidence from Scotland featured strongly in these enquiries. When combined with the perceived inadequacies of voluntarism, the constraints of existing law, and the 'threat' of socialism, their findings began to push moderate reform opinion towards statutory provision. In the Scottish case, the link between poor environment – and especially housing – and children's ill-health received further support, and all in all there seemed little to suggest that Scotland's children were not at least as badly off as their counterparts elsewhere in Britain.

The 1903 Royal Commission on Physical Training (Scotland) was the first official enquiry into the population's condition in the wake of the Boer War. As Ian Levitt notes, it was dominated by Unionists, and viewed the possibility of School Boards supplying meals with trepidation. The Commission's Report wondered whether philanthropy might not carry out the task of feeding with 'more discrimination and consequently less danger than a statutory system', one of the principal claims of the proponents of voluntarism. Nonetheless, the Commission recognised the need to reconcile the national benefit from 'the improved moral and physical state of a large number of future citizens' with 'the evils of impaired parental responsibility'. It therefore recommended that School Boards be obliged to enquire into cases of apparent underfeeding; provide facilities for, and cooperate with, voluntary organisations; and, if necessary, provide meals on their own account, and recoup the costs from parents.[13] While clearly not a wholehearted endorsement of state intervention, the Report nonetheless recognised the limitations of voluntarism, and thus the possibility of School Board action to the benefit of the whole nation.

The Physical Deterioration Committee, which reported in 1904, is the most famous Edwardian enquiry into supposed racial decline. It dwelt extensively on child welfare issues, including school feeding, and a number of witnesses dealt with the Scottish situation. The Medical Officer of Health for Glasgow, Dr Archibald Chalmers, agreed it a 'pretty accurate description of the condition' that in his city no child need ever go to school hungry; and that there was 'systematic provision' for supplying food to the children of the very poor through the efforts of the Poor Children's Dinner Table Society. General Sir Frederick Maurice, whose article on low-quality military recruits had crystallised concerns over 'physical deterioration', agreed that conditions in Glasgow were almost certainly the worst in Britain, a further acknowledgement of the difficulties facing the 'Second City of the Empire'. But it was here, he suggested, that most effort had been made to tackle the problem, notably through joint action between the voluntary bodies, the police, and the COS. These had made it a 'golden rule' that children be fed, and that parents then be reminded of their responsibilities. This had reduced, rather than increased, the number of applications for 'gratuitous food'.[14] It is clear that both Chalmers and Maurice believed in the efficacy of voluntary systems, while the role of the COS and of the police is particularly noteworthy. Once again, however, the recognition by Maurice of the depth of Glasgow's problems and the need to prioritise its children was highly significant.

Others, moreover, took a less sanguine view of the current situation. W. Leslie MacKenzie, Medical Inspector of the Scottish Local Government Board and subsequently its Medical Member, suggested that in Edinburgh's Canongate a 'large proportion of the children ... are certainly half-starved', although he was unwilling to speculate as to how generally applicable this was. He agreed, however, that to 'subject a half-starved child to the ordinary routine of school' was the 'height of cruelty', a point explicitly picked up in the Committee's final report. This echoed his slightly earlier claim that attempting to educate the underfed child was 'a positive evil'. Education could only take place within 'certain physiological limits … primarily determined by the food'. The Physical Deterioration Report, while recognising an important role for philanthropy in school meals provision, also argued for a 'working adjustment between the privileges of charity and the obligations of the community'. As with the comments of the Physical Training Commission, this was a guarded recognition of the limits of voluntarism.[15]

MacKenzie's argument that it was counterproductive to attempt to educate ill-nourished children had a long pedigree, and had been part of the motivation behind both voluntary action and legally dubious School Board initiatives. MacKenzie himself was an important figure in the Scottish campaign for better child welfare services. A sceptic of laissez-faire approaches to welfare, his activism at the Local Government Board exemplified, as Levitt notes, a change of outlook among Scotland's administrative personnel. From the early 1900s onwards policy implementation was to be, Levitt continues, increasingly influenced by those who 'wanted to respond more positively, and more urgently, to an advanced industrial economy'.[16] Again on child welfare, MacKenzie told the Royal Society of Edinburgh in March 1905 that in recent official investigations the schoolchild had been a 'focus of interest', not least because children had for some time 'been under the direct control of the State'. Consequently the schoolchild was 'easily seen, easily examined, easily described'.[17] These comments bear out the point noted earlier, that children were important in the fight against racial decline partly because of their institutionalisation through education. All this implied a greater supervisory role for the state in child rearing.

To the evidence from official enquiries and the change in attitude among the Scottish administrative class we can add at this stage two further factors. First, elements within the Scottish churches were beginning to question a social policy based on evangelicalism, in part a response to the 'rise of labour' and investigations of urban living conditions. As early as 1893, for example, we find the Reverend A. Scott Matheson of Dumbarton arguing that ill-nourished school-children be fed because it was a basic human instinct to do so. Furthermore, children should not suffer on account of their parents; Christian charity dictated that the hungry should be fed; and in any event common sense showed that the underfed children could not be properly educated. This was not a direct recommendation for state action, but it did suggest that society had responsibilities which overrode strictly 'traditional' approaches to social policy.[18]

More explicitly, the Reverend David Watson of Glasgow dealt with the school feeding question as the 1908 Bill was progressing through Parliament and in a way which encapsulated important issues in contemporary child welfare debates. Children, he claimed, were the 'Empire's chief asset, and they must be guarded at all costs'. Watson noted that there was a range of conflicting proposals as to how school meals should be funded, but that there was a general consensus that they should be provided. Only in this way, he claimed, 'can we effectually check that deterioration which is at present threatening the very existence of the Empire'. Watson himself was thus in no doubt as to the importance of school meals. Later in the same work, while discussing education, he suggested that 'Our first care must be to lay a sound physical basis. Therefore the children must be fed, *whoever pays for it.*' 'Every great continental city,' he continued, 'has had to institute some system of feeding school children.'[19] This was clearly some way from the view of welfare to which the overwhelming majorities in the Scottish churches had previously subscribed, and laid the way open for state or municipal action.

Second, it was not only official bodies which gathered evidence on the condition of working-class children. The Dundee Social Union, a middle-class philanthropic organisation, published part of its findings in 1905. Its enquiry was clearly influenced by the Physical Deterioration Report, the evidence to which, the Union remarked, showed that the 'proper treatment of the young constitutes the most promising line of reform for correcting the serious evils of national deterioration'. It further noted that the 'question of feeding school children is now engrossing a large share of public attention', although the Union was itself unwilling to comment on 'particular schemes'. Nonetheless, the unequivocal conclusion was that in Dundee 'there must be a large number of children whose health is impaired and whose development is retarded by insufficient nourishment'.[20]

Prompted by the Physical Training Commission's work, the Edinburgh COS carried out a health survey of the city's child population. This noted the unsatisfactory nature of much Edinburgh housing – as will by now be evident, a key concern of Scottish social investigators and reformers – and correlated children's heights and weights with the number of rooms available to their families. The lessons drawn from this were, typically of the COS, that much child suffering was due to parental indulgence in alcohol; to female employment, which often resulted in children eating 'pieces' (that is, sandwiches) rather than proper meals; and to demoralisation due to indiscriminate charitable relief. Nonetheless it was the evidence rather than the fairly predictable conclusions which was important here, adding as it did to the growing body of data on the poor condition of Scottish children. As Levitt remarks, all this 'continued to underline the call for a re-examination of policy'.[21]

Scotland and the 1906 Act

Momentum was gathering, therefore, for legislation allowing for the problem of underfed children to be addressed directly by the appropriate statutory authorities. And, as we have seen, Bills dealing with both England and Wales and Scotland were introduced by two Labour MPs shortly after the Liberal election victory of 1906. These sought to allow, although not compel, the statutory authorities to provide school meals in cases of need. The Bills were then consolidated, and taken up by the Liberal government. However, Scotland was excluded from this consolidated Bill as the result of a Lords amendment, and in consequence the 1906 Education (Provision of Meals) Act applied only to England and Wales. It is worth stressing that while this Act generated heated discussions during its parliamentary passage, it was in fact modest in its actual provisions. Not only was it permissive rather than compulsory, there was also a limit on statutory authority expenditure on school meals.

How, then, are we to explain Scotland's exclusion in 1906 and the passage shortly afterwards of the more comprehensive 1908 Act; and what does this tell us about the debates over child welfare in the early twentieth century? On one level, the events of 1906 can be explained by the parliamentary deliberations on school meals. There was only one Scottish MP (out of a total of 15) on the Select Committee which considered the 1906 Bill, the Conservative Sir Henry Craik, former Secretary to the Scotch Education Department and committed opponent of state-provided school meals. Although Craik was a shrewd political operator, and almost certainly a key figure in persuading the Lords to take the action they did, what was perhaps more important was the Scottish evidence to the Select Committee. This was overwhelmingly hostile despite memoranda from the Minority on the Glasgow School Board urging that the Bill be adopted and applied to Scotland.[22]

Significantly, the four Scottish witnesses who actually appeared before the Committee – out of a total of 27 – were uniformly against the proposed measure. We have already encountered three of these: Newlands, Mill, and Allan. The fourth against the Bill was Miss K.V. Bannatyne, a member of the Glasgow School Board and of the Council of the Glasgow COS, and a nursing and social work visitor. Bannatyne claimed that in respect of the underfed young, 'voluntary agencies feed these children, or can feed them'. Any investigation carried out by a statutory body could not, she continued, 'reach the real reason of the distress in the same way that a voluntary agency would, and could not deal with the root of it'. Consequently any intervention by a government agency would undermine parental responsibility without improving the overall situation, which indeed might be worsened through encouraging 'drunkenness and general thriftlessness'.[23] Here was a classic statement in support of the efficacy of voluntarism, and the dangers of state action.

The overwhelming majority of the Scottish evidence to the Select Committee, including Flora Stevenson's memorandum, thus upheld the voluntarist, individualist, and moralistic approach to social welfare. Parental responsibility had to be enforced, and any form of state intervention was assumed to promote the demise of the family and the triumph of (socialist) collectivism. R.S. Allan even sought to differentiate Scotland from the rest of Britain by denying, when questioned by the Labour Party's Arthur Henderson, that the findings of the Physical Deterioration Committee applied to Scottish children.[24] The arguments of the Bill's Scottish opponents gave the Lords its rationale for confining the Act to England and Wales. Lord Balfour of Burleigh, former Unionist Scottish Secretary, claimed that no Scottish witness to the Select Committee had been in favour of the Bill and that no public body had passed a resolution of support. He specifically remarked on the attitudes of the Glasgow and Edinburgh School Boards; and that the motion to consolidate the two original Bills in Committee had been opposed by its only Scottish member, Craik. Despite an appeal from government minister Earl Crewe, in which he quite correctly claimed that the measure was supported by the majority (indeed an overwhelming majority) of Scottish MPs, the Upper House removed Scotland from the Bill.[25]

This was a victory for the voluntarist approach to child welfare. Unsurprisingly, it received a rather mixed reception. The COS journal *Charity Organisation Review* noted that some socialists were, quite correctly in its view, welcoming the 1906 Act as 'a step, and a big step too, towards the entire maintenance of all children by the State'. Scotland had, however, escaped the 'scope of this injurious measure'. By contrast *The Liberal Monthly* thought their Lordships' exclusion of Scotland 'the meanest thing' they had done. As a result, the 'Scottish child who comes to school hungry must stay hungry – thanks to the tender mercies of the House of Lords'.[26] Whatever the response, it is clear that part of the explanation for the different treatment of one part of Britain was the ability of the Bill's Scottish opponents virtually to monopolise the evidence to the Select Committee and thereby give the Conservative-dominated Upper House the opportunity to defeat a government-supported measure.

Scottish Particularism and the Coming of the 1908 Act

However, there is more to this matter than parliamentary manoeuvring. It is clear that the arguments of individuals such as Flora Stevenson and organisations such as the Poor Children's Dinner Table Society constituted a powerful voice in the debate over child welfare in Edwardian Britain, and in this they were complemented by the influence and ideological drive of the COS. But this was only one voice. Voluntarism was itself under increasing pressure as the demands of industrial society and international competition showed up its shortcomings, and in certain circumstances forced it into a closer relationship with the state than previously. Furthermore, and particularly in large cities such as Glasgow, there was an existing tradition of municipal action geared solely to the civic good rather than, as was the case in most English cities, profit or rate subsidies. Such an attitude potentially opened the door to municipal action on specifically welfare matters.[27] More specifically on school meals, we have seen that pressure had been building within Scotland itself for greater state intervention and that the overwhelming majority of Scottish MPs were in favour of the 1906 Bill. Scotland was, moreover, a Liberal stronghold and on an ideological level no less prone to the advance of 'new' Liberal ideas than any other part of Britain. Indeed, while it is generally agreed that social reform issues played only a small part in the 1906 general election in England, this seems to have been much less the case in Scotland.[28]

This leads us in to a further important aspect of the Scottish campaign, and how it ultimately resulted in the more comprehensive 1908 Act. The Liberal Secretary of State for Scotland, and hence the individual principally involved in the parliamentary passage of the 1908 Bill, was John Sinclair. His appointment, as Levitt puts it, 'brought a new tone to the politics of welfare'. In particular, Sinclair sought to prioritise the education and physical condition of Scottish children for, as Levitt further remarks, he felt that the medical and social needs of the young 'overrode any consideration of economic utility'. As one of his civil servants later recalled, it was thus 'fitting' that Sinclair was largely responsible for legislation which sanctioned the treatment of 'necessitous cases' among Scottish schoolchildren. The Scottish Secretary was, therefore, very much on the 'new' Liberal wing of his party. He was also anxious, according to his former private secretary, that Scotland 'be governed according to Scottish ideas, and was never enthusiastic about the method of dealing with Scotland by applying a single legislative measure to Britain'.[29]

Crucially, this approach was shared by other leading Scottish Liberals and by the officials of the Scotch Education Department. An internal memorandum of November 1906 – that is, before the Lords amendment excluding Scotland – recommended that the current Bill not be applied to Scotland on the grounds of the paucity and hostility of the Scottish evidence; its permissive nature; and, principally, the fact that it was 'a very incomplete and fragmentary way of dealing with a big social question'. Current drafts of specifically Scottish Bills, the memorandum concluded, dealt with the matter better and were 'more in consonance with Scottish opinion'. This ministerial and departmental attitude helps explain the government's relatively sanguine response to the Lords' action, the annoyance of its Scottish backbenchers notwithstanding.[30] The aim was therefore, and explicitly, that a fuller measure, and one geared to Scottish conditions, be introduced. Scottish particularism was, in other words, a card played not only by the opponents of state intervention in child welfare, but also by its supporters. In the broader political context, the Scottish socialist movement remained weak, to such an extent that the Liberal Party in Scotland saw no need to enter into the electoral pact arrangement which existed in England and Wales. Nonetheless leading Scottish Liberals were, by the mid-1900s, discussing the need to counter any future threat from the left. Social reform was clearly central to this strategy of keeping any such challenge at bay, and in any event embraced on principle by politicians such as Sinclair.[31]

Furthermore, evidence continued to accumulate suggesting that, the efforts of voluntarism notwithstanding, Scottish children remained in a poor condition. An official report of 1907, of which the ubiquitous MacKenzie was one of the two authors and which claimed to be the 'most extensive investigation' of its type ever undertaken in Britain, analysed the heights and weights of Glasgow schoolchildren. It found these to be, on average, uniformly below the standard set by the Anthropometrical Committee of the British Association, and variations within the schoolchild population were correlated with the number of rooms occupied by families. This in turn was as 'a good indication of the child's nutritional environment'. Such an argument took on a further dimension in the light of the point already noted, that contemporary reformers thought Scottish housing conditions particularly poor. However, this was not seen in isolation, and the point strongly made that 'only one conclusion' could possibly be drawn from the data gathered, namely that 'the poorest child suffers most in nutrition and growth'.[32] As with other surveys of the Edwardian period, such analysis was used by proponents of state-sponsored school meals. Findings of this sort also continued to undermine the claims of the supporters of voluntarism, namely that Scotland was in some way better off than England and Wales and that philanthropic organisations had the situation under control north of the border.

Broader Scottish opinion too was increasingly in favour of a school meals measure, and we have already noted the shift in attitude among the Scottish churches. The action of the Conservative-dominated Lords in excluding Scotland in 1906 did nothing to enamour that institution to a country which was overwhelmingly Liberal in politics and which already saw the Upper House as an obstacle to other important Scottish issues such as land reform. More directly on child welfare, it is notable that, early in 1908, the Scottish School Boards demanded the 'power to deal effectively with neglected children'. This is particularly significant given that the 1908 Bill was about to begin its parliamentary passage; and given also the Glasgow and Edinburgh Boards' evidence to the 1906 Select Committee. It is notable too that the vast majority of the correspondence on the 1908 Bill sent to the Scotch Education Department, from School Boards and other interested parties, had little to say about school meals. Instead, it was much more concerned with other provisions of the Bill, such as those relating to teachers' pensions.[33] The wider socio-economic context is also important as the 1908 economic downturn hit Scottish cities such as Glasgow particularly hard, thus forming the backdrop to the Bill's parliamentary passage.

Consequently the school feeding clauses of the 1908 Education (Scotland) Bill passed easily through both Commons and Lords, and in the former at least one Liberal MP took the opportunity to question the efficacy of the voluntary organisations currently providing school meals. But the most obvious change, given that virtually all Scottish MPs had in any case supported the 1906 Bill, came in the Upper House. The Conservative peer who had previously led the opposition to Scotland's inclusion, Balfour of Burleigh, now found 'nothing really controversial' in the 1908 Bill, and his speech contained no reference to the school meals clauses.[34] Thus a mere two years after being excluded from a Bill originally intended to encompass the whole of Britain, Scotland had its own, more comprehensive, measure.

Conclusions

What, then, does the experience of the campaign for state-sponsored school meals in Edwardian Scotland tell us about child welfare and social action? First, there was growing sociological and medical evidence that many children were in an extremely poor state, and this was as true in Scotland as elsewhere in Britain. Indeed given the widely acknowledged problems of Scottish housing, and the apparent correlation between environment and ill-health, there is a strong case that Scottish children were especially at risk. Whatever conclusions were drawn by the particular authors of particular official and unofficial surveys, the mounting volume of empirical data gave increasing support to those in favour of direct state intervention, even in the sensitive area of the care of children. In Scotland the interventionist strategy was clearly favoured by influential individuals such as W. L. MacKenzie, and potentially built on an existing tradition of municipalities using their powers specifically to ameliorate social conditions. In the early twentieth century the arguments favouring some form of positive initiative by the state on the question of school meals were given further support by fears of racial deterioration and the emergence of socialism, and by the perceived problems of voluntarism.

Second, it is clear that some form of provision for needy children had existed in Scotland, as elsewhere in Britain, for some time. This was provided overwhelmingly by voluntary organisations, and was a recognition by philanthropy that something had to be done about the welfare of working-class children. However, rather than seeing the roots of child ill-nourishment in socio-economic circumstances, voluntarism stressed an approach to child welfare which took as its starting point the centrality of the family as a social institution. Saving children was a matter best done through addressing the issue of the personal moral responsibility of individual parents. Where such a sense of responsibility was deemed inadequate, the optimum way to tackle this was through charitable organisations supported by the community and sensitive to particular individual and local circumstances. As in more strictly religious matters parents could thus find personal 'redemption' by, for example, eschewing alcohol and so devoting more time and resources to their children. Philanthropy was thus hostile to state intervention, which was perceived not only as mechanistic and materialist, but also as potentially or actually 'socialist'. The continuing strength of the anti-collectivist approach is evident in the Scottish evidence to the 1906 Select Committee, which in turn formed the basis of the Lords' exclusion of Scotland from the 1906 Act.

What these two points illustrate is that while there was a broad general agreement that something had to be done about the condition of Scottish children, there was profound disagreement as to the way in which the problem should be addressed. This leads me to my third concluding point. I have suggested that Scotland's exclusion in 1906 was a victory for the 'traditional' approach to social welfare. But this is not to argue that the movement for a more collectivist approach to child welfare was weaker in Scotland than elsewhere in Britain. We have already noted the significance of MacKenzie and the Scottish municipal tradition, and this can be extended to the more general tendency within the Scottish administrative structures in favour of interventionism, to 'save' the nation's children.

On the political level, the leading Scottish politician of the period,

John Sinclair, was deeply committed to an interventionist strategy, particularly where it would improve the condition of Scottish children. The approach of 'new Liberals' such as Sinclair was, moreover, designed to subvert the socialist 'threat' by gaining the social policy high ground rather than, as was the case with voluntarism, rejecting any state intervention in matters such as school meals. In addition, there was a strong sense among Scottish Liberals, including Sinclair, and the Scottish civil service that legislation should both be tailored to Scotland's particular circumstances and be more 'progressive' than its English and Welsh counterparts. So while the loss of Scotland from the 1906 Bill was hardly welcomed, and was further proof of the Lords' hostility to social reform, nonetheless it gave the opportunity to advance the more comprehensive measure enacted in 1908. This strongly suggests that historical contingency and Scotland's own particular political situation had a central part to play in the coming of the 1908 Act.

Despite the significance of Scottish particularism, however, it must also be recognised that Scotland was deeply, and willingly, integrated in the British Empire and a major contributor of both manufactured goods and human capital to the imperial project. Thus if the 'children of the nation' held the key to Britain's racial and imperial future then to exclude Scottish children was clearly anomalous. In this respect, Scotland was subject to broader *British* trends in child welfare policy. Furthermore it is evident that child welfare legislation in Scotland and in England and Wales did not exist in isolation, so that, for example, the greater scope of the Scottish 1908 Act acted as a spur for those in favour of extending the school meals service in the rest of Britain.[35]

Finally, a note of caution needs to be sounded. The 1908 Act did not signal the inexorable advance of collectivism in the care of Scottish children. It was certainly the case that a number of School Boards did not fully carry out their statutory obligations. Rather curiously, at least in the light of their activities in the 1880s noted above, the Dundee education authorities were among these. This reluctance to implement a school meals programme was also evident in the rest of Britain.[36] If the tendency was undoubtedly towards some form of state responsibility for school meals, it was nonetheless clearly both slow and uneven. Similarly, the state did not take over wholesale the care of Scottish children: on the contrary, it was still assumed that the responsibility for child maintenance lay in the first instance with the parents, and this was explicitly built into the 1908 Act. On the other hand, the Act did have profound implications for the voluntary sector. As George Newlands of the Poor Children's Dinner Table Society told the 1906 Select Committee, in the event of legislation donations to his organisation would 'stop immediately, because the burden of any such proposal would fall largely upon the class who give us contributions'. This was a prescient analysis. Newlands's Society continued to be the main provider of meals in Glasgow until 1910. By that date, however, voluntary donations were insufficient to continue operations, which were then taken over by the School Board. The decline in voluntary contributions for school meals was part of a broader trend throughout Britain as a whole.[37]

The campaign for school meals in Edwardian Scotland thus reveals a complex series of interrelated and interacting factors. Voluntarism, the main provider of school meals until at least 1908, was almost certainly inspired by individual concern and a sense of Christian duty and charity on the part of those who contributed money and time to charitable work. Nonetheless, voluntarism also promoted a particular view of the role and purpose of social welfare based on the centrality of individual responsibility. While 'traditional' welfare ideology did not disappear under a collectivist tide, the consequences for the 'children of the nation' of urban-industrial living, especially in the context of changing domestic political and international circumstances, appeared to demand some measure of state intervention. However, the nature of the British polity and the political dynamics of Edwardian Britain resulted in different school meals legislation being applied to England and Wales and to Scotland at different points in the early twentieth century. This suggests that an understanding of the relationship between child welfare and social action requires not only an analysis of child-centred campaigns, but also of the specific political and socio-economic circumstances in which these take place.

Notes

1. J. B. Russell, *Life in One Room, or Some Serious Considerations for the Citizens of Glasgow*, Glasgow, James Maclehose and Sons, 1888, pp. 15, 28, 30, and passim.

2. School Boards were abolished in England and Wales in 1902, but remained part of the Scottish educational system until 1918, when they were replaced by elected Education Authorities. These were, in turn, abolished in 1929, being succeeded by local authority education committees. This reminds us that the Scottish education system differs in a number of ways from that of England and Wales.

3. H. Hendrick, *Child Welfare: England 1872–1989*, London, Routledge, 1994, part II.

4. The political aspects of this episode as a whole, and the imperial dimension alluded to in the conclusion to this essay, are dealt with in more detail in J. Stewart, '"This Injurious Measure": Scotland and the 1906 Education (Provision of Meals) Act', *Scottish Historical Review* LXXVIII, April 1999, pp. 76–94.

5. *Report of the Second Annual Scottish Trades Union Congress*, Glasgow, Scottish Trades Union Congress, 1898, pp. 36–37; for a fuller account of labour movement concerns over child welfare, see J. Stewart, 'Ramsay MacDonald, the Labour Party, and Child Welfare, 1900–1914', *Twentieth Century British History* 4(2), 1993, pp. 105–25.

6. On 'new' Liberalism see M. Freeden, *The New Liberalism: An Ideology of Social Reform*, Oxford, Oxford University Press, 1978, which includes a brief discussion of the school meals issue at pp. 224–29; on the idea of 'state maintenance', and how this was used by opponents of socialism, see Stewart, 'Ramsay MacDonald, the Labour Party, and Child Welfare', passim.

7. On the ideology and significance of voluntary welfare effort see F. K. Prochaska, 'Philanthropy', in *The Cambridge Social History of Britain*, III, ed. F. M. L. Thompson, Cambridge, Cambridge University Press, 1990, pp. 357–93; on evangelicalism in nineteenth-century Scotland, see C. G. Brown, *Religion and Society in Scotland since 1707*, Edinburgh, Edinburgh University Press, 1997, ch. 5.

8. Parliamentary Papers 1909, vol. XLII, Report of the Royal Commission on the Poor Laws and Relief of Distress on Endowed and Voluntary Charities in Certain Places, and the Administrative Relations of Charity and the Poor Law, pp. 231, 232, 288; Parliamentary Papers 1906, vol. VIII, Special Report and Report from the Select Committee on the Education (Provision of Meals) Bill 1906; and the Education (Provision of Meals)(Scotland) Bill, 1906, together with the Proceedings of the Committee, Minutes of Evidence, and Appendix, Appendix 8.

9. Special Report and Report, qs. 3075ff.

10. Special Report and Report, qs. 4191ff and 4341ff.

11. O. Checkland, *Philanthropy in Victorian Scotland*, Edinburgh, John Donald, 1980, pp. 314–16. On the problems of the voluntary provision of school meals see, for example, M. E. Bulkley, *The Feeding of School Children*, London, G. Bell and Sons, 1914, pp. 3ff; Parliamentary Papers 1903, vol. XXX, Report of the Royal Commission on Physical Training (Scotland), Report and Appendix, part VII; R. D. Anderson, *Education and the Scottish People*, Oxford, Oxford University Press, 1995, pp. 204–05.

12. J. Scotland, *The History of Scottish Education: vol. II, From 1872 to the Present Day*, London, University of London Press, 1969, pp. 88–89.

13. I. Levitt, *Poverty and Welfare in Scotland 1890–1948*, Edinburgh, Edinburgh University Press, 1988, pp. 47–48; Report of the Royal Commission on Physical Training (Scotland), p. 30 para. 165, and p. 36 para. 210.

14. Parliamentary Papers 1904, vol. XXXII, Report of the Inter-Departmental Committee on Physical Deterioration vol. II, List of Witnesses and Minutes of Evidence, qs. 6173–75, 279–80.

15. Ibid., qs. 6977–80; W. L. MacKenzie, *The Medical Inspection of School Children*, Edinburgh and Glasgow, William Hodge and Co., 1904, p. 196; Report of the Inter-Departmental Committee on Physical Deterioration vol. I, Report and Appendix, paras. 360–61, 365.

16. I. Levitt, 'Introduction', in *Government and Social Conditions in Scotland, 1845–1919*, ed. I. Levitt, Edinburgh, Scottish History Society, 1988, pp. xlii–xliii.

17. W. L. Mackenzie, *The Health of the School Child*, London, Methuen, 1906, p. 51.

18. Brown, *Religion and Society*, ch. 6; A. S. Matheson, *The Church and Social Problems*, Edinburgh, Oliphant, Anderson and Ferrier, 1893, pp. 257–58.

19. D. Watson, *Social Problems and the Church's Duty*, London, A. & C. Black, 1908, pp. 21, 35 (emphasis added).

20. Dundee Social Union, *Report of Investigation into Social Conditions in Dundee: Part I, Medical Inspection of School Children*, Dundee, Dundee Social Union, 1905, pp. 5, 15.

21. City of Edinburgh Charity Organisation Society, *Report on the Condition of Fourteen Hundred School Children in the City*, London, P. S. King, 1906, pp. 1, 3; Levitt, *Poverty and Welfare*, pp. 47–48.

22. Special Report and Report, pp. ii–iii, Appendix 11.

23. Special Report and Report, qs. 4478, 4482, 4497.

24. Special Report and Report, qs. 4383, 4395, 4398, 4448.

25. Parliamentary Debates, 4th Series, vol. 167, cols. 1662ff. Contemporary comment on Craik's role can be found in Stewart 'This Injurious Measure', p. 85.

26. *Charity Organisation Review* 21(121) (New Series), January 1907, pp. 6–7; *The Liberal Monthly* 4(II), January 1907, p. 4.

27. On the problems of early twentieth-century voluntarism, see J. Harris, 'Society and State in Twentieth Century Britain', in Thompson, ed., *The Cambridge Social History of Britain*, III, p. 114, and G. Finlayson, *Citizen, State, and Social Welfare in Britain 1830–1990*, Oxford, Oxford University Press, 1994, ch. 2; on municipal action in Scotland, see H. Fraser, 'Municipal Socialism and Social Policy', in *The Victorian City*, ed. R. J. Morris and R. Rodger, London, Longman, 1993; and T. C. Smout, 'Scotland, 1850–1950', in Thompson, ed., *The Cambridge Social History of Britain*, I, p. 252.

28. R.J. Finlay, *A Partnership for the Good?*, Edinburgh, John Donald, 1997, p. 54.

29. Levitt, *Poverty and Welfare*, p. 49; Lady Pentland, *The Right Honourable John Sinclair*, London, Methuen, 1928, pp. 99–102; 'Our Liberal Leaders: Mr John Sinclair', *The Liberal Monthly*, January 1908, p. 6.

30. Scottish Record Office ED 7/6/5, memorandum 16 November 1906 to the Vice-President, Scotch Education Department.

31. I. C. G. Hutchison, *A Political History of Scotland, 1832–1924*, Edinburgh,

John Donald, 1986, p. 246; Finlay, *A Partnership*, p. 55; Stewart, 'This Injurious Measure', pp. 89–91.

32. Parliamentary Papers 1907, vol. LXV, Report by Dr W. Leslie Mackenzie and Captain A. Foster on a Collection of Statistics as to the Physical Condition of Children Attending the Public Schools of the School Board for Glasgow with Relative Tables and Diagrams, pp. i–vi, and passim.

33. Stewart, 'This Injurious Measure', pp. 86–94; Finlay, *A Partnership*, p. 56; *The Scottish Review and Christian Leader* VI (135), 6 February 1908, p. 146; correspondence in Scottish Record Office ED 14/50–56.

34. Parliamentary Debates, 4th Series, vol. 188, col. 134; and vol. 198, cols. 12–21.

35. Stewart, 'This Injurious Measure', pp. 77, 79–81, 92–94.

36. *Charity Organisation Review* 2(157) (New Series), January 1910, p. 37; for the situation in England and Wales, see B. Harris, *The Health of the School Child: A History of the School Medical Service in England and Wales*, Buckingham, Open University Press, 1995, pp. 77–78.

37. For parental responsibility and the 1908 Act, see Stewart, 'This Injurious Measure', p. 87; Special Report and Report, q. 3170; Bulkley, *The Feeding of Schoolchildren*, pp. 244, 54–55.

9

'Blood is Thicker than Water': Family, Fantasy and Identity in the Lives of Scottish Foster Children

Lynn Abrams

Breaking and Making Families

In his recent and illuminating study of the family, John Gillis has argued that 'we must recognise that families are worlds of our own making'.[1] Today, the family we live by in western society is a mythical, idealised creation vested with profound symbolic importance. The family is assigned to do the emotional work once carried out by other institutions and thus it has become a totem of our identity. This process has proceeded apace since the early nineteenth century and perhaps nowhere is the construction of the family as a fulcrum of identity, emotion and belonging more stark than in Scotland. Here, several waves of rural depopulation, urban transformation and industrial growth and decline have had a profound impact on family forms, causing an exceptionally high degree of family dislocation and reconstitution. The Scottish family has been a flexible institution, expanding, contracting and transmogrifying in response to economic and social upheaval. And at the heart of the family's attempts to make and re-make itself are children, who represent the future and the promise of a family's eventual survival.

At the beginning of the twenty-first century the concept of the blood family has assumed great importance, both in popular discourse and in the policies pursued by child welfare professionals. There are a number of reasons for this. Demographic changes, especially since the Second World War, have accelerated the formation of the self-contained or 'nuclear' family. Declining mortality rates have left fewer orphaned children; rising economic prosperity and, more importantly, the development of a comprehensive welfare safety net has reduced the need for children to be placed in substitute families.

Medical advances in the treatment of infertility have also contributed to the obsession with blood over water. Moreover, economic trends have accelerated the demise of the household containing kin and strangers such as servants, lodgers and apprentices. From the perspective of social policy, the predominant trend since the late 1970s has been to make every effort to keep families together; the removal of children from their blood parents and their placement with a foster or adoptive family is an action of last resort.[2] Accompanying the defence of the birth family has been the recognition that children placed in substitute families need information on their biological and sociological background in order for them to complete their self-image, their identity. The 1975 Children Act enshrined this principle in England and Wales by permitting adopted children over the age of 18 access to their birth records, although in Scotland such access had been allowed under the 1930 Adoption Act.[3] Thus the importance of the blood tie for the identity of the individual and the implication that nature plays as significant a role in identity formation as nurture, has been publicly acknowledged. In the last twenty years or so, thousands of those who were involuntarily or forcibly separated in their childhood from their blood relatives and placed in foster families or residential care have taken steps to discover their roots.

Among those who have taken advantage of the legislation and the support services provided by child-care charities and local authorities in order to find out something about the circumstances in which they were taken into care are a great number of the former 'boarded-outs' – Scottish children, some orphaned, some destitute, some illegitimate, who were placed with foster families by the Poor Law and later local government authorities from the mid-nineteenth century up to the 1970s. Many of these individuals are only now beginning to come to terms with their experiences of separation from birth parents, siblings and wider family members, within a context of heightened public knowledge about Scotland's history of child welfare practice – including boarding out and emigration overseas – and the widespread acceptance of the right of every individual to have access to his or her family history.[4] In this chapter I shall address a number of issues surrounding the identity of the boarded-out child in the family and the wider community primarily by adopting a child-centred perspective, an approach still largely absent from the history of child welfare and social policy.[5]

Many children who became the victims of broken families, those who were orphaned, deserted, neglected or those born illegitimate or simply poor, were forcibly separated from their blood relatives and placed with substitute families, usually some considerable distance from kin and cultural roots. The distinctive Scottish policy of boarding out homeless children with foster parents was universally lauded by child-care workers in the state and voluntary sectors as providing the child with a 'natural' home environment, but the undoubted humanitarian principles underlying boarding out conceal more questionable aims on the part of the authorities and tended to bypass concerns about the identity and experience of the homeless child brought up in an 'unnatural' family. Boarding out was primarily a response to the nineteenth-century fear of urban degeneration and hereditary pauperism. A child removed from his or her destitute mother or father in one of Scotland's cities, for instance, and sent to live with a substitute family in the Highlands was used, both symbolically and materially, to undermine the dependent, urban working-class family in order to bolster the idealised independent and moral rural alternative.[6] Boarding out, according to its supporters, served to sever once and for all the link between the child and its pauper parents, lessening the likelihood that the child would follow the same path. The place of the child in this crude scenario was rarely considered. In short, although foster care can be seen as the humane alternative to the poor house and the orphanage – and it is still the favoured solution for homeless children today – in Scotland, from the early nineteenth century to the 1970s, it was also used as a rather crude method of social engineering which paid little attention to the emotional needs of the children involved.[7] Boarding out was an early form of foster care which placed children in a legal no-man's land. Unlike the adopted child who was given a new legal identity and thus rights, the boarded-out child lived in a grey world, possessing none of the rights of either birth or adopted children.[8]

Historians tend to agree that by the mid to late nineteenth century the middle classes had developed a fairly well-defined ideology of childhood. At its heart 'lay a firm commitment that children should be reared in families, a conviction that the way childhood was spent was crucial in determining the kind of adult that the child would become, and an increasing awareness that childhood had rights and privileges of its own'.[9] The proper place for a child was deemed to be within a 'family', protected and dependent, whether this be the child's natural family or a substitute. Henceforth, children found unattended outside the home, in the streets, wynds and closes of Scottish cities, or ill-attended as a result of poverty and material deprivation, or those born illegitimate, were judged to be at risk, requiring rescue and, if necessary, removal from the source of the problem – the blood or birth family – to a new home untainted by the alleged depravity, immorality and pauperism of the urban environment.[10] Needy children, concurred all the major child-care authorities in the late nineteenth century, were best brought up outside the influence of parents and the environment which had brought them so low. In short, it was believed such children needed a fresh start.[11] The boarding out of city children in the more sparsely populated, rural regions of the country, notably in the Highlands and Islands and the coastal districts, was seen as the ideal solution.[12] Between 1880 and the 1940s the vast majority – up to 90 per cent – of Scotland's pauper children were found homes with foster families, amounting to around 8,000 children every year. It is this enthusiasm for boarding out that distinguishes Scottish child welfare under the Poor Law from the policy implemented in England and Wales where pauper children were more likely to find themselves in a workhouse or a cottage home. It is really only since the Second World War that the child-care authorities throughout the British Isles have progressively rejected residential care in favour of foster placements for those children unable to be cared for within their own homes. In 1946, following two government inquiries for England and Wales and for Scotland into the provision of care for homeless children, the prevailing view was that expressed in the Curtis Committee's report: 'there is probably a greater risk of acute unhappiness in a foster home, but ... a happy foster home is happier than life as generally lived in a large community'.[13]

Nowadays, in the light of a series of allegations of physical, emotional and sexual abuse in children's homes around the country, foster care remains the preferred option for the majority of children in the care system. At least one English local authority has dispensed with children's homes altogether. Yet in Scotland at least, it has recently been noted that foster placements have reached a plateau in respect of the availability of foster families, prompting a reappraisal of the mantra that foster care is almost always preferable to residential care. 'A good experience of group care is better than going to the wrong foster home, and infinitely better than going to a succession of foster homes', stated Roger Kent in the most recent official report into the Scottish care system.[14]

In the mid-nineteenth century, when England was housing the majority of its pauper children in the workhouse, the Scottish solution strikes one as liberal and humane. In Scotland, boarding out was portrayed as a natural solution to the problem of homeless children as the Glasgow City Children's Committee argued in 1864:

> The family circle is the most natural one for the bringing up and training of children ... These children look upon the heads of the family as their parents, and the younger branches as brothers and sisters – the best feelings of the heart are engaged, the affections are cherished and drawn out, not smothered in the child's breast as if among strangers ... [the parish authorities] are satisfied that they are following the arrangements of the Sovereign of the Universe by placing these children in families where the moral, intellectual and physical training is calculated to fit them for that sphere of life which they are likely to occupy.[15]

It was believed that children were in safe hands with the uncompli-cated, hard-working, law-abiding, moral and God-fearing crofting, farming and fishing folk who would take orphaned, destitute and neglected children into their homes and their hearts. City fathers imagined children who had been so removed

> enjoying themselves on the sea beach, playing about the family hearth ... or looking after the cows, or sheep or poultry, helping to plant potatoes, or engaged in any of the many rural avocations of crofters' children – amidst beautiful scenery, and in a healthy climate, with good lodging, wholesome food, and decent and sufficient clothing ...[16]

This tendency to romanticise the Highlands and its inhabitants, frequently described as 'kindly and hospitable', honest and respectable, and to contrast the rural environment with the urban centres and unsuitable areas such as mining villages whose inhabitants, it was said, as 'a class apart, stand very low in the scale of civilisation', served to reaffirm the belief in the value of permanent separation of a child from blood relatives.[17] The reflections of the Argyll officer of the poor in 1893 represented the common view: 'When [children are] left with thriftless guardians, having always before them bad examples, [they] will almost invariably turn out bad members of society; but boarded out with respectable guardians in the country, seeing nothing but exemplary conduct, they will almost always in after life lead useful and industrious lives.'[18] In maintaining an almost evangelical zeal in favour of boarding out, children's officers seriously overestimated the ease with which these children would be absorbed into their new homes and communities – they spoke of children 'melting into the population so that you cannot find a trace of them'[19] – and seriously underestimated the long-term effects of severance of a child from cultural roots. 'We believe that the suffering arising from the loss of their parents is reduced to its minimum' commented the Paisley Poor Law Board in 1866.[20] Such was the concern with a child's physical welfare and so great was the requirement to reduce dependence on the state that children's psychological well-being was overlooked. For those who implemented boarding-out policy, families were flexible, permeable institutions which might reject or accept members on grounds other than kinship. Thus, the removal of a child from one family to another was simply a solution to a problem which, it was believed, conformed to the family model practised by most lower-class families.

Present-day child welfare practice, which places great emphasis on the maintenance of family ties where appropriate and affirmation of cultural identity, throws past practice into stark relief. At least until the Second World War, it was the prevalent practice among child-care workers in the state and voluntary sectors to deny and even destroy the child's previous identity purportedly in the child's own interests.[21] Continued contact with the birth family, it was believed, would prejudice the child's adaptation to a new way of life, as a Glasgow Corporation representative acknowledged in 1945: 'Obviously blood is thicker than water ... The fact remains that if the children are a good distance apart from their original upbringing, obviously the opportunities of intervention by parents are lessened.'[22] Secrecy, deliberate obfuscation and lies by the authorities, ignorance on the part of carers and geographical separation placed many children in limbo in respect of their origins, identity and sense of belonging. Few in authority recognised the dangers, although a more enlightened standpoint did begin to be accepted within the child-care profession in the post-war years. The experience of evacuation, not least the public response to the symptoms of homesick children, highlighted the need for children to understand the reasons for their separation from parents.[23] Moreover, the findings of child psychologists, most notably John Bowlby, whose theory on the strength of bond between parent, and especially mother, and child began to be widely accepted, also influenced child welfare workers.[24] 'If the Homeless child is not to indulge in unhealthy fantasy, or become a prey to the first unfortunate suggestion regarding his parentage,' stated the Educational Institute of Scotland in 1945, 'he should be told the truth about his origin, however unpleasant it may be.'[25] The majority of children taken into care before the war and many in the post-war years, however, were ignorant of the circumstances which placed them there, as were their foster parents who were often left to cope with disturbed youngsters with no inkling as to why the children displayed symptoms of trauma. 'They never told us where they came from, they just left them with us', recalled one former foster parent who described the symptoms of one of her foster children who flinched in fear of being beaten: 'if you lifted anything she'd take fright because she thought you were going to hit her. I'm almost crying now just thinking about it.'[26] This gap in the understanding of both children and carers and in that of others could be prejudicial to children's acceptance by the community, their successful incorporation into their new family and ultimately to the individual's sense of identity or belonging. Today it is generally agreed that children who are not informed of their background and the reasons for their adoption are more likely to develop negative identities, insecurity and anxiety.

The openness now encouraged by child welfare legislation and professional practice has undoubtedly facilitated a new and more nuanced understanding of the experience and identity of the boarded-out or fostered child. The discovery of the truth about their back-grounds, and in some cases the discovery of a family they never knew existed, has enabled some individuals partially to reconstruct some elements of a lost identity. In the remainder of this chapter the personal family stories of three former 'boarded-outs' will be closely analysed. All three have constructed life narratives which are organised around feelings of uncertainty, insecurity and a search for identity.

Family Stories – Fantasy Families

Peter was born in Glasgow in 1934, the youngest son of a family of six. In the summer of 1938 when Peter was not yet four years of age, his widowed mother died and he and two brothers aged 10 and 12 were taken from their home by the Glasgow Corporation Children's Department. The three older children – a boy and two girls – were already working and old enough to be left in Glasgow. Seemingly there was no-one in the extended family willing to look after the three youngest children so the boys were sent by the Corporation to stay with a family on the Black Isle, 200 miles away in the eastern Highlands, effectively severing the youngest children from the rest of their siblings. There was no attempt to maintain contact between the two sets of children, and presumably the Corporation never intended for those boarded out to see their family again. Peter recalled, 'Glasgow Corporation just never followed through, couldn't have cared less.'[27] Some months later, for reasons that are unclear, they were suddenly moved again to stay with a widow in a tiny village on the east coast. 'I can remember myself and my two brothers getting off the bus … there was snow on the ground and we went across into this house and that was where we were to be.' The death of the widow soon after meant that the boarded-out boys in her care were simply shifted to the guardianship of her domestic help. From there on Peter described his childhood as 'purgatory'. The boys' movements within the large house were restricted to the kitchen and their bedroom, they were provided with inadequate food, warmth and bedding, no lights to read by, no radio or comics. The boys were required to rise at 6 a.m. in order to fetch milk from a distant farm and carry out household cleaning chores before school, they were deprived of the luxuries afforded to their guardian's natural son, and they were regularly beaten. 'I mean hammerings were daily, every day without fail you got a belt.' On occasion the punishment was so harshly administered that Peter and his brother suffered serious injury – in Peter's case a broken arm while his brother was left permanently deaf in one ear after being beaten round the head with a brush. Peter remembered his childhood as a time of fear with only school as an escape. At the age of 15 Peter and the other boys remaining were suddenly removed by the Corporation inspector and 'dumped with two spinster sisters' in Inverness. From there, with the encouragement of his brother who sent him the rail fare, Peter ran away to Glasgow.

Clearly Peter's experience bore no relation to that envisaged by the architects of the boarding-out policy and his narrative reflects his anger and disappointment at the treatment he received. Living in an isolated village and forbidden to have much contact with other children Peter could never feel part of his adoptive community. But, as he recalled, the village was not eager to embrace the 'Glasgow kealies'. 'You were known as a Glasgow kealie and anything bad that happened in the village we were the first to get [the blame] … I wouldn't say ostracised, but you were looked on as being different.' However, it was within the 'family' that Peter experienced the greatest anxiety. A loving family environment could go a long way towards redressing any harm wreaked by community attitudes. By the 1940s all child-care professionals were in agreement; normal childhood development was dependent upon three things:

> These three things are parental affection, which calls forth the response of the child and starts normal emotional development; the second thing is the intimate personal interest which parents can take in each child, which encourages it to develop its capacities and train its character, and enables it, in fact, to become an individual in the community ... and the third thing is preparation for and gradual introduction to independent life.[28]

The emergence of a well-developed and secure personality, it was generally agreed, was dependent upon emotional satisfaction in the childhood years. Child-care workers today agree that a secure family environment is crucial to a child's sense of well-being, self-esteem and belonging. For this child, though, there was no bond between 'mother' and child. When asked what he called his foster mother Peter replied, after a long pause, 'I didn't call her anything ... no I can't remember ever calling her anything.' Peter was adamant that his guardian was motivated to accept boarded-out children for purely mercenary reasons:

> Purely money ... material gain because not just what they would be getting from Glasgow Corporation they were obviously gaining something for sending us out to the farm to work, I mean we got nothing for it. We had to slave and do what we had to do so I mean she's bound to have got some reward from that ... I mean there was no love, no...

This was a common and not entirely unfounded criticism, especially of crofters who allegedly took in children as a source of free labour. Peter's foster mother certainly used the children in her care to supplement her income by sending them to work in the school holidays and denying them the meagre fruits of their labours, even demanding they hand over the pennies they received from neighbours for running messages. His guardian instilled in her charges a sense of fear. When asked why he or his brothers had not told anyone of the treatment they were subjected to Peter commented: 'we'd no will of our own. I mean you never queried, you never said why or wherefore, you were told to do something and you just did it. You know it was immediate obedience ... You didn't even question if anyone else was different ... you were brainwashed, completely brainwashed.'

Peter described his experience as a lost childhood. Peter's sense of 'family' and of his own 'childhood' is, in his testimony, confused and problematic. Freud posited that every child has a 'fantasy family' in which his or her true parents are imagined as not the 'real' parents and the child imagines himself or herself as adopted.[29] Peter's testimony unconsciously reworks this psychological process, only in his case the fantasy family is his lost, 'real' blood family. For more than two decades of his adult life this remained a fantasy but in his forties he suffered a heart attack – an event which characteristically requires 'official documentation' of next-of-kin, family medical history and so forth. As a result, Peter sent away for a copy of his full birth certificate and it was only then that he discovered what he called a 'skeleton in the cupboard'. He had been born illegitimate, a fact none of his brothers or sisters had ever revealed to him.

> And it started to answer all of the questions that I'd had over the years. I'm different from them ... and that also explains why they didn't take any interest in me while I was up there, except for [my brother] who got me out of it because he'd been there and experienced it ... Oh I was angry, blazing, really angry, you know that they [his brothers and sisters] were obviously trying to hide it from me ... but I left them in no uncertain frame of mind that I thought it was something worth bothering about and that I should have been told and that explained a lot of actions for instance when I ran away and came down to Glasgow and Donald took me round to our sister ... now I'd never been hugged or kissed in my life up till then but I'm expecting I'm going to meet my sister you know, she's going to hug me, no didn'ae happen.

Instead, the long lost youngest brother who had not seen his sister for twelve years was greeted in a rather matter-of-fact manner; 'hello Peter ... how are you doing?' was the only greeting he received. In retrospect Peter rationalised his disappointment at his sister's lack of outward show of affection in the light of what he termed 'the skeleton in the cupboard'. For him, it must have been his status as the illegitimate child that explained the absence of filial emotion. This he took as a rejection by his 'fantasy family', a wounding experience. He had expected at the moment of meeting his sister to receive a hug – a symbolic restitution, not just of the affection he was deprived of in his foster family, but of his place in his ideal, 'real' family.

As a result, after a childhood that lacked all the things commonly associated with that period in one's life – love, security, encouragement and a feeling of belonging to a family, a community – Peter spent years going about, as he put it, 'with a chip on my shoulder'.

> Why should that have happened to me you know, why should I have been beaten from morning until night, you know I'm just an ordinary human being

but when you came out and saw how other people lived and started mixing with families and made friends and you saw how they lived and were brought up you know it made you feel bitter ...

Yet Peter's discovery about his own parentage, the circumstances in which he was taken into care, and the reaction of his brothers and sisters to his status clearly forced him to rethink his assessment of the boarding-out policy. When asked about the policy in general Peter replied, 'well you're bound to say initially it was terrible but then you think what would have happened if they hadn'ae, where would I have been?' Peter was unable to resolve the contradiction between his unhappy experiences and his imagined childhood as the illegitimate son in a family lacking the resources and maybe the desire to care for him. The discovery of his origins in the words on a birth certificate could not resolve Peter's bitter feelings about a childhood lost, since his fantasy family did not exist in reality. Reality was almost more troubling than his childhood experiences. Neither could it affirm his identity; indeed, the discovery that he was illegitimate, while answering some questions, only served to raise many others. In fact Peter revealed that it was only when he created a family of his own, when he married and had children, that he was able to square the circle, to create the ideal 'fantasy' family, to come to terms with what had happened to him. Yet it still left him deprived of a family history in which he had a place.

A parallel case is that of Robert who, like Peter, was born in 1934 in Glasgow. Both were born illegitimate and both were boarded out in the northeast of Scotland. Robert also had difficulty in coming to terms with his identity. But here the similarities end. Robert, born a Catholic, was placed in the care of Glasgow Corporation at the age of three. He was initially boarded out in Banff but was apparently removed from his first foster family on account of neglect. In 1937, suffering from rickets, he was taken to stay with a widow in the bustling fishing town of Buckie. She was already well known to the Corporation as a reliable guardian. 'Granny G.' had six children of her own but she accepted up to 12 boarded-outs – all Catholic – and Robert was the youngest.[30] Robert remembered his childhood as a happy time. He was made to feel part of the family, 'we referred to each other as brothers and sisters ... it was the only family I ever knew you see', and when his guardian died her eldest daughter – known as 'Nanny G.' – took her place.[31]

However, despite Robert's settled and secure family life, he was aware of his provisional status. The story was told ﾛﾟy that there had been a black child brought to Buckie ﾟﾟn Robert 'and they often used to say to me they wish they'd ﾟﾟn her instead of me like, when I was misbehaving. More than once I was told, now you behave yourself or you'll be away.' At the same time Robert was acutely conscious of his position as a boarded-out child. His narrative is peppered with references to another 'orphan' child in the extended family, one unlike him who was legally adopted. She seemingly became the centre of attention, or at least that was Robert's interpretation: 'it was unbelievable how they accepted [her] and everything centred around [her] and [her] kids'. However, Robert was keen to emphasise how, in his view, he was given a better life than many children who lived with their natural parents.

> We was better looked after than the bloody kids with their mother and father I can tell you that, we really were. I used to stand on a rostrum and tell them that you know and yet you was underdog you know in the playground and that you see, you were a Glasgow orphan (...) In fact you couldn't be bloody jealous right enough because you were better off than they were.

In addition to free health care, clothing and other material help provided by the Corporation, Robert was constantly at pains to affirm his positive experience as a boarded-out child. Not for him the family frictions present in blood families: 'I'd no traumas to go through.' He referred to his childhood as 'happier than most that had their mother and father'. 'As I say,' he continued, 'I'm more cynical and bitter, it makes you kinda more on your guard throughout life which is no bad thing.' Robert's cynicism was presented as a form of protection against the disappointment of not wholly belonging to either a 'real' family or his foster family.

Robert was also made aware of his outsider status within the fishing town of Buckie. At that time considerable numbers of Glasgow children were boarded in the town and local inhabitants made the boarded-outs conscious of their identity as outsiders in a number of ways. At his Catholic school Robert recalled being called names:

> Kids will be kids and you used to get the brickbats at school, Glasgow orphan this that and you were called names and again – it wasn'ae so bad, it was acceptable to you as a kid, it was one kid to another idea but again you see if there was any devilment ... the adult parents 'mine can do no wrong, it's those Glasgow orphans' and that you know that's what you're up against ... there was a differential kind of system there you see.

And when the time came for him to find work he discovered that being an incomer restricted his opportunities in a single-industry town like Buckie, dominated by fishing:

> The thing was there was the slips, the boat-building, there was the fishing, and it's a fishing community you understand, and they were clannish ... and they looked after their own you see; now just take me, I wanted to get in to serve my time as a joiner I did you know, but Willie was taken before Bobby because Willie's dad was maybe in the shipyards, I didn'ae have that push, I didn'ae have that kick your backside into a job, but this is what you're up against and you accept it right enough ...

The treatment of boarded-out children as incomers was an attitude that had long-term and potentially damaging repercussions. In 1945 the director of social service for the Church of Scotland commented on how 'in country places, where everybody knows everybody else, the boarded-out child tends to be regarded as an "in-comer" ... as an unwelcome intrusion into a rather class-conscious community'.[32] Robert eventually found work 'on the message bikes' for the local businesses but after a stint in the army 'I came back to Buckie, naturally it was my home, again there was no work so I had to up roots away ... and I went down south ...'

Robert was prompted to reflect on his roots and his identity on the occasion of his marriage. Before that time he had never been told anything about his birth family apart from the story that his parents had been killed in a car crash. It was clear that his foster mother was 'left ignorant by the authorities'. The culture of secrecy surrounding the removal of these children from the cities was a legacy bequeathed by late-nineteenth-century practice when the Poor Law authorities forcibly separated children from their pauper parents and sent them far away, thus severing all contact, a policy formalised in 1891 when automatic access to a pauper child by a parent was denied. It was widely believed that children would soon forget their families and backgrounds and would be grateful for having been rescued from a destitute existence. Upon receiving his birth certificate, and upon the prompting of the marriage registrar noting that his birth had only been registered by his mother, Robert recalled, 'that set me thinking and made me start a wee bit of researching myself'. The story of the car crash was revealed to be patently false but Robert has not been able to construct an alternative family story for himself. 'According to the certificates [my mother] got married in 1932 and I was born in 1934 which if everything's black and white I'm not a bastard child but given their age differences ... and no father's name makes one wonder you know, so you're left hanging there.'

Robert's narrative is pervaded by self-doubt and confusion about his identity. Unlike Peter, Robert's experience of boarding out was generally positive, or at least he describes it as such, though hardly concealing a repressed anger. Yet at the same time he has been unable to resolve pressing questions about his biological family. His research has not revealed answers about his own status. Robert inhabits a no-man's-land in his mind. Accepting that he was well cared for as part of a family, he still harbours doubts about the degree to which he was truly a member on account of the fact he was never adopted, the reminder that he could have been sent back (to Glasgow) at any time and on account of the knocks he experienced as a schoolchild and as someone looking for work in that close-knit community. It is revealing that Robert's comment in respect of eventually gaining work through a friend of his wife's father was 'I got my own back on society'. Society, one feels, dealt Robert an impossible hand.

In the cases of Peter and Robert a resolution to the problem of identity has not been wholly forthcoming through the discovery of their biological and social roots. For Frances, who has discovered her birth family, the issue of identity is muddier still. Frances was born in 1936 in Glasgow's Stobhill hospital and she was boarded out four months later to a couple in a small village in Aberdeenshire who already had three children of their own. Frances was fully incorporated into family life. She was treated the same as her sisters: 'I was just like any other child.'[33] Frances' mother refused to dress her in Corporation clothes; instead she received cash payments and clothed her the same as the other girls. Until the age of seven Frances had no idea she was a fostered child but the taunts of schoolfriends after a falling out – 'he's not your father in any case, it's not your father' – prompted her to look for her birth certificate in a box under her parents' bed, and 'out came the black book' in which the Glasgow Corporation inspector had registered his visits. All was revealed or, as Frances described it, 'I found out that I didn't belong.' The news perhaps confirmed a niggling suspicion since Frances had always used two surnames: the name on her birth certificate and the name of her foster family which 'was always in brackets after on everything official'. It was only when Frances left school and attended nursing college that she decided to use the name on her birth certificate and when she got married 'I said at least I'll have a permanent name now'. Her foster mother's response – 'is our name not good enough for you?' – revealed that both foster parents and their children could feel troubled about the legal uncertainty inherent in boarding out in contrast with the more fixed legal status of adopted children.

For Frances then, notwithstanding her secure and happy childhood, identity was something to be negotiated ever since the day she discovered her true status. Thereafter events and behaviour which might commonly occur in any family relationship were interpreted in the light of the revelation that she was not the natural child of her parents. One of her sisters, as Frances described it, 'said her nose was out of joint with me'; 'all at once she realised she wasn't the baby you see, her life had been ruined by me, she thought'. When Frances had children of her own she admitted to some curiosity about her birth family, commenting, 'I'd think, I wonder where that one takes, my family ... the looks ... to hold your baby and say "Oh that's uncle's this and that"', but it was not until she suffered an illness and was asked questions about her past history that Frances decided to discover her roots. 'I always vowed I wouldn't do any research until [Mum and Dad] died you know, just for their sake.' It was then she discovered that the family story she had always been told was untrue. 'My foster mother told me, this is what she was told and I know they were told nothing else because that story was told over and over again, "she was only 16 and her mother wouldn't have her".' Frances discovered much more than just her mother's identity. In fact Frances found out that her mother was a single Jewish woman, a boot repairer's assistant from the Gorbals, and her father was an unemployed Protestant. Frances was taken into care just ten days after the birth, her mother having been disowned by her family – 'I mean to go with a non-Jew was terrible' – and some years later Frances' mother, who had not been well for some time, was admitted to a psychiatric institution. Frances' mother died in 1976 before she could meet her.

The consequences of Frances' discovery of her Jewish identity have been profound for her. Raised by a strict Presbyterian family, Frances had no inkling of her 'real' cultural and religious origins. Although Frances acknowledged that she had benefited from being boarded out, as she had been able to take advantage of educational and career opportunities which she would not have had access to if she had been brought up in poverty in the Gorbals – the Corporation paid for her to attend nursing college, a privilege not available to her sisters – nevertheless Frances reflected:

> I tried to understand as much as I could, I also read lots and lots of books on Judaism so I think I'm more understanding about it now ... when I found out I was Jewish I thought now I should've had a chance to follow my culture, that's maybe my only regret after ... being amongst Jewish people and thinking, you should know this, because reading up, you'll never be a Jew.

Frances was initially elated at discovering her roots, finding physical resemblances between herself and a photograph of her mother, and at meeting some distant relatives. However, Frances, like Peter and Robert, is left in a state of limbo, unable to become part of her birth family, partly on account of her relatives' apparent embarrassment at her existence, and partly because she has been unable to discover any more about her mother or her father. At the same time Frances is now ambivalent about the boarding-out system. While acknowledging that she gained in many ways, she is left with the feeling that 'maybe baby Jews didn't mean much to [the authorities]'.

A Life in Three Acts

Peter, Robert and Frances present three variations on a common theme. All three demonstrate how the fostered child is one who knows that he or she holds that rather ambiguous status within the family and the wider community. In the foster family, domestic arrangements, differentiation in treatment from birth children in the household, and the system of payment and regular inspections by the authorities, could act as constant reminders of the child's special status. Similarly, in the community, and especially in parts of the Highlands and Islands where considerable numbers of children were sent, the fostered child was known. In school, in the local shops and on the streets, boarded-out children were identified as neither true members of a family nor of the community. In some communities language difficulties also served to isolate the boarded-out child. A child with a Glasgow accent was immediately noticeable anywhere else in the country, but some of those sent to parts of the Highlands and particularly the Western Isles and the Hebridean Islands found they had to learn a new language – Gaelic. 'I remember my first day at school,' recounted one woman who was found a home with her sister on Barra in the Western Isles. 'I couldn't speak Gaelic and I felt different from the others ... I made sure I learned and worked out the meaning of every word so that I could speak Gaelic and be like the others at school.'[34] On Tiree, on the other hand, English was widespread in the 1930s and 1940s on account of the large influx of boarded-out children to that small community. As a result, in school 'there was one lot spoke Gaelic and the other lot spoke English because there was a bigger percentage of boarded-out children on the island than there was of native speakers ...'[35] Not that there was necessarily strength in numbers. 'I was only very young at school when I realised that these children were different from the island children,' recalled one Tiree resident:

> Day after day the island children mistreated the children from Glasgow. And everyone, teachers too, made fun of these children and never stopped teasing them. You can't do that to little children without causing them terrible mental suffering. That child will never ever forget how people despised him or her.[36]

Each boarded-out child revealed what might be termed a 'foster-mentality' in their family stories. They become preoccupied with the definition of 'family' and of 'belonging'; they construct stories which both accentuate and question their own position within the foster family. Betty, who was fostered on a small Hebridean island, clearly demonstrated this contradictory position. Betty was taken to Tiree by Glasgow Corporation in 1943. Along with other children needing homes she was driven around the island in a black taxi and described how 'I was the last to go to be taken. They just came out and shook their heads and went away again.'[37] Finally Betty was provisionally taken in by a couple who, she believed, had really wanted a boy to work on the croft, yet she stayed until she was 19. Of her foster mother she remarked, 'I mean she was very very kind ... I mean she was just over the moon about getting me, that must have been just what she wanted, she got this wee girl...'[38] And yet Betty's description of the reaction of another set of foster parents on the island to the death of their foster child is revealing: 'And on the [head] stone it says beloved daughter and they broke their hearts over it, in fact they say he never got over that. Now that was a wee girl that they brought up and yet they had family of their own.'[39] Surely the subtext here was Betty's anxiety over her place within her own foster family.

Concepts of 'real' and 'imagined' or 'fantasy families' grow steadily in the foster child's consciousness until a chance event or unwitting discovery causes them to expose the wound of non-belonging. At that point real families and fantasy families become fields of cautious exploration. For some the voyage of discovery begins and ends with a birth certificate; others may meet members of the family that has long been an object of fantasy. However, in the three cases analysed here and in many others involving persons only researching their families in later life, the discovery of the truth about one's origins may not bring about a resolution of the identity crisis. Indeed, as Peter, Robert and Frances all show, it may create another parallel world which is no more comfortable than the old. For Betty, the discovery of a brother and a family history only served to reinforce this confusion. 'Well I think compared to what my brother had I had a far happier childhood ... well he stayed with my mother ... alright he lived with his mother which I didn't which you'd suppose was better for him but on the other hand I had a happier childhood.'[40] What was more important, happiness or a 'mother'? Betty was unable to resolve this apparent contradiction.

The construction of life narratives of those separated from their birth families when young tend to conform to the model of the three-act play with each act divided from the other by moments of supreme personal drama. The first act consists of an almost entirely forgotten but hazily imagined childhood with the birth family when the circumstances which necessitated the child being removed are reconstructed from limited knowledge of deprivation or of abuse. This stage is interrupted by the abrupt removal to the new family, usually in circumstances little understood. This 'memory' of trauma invokes a sense of displacement from family and culture but it is often recalled in later years through name calling – 'Glasgow kealies' – or veiled references to being 'sent back'. This stage is punctuated by a second turning point – which may be the confirmation that one is fostered, or a life-cycle event such as marriage or an illness which calls for an invocation of a family history. At this point an attempt may be made to turn the fantasy family into something more concrete. Yet, whatever the results of this exercise, the effect is to sustain and even accentuate the individual's sense of personal loss since they can never really know their birth parents, never become fully part of the culture they have lost. Thus, the boarded-out child becomes an itinerant player without a home in any family history. Some resolution may come with their own construction of a family which comes with marriage and children. This provides some with the opportunity to live a 'real' vicarious childhood through their own children and to form a family to take the place of the fantasy family.

Latterly the issue of identity has influenced child-care policy and practice, and especially those aspects relating to foster care and adoption. In the last few years we have witnessed a vociferous debate between the advocates of transracial adoption and those who argue that to place a child of a particular race with parents of another would be tantamount to denying that child the right to its own culture. In Scotland, notwithstanding religious sensitivities which consigned many Catholic children to orphanages owing to the shortage of Catholic foster families, boarding out never aroused similar concerns. As we have seen, however, the naïve assumption that one could create new, healthy families from the debris of old dysfunctional ones ignored some basic truths concerning cultural belonging and identity. Many former boarded-outs have long had the sense of inhabiting a no-man's-land where the signposts to one's cultural identity are confusing or absent. 'I have often experienced problems with "acceptance" and have at times felt I have had to work harder than others to justify my position in various areas of life', wrote one man who was happily boarded out with an affectionate guardian.[41]

The transparency of present-day social work practice goes some way towards relieving these contradictory impulses in children placed in adoptive and foster care today, and proffers the hope that in future children separated from their birth families will not suffer the same confusion of identity as their predecessors. Boarding out was a policy designed in the nineteenth century permanently to separate children from their blood ties in the service of economic efficiency and social engineering. The aim was to give children a fresh start with new identities. As the personal narratives analysed in this chapter demonstrate, the experience of being a boarded-out child could be fraught with tensions and anxieties which were, in no small part, the result of being denied information about biological parenthood and social origins.

214   **Rethinking Philanthropy**

Notes

1. J. R. Gillis, *A World of their Own Making: A History of Myth and Ritual in Family Life*, Oxford, Oxford University Press, 1997, p. 240.

2. On the trends in child welfare and protection practice see L. Fox Harding, *Perspectives in Child Care Policy*, London, Longman, 1991.

3. On some of the consequences of the Scottish policy see J. Triseliotis, *In Search of Origins. The Experience of Adopted People*, London, Routledge & Kegan Paul, 1973.

4. The broadcast media have been especially influential in this regard. The BBC Scotland television programme *Air Fasdadh* (Boarding Out) broadcast in 1997 raised awareness of the policy and extent of boarding out and alerted many of those who experienced the policy to the fact that they could trace their natural parents and find out why they were taken into care. Other programmes and newspaper reports on child emigration have had a similar impact. Margaret Humphreys' emotive account of her crusade to help former child migrants in her *Empty Cradles*, London, Transworld Publishers, 1994, is widely cited but perhaps exaggerates the number of children involved in the Australian emigration schemes.

5. See Harry Hendrick's advocacy of and attempt to adopt a child-centred perspective in his *Child Welfare: England 1872–1989*, London, Routledge, 1994.

6. See H. Macdonald, 'Boarding Out and the Scottish Poor Law, 1845–1914', *Scottish Historical Review* LXXV, 1996, pp. 197–220.

7. For an elaboration of this argument see Lynn Abrams, *The Orphan Country: Children of Scotland's Broken Homes, 1845 to the Present Day*, Edinburgh, John Donald, 1998.

8. For example, the boarding-out authorities might remove a child from a foster family at any time and resumed guardianship rights when the child reached employment age.

9. H. Cunningham, *Children and Childhood in Western Society since 1500*, London, Longman, 1995, p. 41.

10. The history of the emergence of this child welfare policy is well known, although most studies are restricted to England. See Hendrick, *Child Welfare*; Cunningham, *Children and Childhood*; G. Behlmer, *Child Abuse and Moral Reform in England 1870–1908*, Stanford, CA, Stanford University Press, 1982; Jean S. Heywood, *Children in Care: the Development of the Service for the Deprived Child*, London, Routledge & Kegan Paul, 1978.

11. For example, one report in 1870 spoke of rescuing children from 'profligate parents or evil associations … in either case the children are removed (with their consent) and boarded out far away from the evil influences, so as to have the opportunity of starting a new life.' B.P.P., 1870, Vol. LVIII, Report on the Boarding Out of Pauper Children in Scotland, p. 81.

12. For a fuller survey of child welfare and protection in Scotland see Abrams, *Orphan Country*.

13. B.P.P., 1945–6, Cmd. 6922, Report of the Care of Children Committee (England and Wales), paragraphs 418–22.

14. R. Kent, *Children's Safeguards Review*, Edinburgh, Stationery Office, 1998, p. 23.

15. Glasgow City Archives, D-CH 1/1: Glasgow City Parish Children's Committee Minute Book No.1, 25 August 1864.

16. B.P.P., 1863, Vol. XXII App (A), No. 4, Report on Pauper Children Boarded Out on Arran, p. 650.

17. Glasgow City Archives, D-HEW, 24/7: Reports by visiting members for 1889.

18. B.P.P., 1893, Cmd. 7140: Report on the System in Scotland of Boarding Pauper Children in Private Dwellings, p. 8.

19. B.P.P., 1870, Vol. LVIII, p. 80.

20. B.P.P., 1870, Vol. LVIII, p. 79.

21. This was particularly true of emigrated children and continued after 1945. See Humphreys, *Empty Cradles.*

22. Scottish Records Office (SRO), ED 11/266: Councillor Brown to Clyde Committee, 1945.

23. On evacuation in Scotland see W. Boyd, ed., *Evacuation in Scotland: A Record of Events and Experiments*, London, University of London Press, 1944. On the role of child psychologists during the war see Abrams, *Orphan Country*, pp. 173–77, and D. Thom, 'Wishes, Anxiety, Play and Gestures: Child Guidance in Inter-war England', in *In the Name of the Child*, ed. R. Cooter, London, Routledge, 1982, pp. 200–19.

24. J. Bowlby, *Child Care and the Growth of Love,* Harmondsworth, Penguin, 1953; *Attachment and Loss. Vol. 2: Separation, Anxiety and Anger*, London, Hogarth Press, 1973.

25. SRO, ED 11/159; memorandum from EIS to Clyde Committee, November 1945.

26. *Air Fasdadh*, BBC Scotland, 1997 (respondent: Hannah NicAsgaill, South Uist).

27. Interview with Peter (all subsequent quotations from the same source). All names are pseudonyms. Transcript in Scottish Oral History Centre Archive (SOHCA), University of Strathclyde.

28. SRO, ED 11/266: Dr Seymour, Department of Health for Scotland to Clyde Committee, 1945.

29. S. Freud, 'Family Romances', in *The Standard Edition of the Complete Psychological Works of Sigmund Freud*, IX, trans. James Strachey, London, Hogarth Press, 1959, pp. 235–41. Anna Freud also developed the idea of the 'family romance' in her work on adolescence in the inter-war period. See J. Sayers, *Mothers of Psychoanalysis*, New York, Norton, 1991, p. 165.

30. Catholic foster homes were thin on the ground and the majority of Catholic children taken into care were placed in Catholic-run orphanages.

31. Interview with Robert (all subsequent quotations from the same source). Transcript in SOHCA.

32. SRO, ED 11/159: Revd L. L. L. Cameron to Clyde Committee, Sept 1945.

33. Interview with Frances (all subsequent quotations from the same source). Transcript in SOHCA.

34. *Air Fasdadh* (Caidlin Bhoid, Barra).

35. Interview with Betty. Transcript in SOHCA.

36. *Air Fasdadh* (Eachann MacPhail, Tiree).

37. Interview with Betty.

38. Interview with Betty.

39. Interview with Betty.

40. Interview with Betty.

41. Author's correspondence with Frank.

IV
'Welfare States' and Child Welfare

10

'Fixing' Mothers: Child Welfare and Compulsory Sterilisation in the American Midwest, 1925–1945

Molly Ladd-Taylor

For most of the twentieth century, child welfare policy in the United States focused on fixing parents, especially mothers. For the most part, this meant providing education and training, instead of resources, to impoverished parents. To combat infant and maternal mortality, for example, the 1921 Sheppard-Towner Act provided education in hygiene and nutrition, but no medical care or financial assistance. The 1935 Social Security Act, which guaranteed financial assistance to needy families through Aid to Dependent Children, permitted states to supervise housekeeping practices and to limit welfare payments to mothers who had a 'suitable home'.[1] Even in the 1960s, in the midst of President Lyndon Johnson's War on Poverty, greater emphasis was placed on education and individual rehabilitation than on economic support for poor families.[2]

Government efforts to 'fix' parents were not limited to education, however. Compulsory sterilisation, although far from routine, was an integral part of American health and welfare policy for much of the twentieth century. Numerous activists and scholars have commented on the connections between sterilisation and welfare, but most studies have focused on the 1960s and 1970s, when a grassroots movement and several highly publicised lawsuits brought about federal guidelines that halted the most flagrant abuses.[3] Little attention has been paid to the period before the Second World War – although 30 American states permitted the compulsory sterilisation of the insane or feebleminded, and at least 38,000 persons had been surgically sterilised by 1941.[4] These early state sterilisation programmes, while legally justified on eugenic grounds, served several purposes – reducing the perceived burden on the public purse being foremost among them. The disproportionate number of sterilisations among young women was due in large measure to such fiscal concerns.[5]

This chapter focuses on the state of Minnesota to examine the place of 'eugenic' sterilisation in the history of American welfare. Located in the upper midwest near the Canadian border, Minnesota is a useful site for a case study because of its relatively homogeneous population and liberal reputation. Unlike studies which emphasise the racist motivations and 'Nazi connections' of American sterilisation supporters, Minnesota's history tells a more mundane tale of fiscal politics and family woes.[6] The physicians and social workers who ran the state's sterilisation programme saw it as a humane and progressive social welfare measure. They rarely authorised operations over the objections of family members and did not sterilise very young children. Minnesota was highly regarded for its enlightened social programmes, including its programmes for people with mental disabilities; yet it had one of the nation's most active sterilisation programmes in the inter-war years.[7]

The numbers were small when compared with Nazi Germany or the state of California, but at least 1,843 people (79% of them women) were sterilised under the state's sterilisation law between January 1926 and June 1946.[8] The programme took off in the mid-1930s – not coincidentally, at the same time that relief rolls expanded because of the Depression. The number of operations dropped off during and after the Second World War, mainly because of a shortage of medical and nursing personnel, but there is evidence that the operations continued, although in vastly reduced numbers, at least until 1975.[9]

Ironically, surgical sterilisation emerged as a vital part of Minnesota's welfare system just as the state's child welfare system as a whole was becoming less punitive. In Minnesota as elsewhere in the United States, the first decades of the twentieth century brought what one scholar has called the 'start of a new era' in American social welfare.[10] Repudiating the nineteenth-century strategy of preventing child neglect and 'saving' children by breaking up impoverished families, progressive social reformers sought ways to keep needy families together, albeit under supervision.

The 1909 White House Conference on the Care of Dependent Children had marked the symbolic beginning of the new era. The reformers and social workers who gathered at Theodore Roosevelt's White House articulated the new consensus on child welfare. Extending sentimental ideas about childhood innocence and mother love to the working class, they avowed that institutions were bad for children and that the government bore some responsibility for children's well-being. 'Home life is the highest and finest product of civilization,' the delegates resolved.

> Children of parents of worthy character, suffering from temporary misfortune and children of reasonably efficient and deserving mothers who are without the support of the normal breadwinner, should, as a rule, be kept with their parents ... Except in unusual circumstances, the home should not be broken up for reasons of poverty, but only for considerations of inefficiency or immorality.[11]

The catch, as many scholars have observed, was in the phrase 'considerations of inefficiency or immorality'.[12] These vague and subjective terms, which social workers used to decide whether families should be broken up or kept together, laid bare the immense (and arbitrary) power individual caseworkers wielded over impoverished parents.

The White House Conference stimulated the reform of child welfare systems at every level of government. The federal government established a Children's Bureau in Washington DC to study and report on children's issues, and a number of states reorganised their child welfare programmes. In 1917, the Minnesota legislature introduced its Children's Code, a package of 35 laws which strengthened and streamlined the state's authority over child welfare.[13]

The White House Conference also stimulated lobbying efforts in the states for mothers' pensions. By the end of 1913, 20 states, including Minnesota, had passed mothers' aid laws permitting counties to provide economic assistance to needy single mothers. Usually administered through the juvenile court to mark them as child welfare measures and not poor relief, mothers' pensions were modest stipends intended to enable impoverished widows and other 'deserving' mothers to keep their children at home (and out of institutions). The 1935 Social Security Act made the programme, then called Aid to Dependent Children, national in scope.[14]

The mothers' pensions movement departed from nineteenth-century child-saving practice by redefining impoverished widows as mothers deserving of aid. However, the older, more punitive approach to child welfare persisted for parents perceived as unfit. There were, in effect, two strands of child welfare policy in early twentieth-century Minnesota: one for the children of the (newly) deserving 'normal' mothers and another for those still considered undeserving:

the inefficient or immoral – and 'defective'. The two strands were closely connected; indeed, mothers' pensions might not have been instituted for widows and 'deserving' mothers had not more punitive programmes continued for the rest.

Some readers may find it surprising to see mothers' pensions described here as liberal when most scholars have convincingly shown them to be stigmatised and stingy. Indeed, mothers' pensions are typically portrayed as the inferior track in America's two-track welfare system. (The better track is social insurance, including workers' compensation and unemployment insurance, which mainly benefits male wage-earners.)[15] There is much truth to this view, for mothers' pensions never really escaped the stigma of charity. Benefits were low, immigrants and women of colour faced extra discrimination, and work requirements marked all pension recipients as inadequate mothers (i.e. wage-earners). Indeed, the worthiness of all poor mothers was so precarious that even those considered most deserving – widows on mothers' aid – were constantly monitored. Social workers attempted to 'fix' pensioned mothers by improving their house-keeping, child care, and money management skills. Despite many inadequacies, however, mothers' pensions offered higher benefits with less stigma than the other forms of public assistance available to single mothers.[16]

While the inadequacies and injustices in the mothers' pensions programme have been much discussed, scholars have paid surprisingly little attention to what happened to children whose parents were deemed too immoral or inefficient to be eligible for mothers' aid. In Minnesota at least, many of these parents were identified as mentally deficient, or feebleminded. For them, Progressive-Era child welfare programmes differed little from the punitive child-saving methods of the nineteenth century. Although in the abstract the policy of family preservation still applied, many 'defective' families were broken up, at least temporarily. Social workers worked closely with law enforcement officials to ferret out neglectful parents (and feebleminded parents were virtually presumed to be neglectful). Wives and children were often placed in institutions. Long after social workers rejected institutions for 'normal' children on the grounds that they destroyed individuality, stunted intellectual and social growth, and prevented youth from developing independence and self-control, institutional-isation remained the strategy of choice for feebleminded children and their mothers.

The Progressive-Era changes to child welfare significantly expanded the number of 'deserving' mothers (and the number of children thought worth saving), but they probably widened the gulf between the 'normal' poor and those considered feebleminded. As social workers began to see family dysfunction as the result of inadequate surroundings or emotional difficulties, they could envision improving the parenting skills of 'normal' people through casework, therapy, or a change in environment. By contrast, mothers who were mentally deficient seemed hopeless cases – and hopeless cases seemed mentally deficient. When ineptitude seemed to have a biological basis, as it did with feeblemindedness, social workers tried drastic measures, such as surgical sterilisation, to 'fix' problem families.

Eugenics, the science of the improvement of the human race by better breeding, provided a useful justification for this two-strand child welfare policy. Eugenics furnished policy-makers and social workers with a compelling – and scientific – explanation for the persistence of family dysfunction and poverty amid improvements in education and the environment. By the 1910s, when the mothers' pensions movement was at its peak, eugenists had produced countless scientific studies 'proving' that hereditary feeblemindedness caused pauperism, illegitimacy, and crime, and that it posed a huge burden on the taxpayer. They lobbied to reduce the 'inferior' part of the US population through restrictive immigration policies, the institutional-isation of defectives during their childbearing years, and compulsory sterilisation.[17]

Sterilisation was a cornerstone of American eugenics, and the United States has the dubious distinction of being an international leader in its legalisation. The nation passed its first sterilisation law in Indiana in 1907; ten years later, 15 states permitted the sterilisation of institutionalised persons. Only California operated an active sterilisa-tion programme, however; in most states, eugenic sterilisation was not firmly established until the late 1920s – when the social welfare programmes enacted during the Progressive Era were coming under attack by social spending conservatives and right-wing groups. In 1927, the US Supreme Court ruled in the landmark case *Buck v. Bell* that eugenic sterilisation was constitutional. By 1931, 28 states had legalised eugenic sterilisation.[18]

Minnesota enacted its sterilisation law in 1925, after intensive lobbying by the state Eugenics Society. The Minnesota law permitted the sterilisation of feebleminded and insane persons who were under the guardianship of the State Board of Control. As in most states, sterilisations could only be performed after careful investigation and expert consultation. Unlike most states, the Minnesota law was 'voluntary'; that is, an operation could be performed only with the written consent of the spouse or nearest kin. If no relative could be located, the Board of Control as the legal guardian could give consent.[19]

Minnesota's sterilisation programme can only be understood in the context of the 'child protection' and guardianship systems that grew out of the 1909 White House Conference on Children. Even before sterilisation was legalised, the 1917 Children's Code gave the State Board of Control broad powers of legal guardianship over illegitimate, dependent and neglected children, and over 'defective' individuals regardless of age. County or probate courts were empowered to commit feebleminded individuals to state guardianship, even without the consent of a parent or guardian. (The guardianship was for life, unless the person was specifically discharged.) To help the judges ascertain who was feebleminded, the Board of Control provided mental examiners to give IQ tests to people who came before the court on a variety of charges, including delinquency, illegitimacy, child neglect or dependency, and inability to do school-work. Once committed as feebleminded, an individual became a ward to be 'protected' by the state. He or she had no civil or political rights; a ward could not vote, own property, manage his or her own financial affairs, or marry without the state's permission. The Board of Control decided whether the ward should be institutionalised or remain under supervision in the community.[20]

The structure of Minnesota's child welfare agencies also contributed to the arrangement of its sterilisation plan. The Board of Control, as well as being the legal guardian of Minnesota's neglected and dependent children, ran the state's child welfare services, its programmes for people with mental and physical disabilities, and (during the New Deal) general relief. County child welfare boards carried out the state Board's work at the local level, cooperating with county relief administrators and supervising other agencies that worked with children.[21]

In the 1920s, the expanded authority of the courts to make commitments, combined with the increased use of intelligence tests and the massive publicity regarding the 'menace of the feebleminded', led to a significant increase in the number of Minnesotans found to be feebleminded and committed to state guardianship. Most of the increase, and most of those who were sterilised, were the 'high-grade' feebleminded, or morons, and many would not be considered to have a mental disability today.[22] Because the statutory definition of a 'feebleminded person' – as someone 'who is so mentally defective as to be incapable of managing himself and his affairs, and to require supervision, control and care for his own or the public welfare' – was vague, county judges had wide latitude in making commitment decisions.[23]

In many cases, commitment to state guardianship had as much to do with a feebleminded person's 'bad behaviour' as with the results of an intelligence test. This is especially true because county judges – who had the authority to commit someone as feebleminded – mainly encountered people already in trouble with the law. Thus, more than half of the 120 morons committed in Minneapolis's Hennepin County in 1927 had been 'grossly delinquent', while another 20 per cent had been charged with incorrigibility![24] In making commitment decisions, judges considered a range of factors beyond IQ, including the person's health, family background and environment, school or work record, and personal deportment. No doubt some followed the definition of the Board of Control, which characterised mentally deficient adults as those who 'lack common sense, foresight, are unable to resist ordinary temptations, act on impulse, and have little or no initiative. They have about the same desires as normals, including sexual, but lack ability to control them. They usually have poor homes.'[25]

The large increase in the number of people found to be feebleminded and committed to state guardianship precipitated a crisis in state institutions. Officials at Minnesota's School for the Feebleminded, for example, complained that 'high-grade' morons were discontented and rebellious and had a 'very bad' influence on other residents in the institution. Their presence also exacerbated the growing problem of overcrowding.[26]

One way state officials attempted to deal with these problems – and save money – was by releasing, or 'paroling' inmates into local communities. Some were discharged from guardianship, but most remained wards of the state. They were supervised directly by the Board of Control or by county welfare boards, which served as agents of the state Board at the local level. The majority of parolees were women who worked in domestic service, laundries, factories, or, occasionally, on farms. In many respects, Minnesota's sterilisation law – or at least professionals' support for it – grew out of these plans for community living. Sterilisation made possible 'many paroles which could not otherwise have been planned for', the Board of Control explained, for it eliminated the possibility that a feebleminded person living in the community would have children.[27]

For a variety of reasons, then, most Minnesota social workers stressed the 'sociological advantages' over the 'eugenic benefits' of sterilisation. 'The genetic argument for sterilisation is plausible,' one explained, 'yet the stronger reason is that they [morons] are unfit for parenthood.' The Board of Control repeatedly rebuffed the efforts of eugenists to broaden the sterilisation law to include all the 'unfit'; they chose instead to take a more cautious approach based on the social work principles of individual casework. (Of course, the emphasis on the need for casework and supervision was in their professional self-interest.) A memo distributed by the Board in 1939 criticised the 'over-zealous' claim that sterilisation was 'wholly justified by the eugenic factors' and rejected 'wholesale sterilization' as impractical and inadvisable. Instead, it endorsed 'selective sterilization' in individual cases. For those charged with administering the state's eugenic sterilisation law, the 'socio-economic justification of sterilization, that the feeble-minded parent cannot provide a stable and secure family life for his children', was paramount.[28] Minnesota sterilisation policy was as much about preventing child-*rearing* by the so-called feebleminded as it was about preventing child-*bearing*.

The 'sociological advantages' of sterilisation – and the centrality of feebleminded commitments to the state's welfare and juvenile justice systems – are abundantly clear in the state archives. Although the wide range of cases warns against too easy generalisation, the admissions and medical records of the Faribault State School and Hospital for the Feebleminded, where the sterilisations were performed, reveal the close connection experts perceived between economic dependency, sexual impropriety, and mental deficiency. Most sterilised women in Minneosta during the inter-war years were either young sex 'delinquents', often unmarried mothers, who were committed as feebleminded through the probate court system, or slightly older women with a number of children on public assistance. Immoral or inefficient (or both) – and therefore ineligible for a mother's pension – they were considered defective mothers in part because they had no breadwinner to support them.

The majority of sterilised women were sex 'delinquents', unmarried but sexually active women who either had children or might have children they could not support. Historians intent on restoring agency to unmarried mothers have often seen sex delinquency as resistance to repressive sexual norms, but the Minnesota sterilisation records tell a sadder tale.[29] Many of the young women labelled feebleminded and subsequently sterilised in the state were victims of incest or sexual abuse; had untreated (and often undiagnosed) physical, mental or learning disabilities; or came from families unable (or unwilling) to support them during economic hard times. Take the case of Lola, who was sterilised in 1938, one month before her 21st birthday. Lola's father had committed suicide, and social workers described her mother, a victim of polio, as a 'very incompetent person'. Lola herself had been sent to a correctional institution when she was just 16 years old for 'excessive indulgence' with middle-aged men. Although never actually delinquent, Lola was considered 'very stubborn, even refusing to go to a doctor when necessary'. She was 'a girl who needs a family', a social worker observed; she got sterilised instead.[30]

While Lola was seen as too stubborn and aggressive for motherhood, most feebleminded women were considered too passive. Ada, an unmarried mother who left school after flunking 8th grade, was typical. Faribault hospital staff described Ada as attractive, agreeable and cooperative, but overly susceptible to influence and unable to make decisions. (This is despite her refusal to take a job that required supervision – after her employer got her pregnant!) Similarly, Mary, a 36-year-old mother of ten children, was determined to be 'inadequate' in the home and unable to care for her children. Although her conduct was acceptable and she did not use alcohol or drugs, Mary's 'dull and rather slovenly' appearance and the fact that her school work had been poor (more than ten years in the past) convinced the hospital staff that improvement was unlikely. Therefore, they considered sterilisation.[31]

Whether too domineering or too weak, the feebleminded mothers (or potential mothers) portrayed in the records of the Faribault Hospital carried to an extreme the image of the dangerous mother who emerged in the psychiatric and child guidance literature of the inter-war period. Prior to the First World War, child psychologists attributed juvenile delinquency to a range of causes, including ignorance, a bad environment, or even heredity. By the 1920s, however, they saw flawed mothering as the explanation for virtually all behavioural problems. Middle-class housewives might smother their children; working-class mothers rejected them by going out to work.[32] But the most ruinous condemnation was saved for feeble-minded mothers, who were neglectful almost by definition. Too much aggression and too little initiative were both considered evidence of feeblemindedness in women; as well, they were indications of a pathological or rejecting mother – signs of a mother who posed a danger to the child. This is why, in spite of a general policy of family preservation, social workers frequently tried to take children away from feebleminded mothers. In expressing special concern for the normal children of mentally deficient parents, social workers revealed both their bias against the feebleminded and their rejection of the eugenist assumption that mental deficiency was almost always trans-mitted to the next generation.[33]

As traditional familial supports broke down during the economic crisis of the 1930s, social workers worried that feebleminded mothers lacked the authority and intelligence necessary to rear economically productive law-abiding citizens. 'Mental defectives have undiminished powers of procreation,' a children's aid official explained in 1934, 'but often have not the power to support children and generally have little or no ability either to guide or to discipline them. Often the children of a feebleminded mother by the time they are 10 years old have more intelligence than their mother and consequently dominate her.'[34]

This is well illustrated in the case of Martin X, an illegitimate and allegedly neglected child of a feebleminded woman whose case history was 'fairly typical'. The fifth of seven children, Martin had no respect for his mother because he was smarter than she was – and knew it. School officials considered him neglected: he was dirty, often absent, and uninterested in his studies. A visiting nurse described Martin's mother Katie as 'simply impossible' and worried what would become of the boy if he continued to live with 'this woman in this environment'. In the spring of 1933, when Martin was ten, the nurse's fears were realised. Martin joined a gang, looted automobiles and broke windows, and stole money from his mother's purse. When a social worker advised Katie to hide her money, the boy sneered, 'I am smarter than her, she can't hide her money where I can't find it.' The case worker concluded that the boy's delinquency was 'a natural result of his mother's inadequacy'.[35]

Martin's case was written up to illustrate another point: social workers were powerless to *prevent* Martin's delinquency. It was only after he got in trouble with the law and had to go before the Juvenile Court that the state was empowered to remove Martin from his mother's custody. For the social worker who wrote up his case, the system had failed Martin; social workers needed more power to intervene. Removing children from the care of feebleminded mothers might help, she believed, but the most effective way to 'protect the child handicapped by being born to mentally deficient parents' was to prevent the feebleminded from having children at all.[36]

Behavioural and fiscal considerations thus merged with eugenic ones to make sterilisation a basic part of Minnesota welfare policy in the inter-war years. Frustrated by disjointed relief policies, high case-loads, and limited resources, a significant number of Minnesota social workers saw 'eugenic' sterilisation as a viable and indeed humane solution to the seemingly endless cycle of family poverty, dysfunction and delinquency. 'The number of children, their doings, the whole thing piles up so terribly that one cannot face it,' another social worker sighed despondently. 'We don't know what the answer is. I think it is not so much a matter ... of getting the feebleminded committed, but of ... catching the feebleminded girls and boys before they can marry and establish homes.'[37]

Such sentiments grew more intense as the economic crisis deepened, relief costs skyrocketed, and high unemployment made it difficult even for a 'normal' person to earn a living wage. Social workers who themselves faced pay cuts and the possibility of job loss worried that welfare agencies – and their own tax dollars – would have to permanently subsidise 'literally thousands' of feebleminded individuals. In the minds of many, providing help for the feeble-minded without attempting to curb their fertility was 'nothing short of developing a program to preserve the unfit'.[38]

Not surprisingly, feebleminded commitments and sterilisation operations increased significantly during the difficult Depression years. County welfare officials, wanting to limit the number of people who had to go on relief, gave IQ tests to families living in particularly 'deplorable' conditions. In many instances, entire families were committed as feebleminded. Perhaps, as a social worker with the Board of Control suggested years later, placing entire families under state guardianship made the harried and underfunded county welfare boards feel 'satisfied that they had taken some kind of action'. More likely, county officials committed large numbers of people to state guardianship because doing so obliged the state to share the cost of their support – not only if the ward were institutionalised, but also if he or she remained in the county. In any case, many people committed as feebleminded during the Depression were not really retarded, and, as the social worker conceded with grand understatement, 'their frustrating experiences made them resentful'. However, court action was required to reverse the commitment; not even the State Board of Control had that power.[39]

The history of sterilisation in Minnesota is not simply a tale of victimisation, however, for many families resisted the state's intrusions. Some engaged legal counsel and petitioned the state to have their loved ones 'restored to capacity' and discharged from state guardianship. Others simply ran away, becoming lost from the authorities (and the historical record). A few tried to turn the system to advantage. Thus, a social worker who thought that sterilisation was a 'questionable remedy' for most problems of feeblemindedness observed that it 'has worked out well in families where there were already enough children and the mother and father were convinced that there should not be any more'. Unfortunately, the records are silent on how often 'eugenic' sterilisation was really contraceptive in purpose. But there are tantalising hints. Faribault admissions records reveal a small number of women, such as Annie, the wife of a farm labourer on public assistance and mother of ten living children, who entered the institution expressly 'for sterilization' and expected to return home upon recovery.[40] But state-funded contraceptive sterilisation required an extraordinary sacrifice on the part of the woman, for the operation could legally be done only on individuals who had been committed as feebleminded (or insane) wards of the state – thereby losing their political and civil rights. It is tragic that some Minnesota women were so desperate for health and contraceptive care that they permitted – and in some cases even asked – social workers to find them feebleminded and hence 'unfit' mothers so they could be sterilised under a eugenics law.

Eugenic sterilisation served many functions within Minnesota's welfare system. For eugenists, it was a stepping stone to more sweeping laws that would curb the fertility of all the unfit. For county welfare officials and the voting public, it was a way to cut public expenditures, or at least to shift the costs of child welfare to another level of government. For front-line social workers with high case-loads and limited resources, it was a way to reduce the numbers of feebleminded and maybe make their jobs manageable and secure. And for a few family members, eugenic sterilisation was a form of birth control at a time when other types of contraception were unavailable.

Although surgical sterilisation has now faded from American welfare politics, the fiscal, social, and eugenic impulses that under-girded it remain all too strong. Politicians still portray reducing the numbers of poor people (via draconian welfare and immigration policies or eliminating their reproductive rights) as a simple – and cost-effective – solution to perplexing social problems. Yet, as history shows, family poverty and dysfunction are not so easily 'fixed'.

Notes

1. M. Ladd-Taylor, *Mother-Work: Women, Child Welfare and the State, 1890–1930*, Urbana, IL, University of Illinois Press, 1994; M. Ladd-Taylor and L. Umansky, eds, *'Bad' Mothers: The Politics of Blame in Twentieth-Century America*, New York, New York University Press, 1998.

2. M. B. Katz, *The Undeserving Poor: From the War on Poverty to the War on Welfare*, New York, Pantheon, 1989.

3. See, for example, the classic studies by A. Davis, *Women, Race and Class*, New York, Random House, 1981, and R. P. Petchesky, '"Reproductive Choice" in the Contemporary United States: A Social Analysis of Female Sterilisation', in *And the Poor Get Children*, ed. K. Michaelson, New York, Monthly Review Press, 1984.

4. In this article, I use terms such as 'feebleminded' and 'defective' freely, usually without quotation marks. Although highly offensive today, these words capture the popular understanding of mental retardation in the early twentieth century. They are also more inclusive than current terminology, often referring to people who would not be considered to have a mental disability – or even a behavioural problem – today. The statistics are from P. R. Reilly, *The Surgical Solution*, Baltimore, MD, Johns Hopkins University Press, 1991, p. 97.

5. Initially, the majority of sterilisations were performed on men, but after the onset of the Depression the percentage of sterilised women increased significantly. Reilly, *Surgical Solution*, pp. 96–97.

6. A. Chase, *The Legacy of Malthus: The Social Costs of the New Scientific Racism*, New York, Knopf, 1976; T. M. Shapiro, *Population Control Politics: Women, Sterilization, and Reproductive Choice*, Philadelphia, Temple University Press, 1985; S. Kuhl, *The Nazi Connection: Eugenics, American Racism, and German National Socialism*, New York, Oxford University Press, 1994.

7. R. J. Levy, 'Protecting the Mentally Retarded: An Empirical Survey and

Evaluation of State Guardianship in Minnesota', *Minnesota Law Review* 49, 1965, pp. 821–87; M. Thomson, 'Social Aspects of Minnesota's Program for the Feebleminded', *Proceedings from the American Association on Mental Deficiency* 44, 1939, pp. 238–45.

   8. E. J. Engberg to Carl Swanson, 22 June 1946, Superintendent's Correspondence, Records of the Faribault State School and Hospital, Minnesota Historical Society [hereafter FSSH].

   9. Reilly, *Surgical Solution*, pp. 140–43.

   10. M. B. Katz, *In the Shadow of the Poorhouse: A Social History of Welfare in America*, New York, Basic, 1986, p. 113.

   11. Quoted in Ladd-Taylor, *Mother-Work*, p. 137.

   12. J. Goodwin, *Gender and the Politics of Welfare Reform*, Chicago, University of Chicago Press, 1997; L. Gordon, *Pitied But Not Entitled: Single Mothers and the History of Welfare*, New York, Viking, 1994.

   13. E. Benson, 'Organization of Public Welfare Activities in Minnesota', unpublished MA thesis, University of Minnesota, 1941, pp. 80–85.

   14. US Children's Bureau, *Public Child-Caring Work in Certain Counties of Minnesota, North Carolina, and New York*, Washington, DC, Government Printing Office, 1927, pp. 30–31. See also T. Skocpol, *Protecting Soldiers and Mothers: The Politics of Social Provision in the United States, 1870s–1920s*, Cambridge, MA, Harvard University Press, 1992.

   15. On the gendered two-track welfare system, see Gordon, *Pitied But Not Entitled*, and B. Nelson, 'The Origins of the Two-Channel Welfare State: Workmen's Compensation and Mothers' Aid', in *Women, the State, and Welfare*, ed. L. Gordon, Madison, WI, University of Wisconsin Press, 1990, pp. 123–51.

   16. Goodwin, *Gender and the Politics of Welfare Reform*; Ladd-Taylor, *Mother-Work*, pp. 135–66.

   17. See D. Paul, *Controlling Human Heredity, 1865 to the Present*, Atlantic Highlands, NJ, Humanities Press, 1995, p. 52; D. Kevles, *In the Name of Eugenics: Genetics and the Uses of Human Heredity*, Berkeley and Los Angeles, University of California Press, 1985; N. H. Rafter, *White Trash: The Eugenic Family Studies, 1877–1919*, Boston, Northeastern University Press, 1988.

   18. M. Haller, *Eugenics: Hereditarian Attitudes in American Thought*, New Brunswick, NJ, Rutgers University Press, 1963; Reilly, *Surgical Solution*.

   19. The Minnesota law is reprinted in C. Dight, *History of the Early Stages of the Organized Eugenics Movement*, Minneapolis, Minnesota Eugenics Society, 1935, pp. 9–10. See also Reilly, *Surgical Solution*, and J. H. Landman, *Human Sterilization*, New York, Macmillan, 1932.

   20. Levy, 'Protecting the Mentally Retarded'; Benson, 'Organization of Public Welfare Activities in Minnesota', pp. 84–85.

   21. Benson, 'Organization of Public Welfare Activities'.

   22. J. W. Trent, Jr, *Inventing the Feeble Mind: A History of Mental Retardation in the United States*, Berkeley and Los Angeles, University of California Press, pp. 131–224.

   23. Quoted in Levy, 'Protecting the Mentally Retarded', p. 826.

   24. Faribault School for the Feebleminded, *1922 Biennial Report*, pp. 5–6, FSSH; Hennepin County Child Welfare Board, *1927 Annual Report*, Minnesota Historical Society [hereafter MHS].

25. 'Report on Census of the Feeble-Minded', typescript, n.d., Psychological Services Bureau, Dept. of Public Welfare, MHS.

26. See the Faribault School for the Feebleminded, *Biennial Report* for 1912, 1922, and 1932, MHS; and Trent, *Inventing the Feeble Mind*, pp. 184–224.

27. Minnesota State Board of Control, *Biennial Report 1924*, p. 18; idem, *Biennial Report 1928*, p. 19, MHS.

28. C. Perkins, 'Summary of the Following Papers', n.d. [1934] Dept of Public Welfare Library, MHS; 'History of the Sterilization of the Feeble-Minded', typescript, n.d. [1940?], Superintendent's Correspondence, FSSH.

29. M. Odem, *Delinquent Daughters: Protecting and Policing Adolescent Female Sexuality in the United States, 1885–1920*, Chapel Hill, NC, University of North Carolina Press, 1995; R. Kunzel, *Fallen Women, Problem Girls: Unmarried Mothers and the Professionalization of Social Work, 1890–1945*, New Haven, CT, Yale University Press, 1993.

30. 'Supervision of the Feeble-Minded by County Welfare Boards', paper given by Mildred Thomson to American Association of Mental Deficiency, May 1940, Dept of Public Welfare Library, MHS.

31. Medical Staff Minutes, 7 December 1937 and 28 September 1936, FSSH.

32. K. Jones, '"Mother Made Me Do It": Mother-Blaming and the Women of Child Guidance', in Ladd-Taylor and Umansky, eds, *'Bad' Mothers*, pp. 99–124.

33. F. Davis, 'The Neglect of Children as Related to Feeble-Mindedness', typescript, 21 September 1934, Dept of Public Welfare Library, MHS.

34. C. E. Dow, 'The Problem of the Feeble-Minded III', typescript, 9 August 1934, Dept of Public Welfare Library, MHS.

35. Davis, 'The Neglect of Children'.

36. Davis, 'The Neglect of Children'.

37. Minutes of the 4th Meeting of the Committee for the Discussion of Problems of the Feebleminded, 2 May 1934, Dept of Public Welfare, MHS.

38. L. M. Clevenger, untitled typescript, 1 March 1935, Dept of Public Welfare, MHS.

39. M. Thomson, *Prologue: A Minnesota Story of Mental Retardation*, Minneapolis, Gilbert, 1963, p. 80.

40. Dow, 'The Problems of the Feeble-Minded III'; Medical Staff Minutes, 10 May 1937, FSSH.

11

A Spirit of 'Friendly Rivalry'? Voluntary Societies and the Formation of Post-War Child Welfare Legislation in Britain

Julie Grier

In recent years, historians have paid increasing attention to the role of voluntarism in welfare policy.[1] Attempts have been made to describe the relationship between the state and the voluntary sector and most of these descriptions are based on the concept of a 'boundary' between two separate spheres. This chapter argues that such a model is misleading and that the relationship between the state and voluntary sector has been (and is) far more fluid and dynamic than the concept of a 'boundary' would suggest. To illustrate the complexity of this relationship the role of two of Britain's largest voluntary children's charities, the National Children's Home (NCH) and Barnardo's, will be considered during the period 1944–53. This period is particularly significant because it is often seen as one of barrenness for the voluntary sector; indeed in many areas voluntary effort was completely superseded by the state. The period from 1945 to the 1970s has been described by Digby, Lowe and others as the period of the 'classic welfare state'.[2] During this period the voluntary societies have been described as being in the doldrums, or as the Wolfenden Committee commented, to be 'marking time'.[3] A study of voluntary child-care provision in this period questions this assumption.

Finlayson has described the relationship between the state and the voluntary sector as 'a moving frontier', and argues that historians studying welfare provision have tended to trace the progression from '"active citizen" to "active state" [which] overlooks the continuing presence of voluntarism'.[4] While Finlayson acknowledges that by 1949 greater responsibility for welfare had shifted to the state, he argues that there was still a significant role for the voluntary sector to play. He outlined the choices for the voluntary societies in stark terms: either they converged with the state and benefited from the increased resources this would bring, or else they diverged, maintaining their independence but facing an uncertain financial future.[5] However, children and child welfare have never been the concern of any one single agency, and this has meant that the sphere of child care represents the voluntary–state boundary at its most plastic. The choices facing voluntary children's societies were more complex than Finlayson suggests. Deakin has also noted that the effect of Labour's post-war welfare legislation was to 'change the size and shape of the space within which the voluntary sector had to operate'.[6] While this study supports this view, it will be argued that the voluntary children's societies were able to defend and retain their space to a considerable degree. The organisations in this study were active participants in shaping post-war child-care provision, and not simply the passive recipients of government policy.

The constraints of budgets, differing models of child care, and the political complexion of local authorities all interacted to determine forms of child-care provision. Before the 1948 Children Act, the Ministry of Health, Board of Education, and Home Office all had an interest in child welfare and each department claimed a particular expertise in the area. The voluntary organisations had to deal with all these departments of central government (with their differing priorities) as well as local authorities. Clearly there were areas where responsibilities overlapped. It was open to the voluntary agencies, therefore, to appeal to one department over (or against) another, or to appeal to central government over a local authority. This variety of authority did not decrease after 1948 (although the pattern of authority did change as the Home Office assumed responsibility for 'ordinary' child-care work) and the various ministries continued to be responsible for different groups of children. The ideas and patterns of care advocated by the various ministries continued to be different, and the voluntary child-care societies were sometimes able to exploit these differences to their own advantage. However, when the ideas of a government department conflicted with the priorities of the society, the influence of the department was irresistible.

Child-Care Provision and the Effects of War

In 1945 Lady Astor observed that 'the country has become child conscious'.[7] Six years of war focused attention on the child in perhaps an unprecedented way. Children became appreciated as an important national asset and anxiety was expressed that those children who had been psychologically damaged by the experience of war were in danger of becoming the maladjusted and unstable adults of the future.[8]

The disruption of war presented child-care professionals with a unique opportunity to study children in a variety of settings: day and residential nurseries, evacuation billets, children's homes and hostels. The experience of evacuation looms large in the historiography of the establishment of the post-war welfare state, and child-care workers hoped that evacuation would enable them to establish a body of knowledge about children that they could apply in the post-war world. Overestimates of the number of orphaned and displaced children who would have to be cared for after the war added to the urgency of the situation, as did concern for the stability of the family and the rising divorce rate.[9]

The campaign waged by Lady Allen for the reform of welfare provision for children deprived of a normal home life has been well documented.[10] In 1944 Allen's letter to *The Times* provoked a flood of correspondence, most of which was critical of the existing provisions for children. In particular, the division of responsibility for children caused concern. A child living apart from his or her family might be placed under the care of the Ministry of Pensions, the Ministry of Health, the Board of Education, the Home Office, or a voluntary society, depending on how and to whom the child was referred. Such a division of administrative responsibility caused confusion and the child's welfare was in danger of being overlooked. In January 1945 the death of Dennis O'Neill (a child who had been boarded out with insufficient supervision and subsequently killed by his foster father) demonstrated how dangerous the lack of co-ordination could be.

The need to consider the position of orphaned and deserted children after the dismantling of the Poor Law functions of the local authorities culminated in a public enquiry. A committee, chaired by Myra Curtis, was appointed and reported in 1946. The committee investigated all forms of child-care provision, both by the state and by the voluntary societies. The most damning criticisms were reserved for those local authorities that had placed young children in adult Public Assistance Committee institutions, sometimes with elderly infirm adults.[11] However, almost uniformly the committee found a lack of personal, nurturing interest in children cared for away from their parents. The Curtis report made over sixty recommendations concerning administration and child-care practice. The committee called for central responsibility for all children in need of substitute care to reside in one central government department to avoid the confusion of responsibility which existed. At the local authority level, the committee advised that the children should become the sole responsibility of an ad hoc committee, cared for by a Children's Officer who would be answerable to this committee.

The recommendations of the Curtis committee concerning child-care practice were to have repercussions for the voluntary sector. The Curtis report claimed that the best way of providing for children without families was by adoption. If this was not possible, children should be boarded out. While the committee recognised the dangers of inadequately supervised foster placements (as evidenced by the O'Neill case) it was felt that, with careful selection of foster parents, this method of care provided the personal care and interest that so many children in children's homes lacked. The final and least favoured method of care was to be within children's homes, the type of provision which dominated the voluntary sector.

Attitudes towards the Voluntary Societies

During her campaign, Lady Allen had argued strongly against the involvement of the voluntary sector in residential child care. Allen feared that children in the voluntary homes would be subject to the 'chill winds of charity' and she claimed that to allow a parallel system of voluntary child care to exist alongside the state system would result in wasted effort and resources.[12] Allen called for all children in care to be made 'wards of state' and made clear her attitude to the voluntary sector. 'May it not be that private philanthropy belongs to a youthful stage of our society out of which we are growing as we reach a maturer outlook?'[13]

As the wife of a Labour peer, Lady Allen reflected a strand of thought within the Labour movement which regarded philanthropy as outmoded and undesirable, an anachronism within a welfare state. Many within the voluntary sector feared that the welfare reforms of the post-war Labour government meant the end of voluntary welfare provision. That this did not happen requires some explanation.

Recent studies of the post-war Labour government have highlighted the role of 'ethical socialism' in Labour thinking.[14] Fielding, Thompson and Tiratsoo have argued that for many within the Labour government, the aim was to bring about a new society, based on an active participatory citizenship. The welfare state and full employment 'was only half of what was on offer in 1945'.[15] Furthermore, they argue that the Labour government wished to promote an idea of 'active citizenship', where service and responsibility would be the hallmark of a new social order. Within this vision, far from being outdated, voluntary societies could promote a greater participation of the population in the creation of this society, and foster an enhanced sense of community and social cohesion.

The post-war Labour government was aware of the advantages of supporting and maintaining the voluntary sector. Attlee, who had had personal experience of settlement work, claimed that 'the voluntary societies ... humanise our national life'.[16] Herbert Morrison also spoke of the 'voluntary spirit' and warned 'if it dies in this country, British democracy is dead'.[17] The voluntary sector was portrayed as intrinsically British and democratic. Ideologically, therefore, the government was able to work with the voluntary sector. A healthy voluntary sector, it was hoped, would promote popular participation in the creation of a new society, encouraging an ideal of active citizenship, and would act as a spur to improve state provision. Just how democratic societies such as Barnardo's and the NCH were in practice is, however, debatable.

The Labour government did not wish to abolish or nationalise the voluntary children's societies. For the Labour administration the problem of the voluntary sector was not ideological, but rather a problem of regulation. In meetings with the children's charities, the Home Office reassured them that 'the ... intention was not to restrict the activities [of voluntary organisations] but to regulate them'.[18] In the aftermath of the O'Neill case and the vigorous campaigning of Allen, the larger voluntary societies welcomed increased regulation as a public guarantee of standards.[19]

The composition of the Curtis committee reflected the Labour government's intentions. It was surprising that Lady Allen was not asked to chair or even to be a part of this committee, and this was significant. As has been noted, the Home Office had reassured the voluntary societies that their work would continue, and this reassurance was reflected in the membership of the Curtis committee. The appointment of a Committee of Enquiry has a political dimension. Lady Allen was greatly disappointed by her exclusion, and challenged Herbert Morrison, the Home Secretary, concerning it. He replied that Allen would not be objective enough because she had 'already made up [her] ... mind about the voluntary societies'.[20] As the voluntary sector was represented on the committee it is clear that the Labour government did not intend to exclude the voluntary sector from residential child care. Revd John Litten, as a member of the committee and principal of the NCH, ably defended the voluntary principle in residential care and other members of the committee were also sympathetic to the voluntary principle. The Curtis committee had found examples of good and bad practice in both the voluntary and state sectors and, to be fair, would have had to condemn both sectors or neither. It chose to condemn neither, but stressed the need to bring all children's homes up to the standard of the best. As the Curtis report concluded, '[w]e ourselves have seen excellently conducted Homes run by organisations that have been attacked. We do not therefore, feel justified ... in forming conclusions adverse to the general administration of child care in any organisation or group of institutions.'[21]

The Curtis committee did appreciate the work of the voluntary societies, but was aware of the public outcry there would have been if the committee had supported voluntary care exclusively (even the 'middle course' proposed by the committee was condemned by Lady Allen). Curtis recommended that both the state and the voluntary sector should continue to provide residential care, and stated 'we see much advantage in continuing a friendly rivalry between the two types of home'.[22] The recommendations of the Curtis committee failed to address some key issues. First, as the best method of care for children was deemed to be adoption or 'boarding out', the numbers of children needing residential care would presumably be small and dictated by the availability or otherwise of foster homes. There was no consideration of the possible numbers of children that would need residential care in the future which made planning difficult. Secondly, the committee seemed to suggest that if a foster home was unavailable, a child should be placed in a voluntary residential home in the first instance and a publicly managed home only when a place in a voluntary home was not available. In practice a local authority would be unlikely to use a voluntary home if there was a place in its own children's homes. Thirdly, the report failed to prescribe the appropriate relationship between the state and the voluntary sector. The report called for co-operation between the two, but no formal mechanism was suggested to enable this to be achieved.

Influence of the National Council of Associated Children's Homes

Although there was goodwill in Parliament towards the voluntary sector, in 1946 this was by no means obvious to the voluntary children's societies. Many feared that they would be excluded from child-care provision and that residential child care would be the sole preserve of the state. That this did not happen, as we have seen, was due partly to the enthusiasm of the Labour government for voluntarism. It was also due to the efforts of the voluntary societies themselves to promote their own interests.

During the Second World War the voluntary societies had been beset by many common problems; for example, the evacuation of some of their residential branches had caused severe accommodation problems. Barnardo's evacuated the large communities at the 'Girls Village Home' and the 'Boys Garden City' and had to find over 2,000 places in other parts of the country. Arising out of these shared problems, a closer relationship between the various children's societies was forged. Informal meetings between the six largest children's charities (which included the NCH and Barnardo's) resulted in the formation of a more formal organisation, the Council of Associated Children's Homes (later known as the National Council of Associated Children's Homes, NCACH).[23] In the early post-war years, therefore, when the criticism of the voluntary children's homes increased, the voluntary children's societies already had a mechanism in place to defend themselves and a platform from which to promote the cause of voluntary child welfare provision. The NCACH was funded by the constituent societies and lobbied Parliament energetically during the passage of the 1948 Children Act, employing parliamentary agents to put their case.[24]

The NCACH watched with great attention the passage of the

Children Bill, and made representations to government on behalf of the voluntary sector. They also prepared a memorandum which was sent to politicians in both Houses and to all chairmen of county and county borough councils. It was noted with satisfaction in March 1948 that 'the government's policy is to work through two systems, of voluntary organisations and local authorities in the work of child care'.[25] It is clear that the voluntary homes had been stung by some of the public criticism that they had received since 1944, and in their publicity they stressed that most of the recommendations of the Curtis report were already common practice in the voluntary homes. The voluntary societies sought to set a standard for the state to follow.

The NCACH was clearly an influential body by the late 1940s, and as far as the 1948 Children Act was concerned had successfully promoted the interests of the voluntary societies. The need for a body to represent their interests was appreciated by the societies, and eventually the Council became the body for communication and negotiation with central and local government.

The 1948 Children Act

The 1948 Children Act, based on the recommendations of the Curtis committee, failed to address certain key issues. The voluntary societies retained a great degree of autonomy and the proper relationship between the state and voluntary sector was not defined. It also appeared that children in the care of the two sectors could be treated differently. In the parliamentary debates this anomaly was most clearly demonstrated by Lord Beveridge. Beveridge was a staunch defender of the voluntary principle in most spheres; however, he pointed out that the Children Bill failed to define the position of the voluntary homes in relation to the state. 'Where do the children who are now in homes managed by the voluntary organisations stand in this matter? Are they children without parent or guardian, so that they automatically come within the scope of the local authority or are they not?'[26] Beveridge called for greater state control of the voluntary sector and for a uniform code of care; for example, the Bill did not empower the Home Secretary to compel voluntary organisations to board out their children although the local authorities were called upon to do this.[27] A further anomaly was that while the Bill required local authorities to try to maintain links between the child in care and his or her parents, this did not apply to voluntary organisations.[28] Such criticisms were all the more forceful coming from a supporter of the voluntary sector. Perhaps Beveridge's most astute observation was that the Bill was 'not merely dealing with children but it is making a new experiment in the relations between public authorities and voluntary agencies'.[29]

The 1948 Children Act did indeed establish a new relationship between the state and the voluntary sector. However, the legislation did not resolve the anomalies which Beveridge had highlighted. Instead the voluntary societies were given parity with local authorities under the control of the Home Office. While the local authority Children's Officers had the right to visit children placed with voluntary societies, they had no right to inspect voluntary homes. That power lay with the Home Office inspectorate, which was also responsible for inspecting the public sector homes. Voluntary societies were not compelled to board out their children, nor did they have to encourage links between parents and children. While a local authority had to obtain the permission of the Home Secretary before arranging child migration, a voluntary society did not. Such anomalies no doubt encouraged an atmosphere of suspicion between the two sectors rather than 'friendly rivalry'. Local authorities were free to place children they had accepted under the Children Act in voluntary homes and were free to negotiate the level of maintenance paid with the individual society. This arrangement caused serious underfunding of the voluntary homes in the early post-war period and was a continuous source of conflict between the societies and the local authorities even after the NCACH had negotiated a formula for funding with the Home Office.[30]

The central authority for overseeing the new service for children was vested in the Home Office and it was thought that this would end the confusion of authority that had existed before the war. However, the Ministry of Health and the Ministry of Education retained responsibility for certain groups of children that were cared for by the voluntary organisations. For example, residential special schools came under the Ministry of Education, no matter that a number of the children cared for in the schools may have been 'deprived of a normal home life'. Thus, the voluntary societies would be able to alter the description of their homes and so come under the authority of another government department.

The lack of guidance that the Children Act offered as to the correct relationship between the voluntary and state sectors safeguarded to a great degree the autonomy of the voluntary societies. However, had more guidance been given, for example if the voluntary societies had been given a more clearly prescribed relationship with the local authority Children's Officer, and had some mechanism been set up for consultation between the two systems, a better working relationship might have been established.

Reactions of the Societies to the 1948 Children Act

The new emphasis of the Children Act was on adoption and fostering in preference to residential care. When residential care was deemed to be unavoidable, or judged to be in the best interests of the child, it was recommended that the residential home was to be small and the child integrated into the life of the community as far as possible. The voluntary societies had, like the local authorities, hitherto cared for children in large groups and had inherited an outdated infrastructure of large homes or groups of homes forming isolated communities. These were clearly out of step with the spirit of the 1948 Act. However, by altering the category of child to be accommodated, the societies could continue to use large homes. One example of this change in direction (which was to be repeated) occurred at the Edgworth (Lancashire) branch of the NCH.

The development of the Edgworth branch into a residential special school for (to use contemporary terminology) 'educationally subnormal' children involved considerable negotiations with both central and local government. The branch was large and before the war had provided accommodation for 273 'normal' children. The NCH had planned to develop the home into a branch for children aged 11 plus and to continue to provide education on site, but such a plan was clearly out of step with post-war thinking on child-care provision. The NCH, after much discussion, concluded that the education they could provide for the children would be inferior to that provided by the state under the 1944 Education Act. It was felt that the children would benefit more from mixing with other children in state schools than by being educated in isolation. However, the Edgworth branch was not closed. In 1950 the executive of the NCH opened negotiations with the Ministry of Education seeking to convert the school into a residential special school. In a letter to the

Home Office it was claimed that the matter had already been discussed with local authorities in the area and that they would welcome the scheme.[31] The NCH discussed its plans informally with a supportive Home Office inspector, who helped the society to contact an inspector from the Ministry of Education. In December 1950 a representative from the Ministry of Education viewed the branch and made recommendations. He advised that the NCH should not accept children with an IQ below 50 and perhaps ought to set the lower limit at 55 to 60.[32]

The difficulties surrounding the change of function for the Edgworth branch were eventually overcome. However, the NCH plans were modified by the Ministry of Education. The NCH had hoped to care for children with special educational needs in mixed groups, but the Ministry would not agree to this on the grounds that if the accommodation was for a single-sex group, there would be no need to provide separate sanitary arrangements and the dormitories could sleep up to eight children as they would not require partitioning. To underline their point, the Ministry of Education would not sponsor a building licence for the work involved in adapting the houses for mixed occupation, as this would be less economical. The NCH had little option but to agree to the ministry's wishes. The NCH was then pressed to increase the number of children they would accept. This caused problems with the residential staff who had been promised by the executive of the NCH that, in recognition of the greater demands that caring for special needs children would entail, the size of the family groups in each of the houses would be reduced from 15–20 children to eight to ten children in each group. The Ministry of Education pressed the society to accept groups of around 13 children to be accommodated in each house. Staff resignations followed. In this way the Ministry of Education was able to override and change the policy that the NCH had been pursuing in co-operation with the Home Office. By 1955 the residential special school was well established and had 102 pupils resident, the majority of whom had been referred by local education authorities and came from as far afield as Kent and Berkshire. The fees were set at £312 per annum for children referred by education authorities, and the branch ceased to be inspected by the Home Office and came under the auspices of the Ministry of Education. The Home Office no longer had any authority to inspect the branch, and the state funding for the children referred by the education authorities was greater than the funding of children placed with the voluntary societies by local authority Children's Officers.[33]

Although many of those resident at the Edgworth branch could be considered to be children 'deprived of a normal home life', the standards applied to their care under the Ministry of Education differed greatly to those applied to normal children under the supervision of the Home Office. While for several of the children the Edgworth school was purely a boarding school and they could look forward to going to their relatives for holidays, for others the school was their home. The 1948 Children Act had sought to end the confusion of authority for children living apart from their parents; however, it was still possible for such children to be the responsibility of different central government departments. Consequently, it remained possible for different standards and priorities to be applied to these different groups of children. The infrastructure of the Edgworth branch, accommodating as it did over 100 children, was frowned upon for the care of 'normal' children under the supervision of the Home Office, but was perfectly acceptable for 'educationally subnormal' children under the Ministry of Education.

While the Children Act had encouraged the fostering of children, the executive of the NCH remained committed primarily to residential care. However, the ambitious programme of building work that had been planned during the war, to replace older large properties with small houses and flats, ran into difficulties. There was a suspicion within the voluntary societies that local authorities were looked on more favourably when applications for building permits were considered. Government grants which were theoretically available under the 1948 Act were in practice almost unobtainable. It was feared that as central government met half the capital costs incurred by the local authority children's committees the standard of local authority homes would eventually be far higher than anything the voluntary sector could provide.[34]

Barnardo's shared many of these preoccupations as it also tried to replace its larger homes with smaller properties. However, the society also had other unique concerns. Encouraged by the 1948 Act, and by the appointment of a dedicated social worker, the organisation sought to increase the number of children who were boarded out. Here the ill-defined relationship between the state and the voluntary sector caused great problems. Miss Dyson, the officer in charge of Barnardo's boarding-out arrangements, attempted to make personal contact with as many of the new Children's Officers as she could. She found great variation between the local authorities in the interpretation of the boarding-out provisions of the Act. The 1948 Act appeared to allow voluntary societies to supervise their own foster homes where they had the resources to do so, but delegated supervision to the local authority where resources were inadequate. It was unclear whether the onus was on the voluntary society to ask for help or for the local authority to ensure for itself that a voluntary society could fulfil this task. Barnardo's also found it difficult to compete with local authorities to find foster homes and to match local authority payments to foster parents. In an effort to encourage the greater recruitment of foster parents, Barnardo's reversed its previous policy and became a registered adoption society (the rationale being that anyone thinking of becoming a foster parent would be more likely to approach a children's society that could also arrange for the fostered child to be adopted should this become the wish of foster parents and child).

By 1949 the deputy general superintendent of Barnardo's had reached the conclusion that in the future the local authorities would assume increasing responsibility for 'normal' child-care work. In this he echoed the concerns of the NCACH. The reports of the deputy superintendent for the early 1950s reveal areas of antagonism between the organisation, the local authorities and central government. The admission figures for 1952 show that although the Children's Officers may have considered 'normal work' to be their own particular, exclusive preserve, in practice this was far from the case. During that year 215 children were received by Barnardo's from local authority children's departments throughout England, Wales and Scotland. Added to that were a further 68 children referred by the local authority education and welfare committees and regional hospital boards. Local authority use of Barnardo's was very uneven in distribution and several authorities referred only one or two children. However, some authorities relied to a far greater extent on the society; for example, Kent referred 15 children, Middlesex 31 children, Bradford 11 children, Wigan 10 children, Wiltshire and Worcestershire 11 children each.[35] These referrals by the local authority children's departments and the voluntary society's relatively high levels of private admissions may have encouraged the society to continue to see its role in terms of 'normal cases', and may have acted to discourage a more rapid extension of its work into other areas.

There was also unease as to the degree of intervention that a Children's Officer could exercise in relation to 'local authority' children. Barnardo's wished to retain an interest in decisions surrounding such children and feared that the society would become regarded 'as a mere children's Hostelry'.[36] Barnardo's felt that in decisions concerning the restoration of children to their parents or the suitability of a child for fostering, the society should be consulted.

By 1953 Mr Lucette, general superintendent of Barnardo's, observed that the children's departments were becoming the mainstay of 'normal' child-care work and he called upon the organisation to increase its work for 'special cases' and to investigate new forms of provision. It is clear from his reports that he had a distinct idea of the future for Barnardo's; however, the council of Barnardo's could and did act to inhibit his plans.[37] In 1952 Barnardo's introduced a degree of 'regionalisation', a proposal which had been discussed and supported by the staff, but not by the council, since 1942. This reorganisation was an attempt to improve the relationship with the local authorities, and to maintain a child in his or her own locality. The work of the organisation was no longer divided into categories such as 'boarding out', and 'girls and toddlers', but into five geographical areas with an executive officer overseeing the work in each region. It was hoped this would improve communications with the local Children's Officers. The results of the scheme, however, were disappointing in terms of local authority referrals.[38]

By the end of 1953 certain trends had become apparent to the council of Barnardo's, and these reflected the experience of most voluntary children's societies. There was a reduction in the need for residential care for 'normal' children.[39] Boarding out was increasingly difficult to arrange, as it became difficult to recruit foster parents, and to compete with local authority boarding-out rates. The demand for places for special needs and maladjusted children seemed to increase, although the local authorities denied that they referred their most disruptive children to the voluntary societies. Barnardo's also experienced difficulties in recruiting staff and in matching local authority rates of pay. The average period for a child to stay in residential care gradually reduced as reception into care did not necessarily mean that the child would never be restored to his or her parents. There was also concern that local authorities were exploiting the voluntary societies by using the voluntary homes as a source of temporary accommodation, and recalling children when a place became available in their own children's homes. This improved the cost-effectiveness of their own provision.[40]

Barnardo's and the NCH both experienced financial difficulties during the early post-war years. Some local authorities, such as Worcestershire, which had given annual grants to the voluntary societies in appreciation for the child-care work they did, cancelled these grants following the 1948 Act, or else demanded to know the details of children in the care of the organisations from their area who might otherwise become cases for their care before they would consider continuing to make a grant. This reflected the confusion that existed over who had ultimate responsibility for children in the care of the voluntary societies. Both societies fell foul of rising costs of living, static voluntary income, an increasing wage bill, inadequate state payments, and the increased expenditure involved in offering additional care to special groups (such as physically disabled children). Both societies also faced the need to employ more field staff to deliver improved after-care to the children and family case work. The chairman of Barnardo's finance committee observed that the average cost of keeping a child in Barnardo's residential homes was increasing each year, and by 1953 new salary scales for super-intendents and matrons added around £25,000 to the wages bill.[41] Concern was also expressed that, as a consequence of making good shortfalls between expenditure and income, the level of accumulated income which in 1946 had stood at four times the annual expenditure of the society had by 1953 been reduced to one and three-quarters the annual expenditure. Barnardo's was also anxious to record that, while the voluntary income of the society appeared to be healthy, an increasingly large proportion of this came from legacies rather than regular, reliable donations from supporters.[42] The NCH reflected a similar position. While voluntary income grew slowly, expenditure continued to climb.[43] To meet the excess expenditure, the society was obliged to take money from the 'reconstruction fund', which had been set aside to finance an ambitious rebuilding programme.[44]

When the Select Committee on Estimates met in 1952 to consider the costs of the local authority children's services the voluntary societies were held up as shining examples of sound financial management. Local authority Children's Officers were asked by the committee if 'financial control was rather looser with public money than with voluntary contributions'.[45] The recommendation of the Select Committee was to encourage an even greater use of boarding out on the grounds that it was both economical and in the best interests of the child. The Select Committee stopped short of encouraging local authorities to place more children with the voluntary societies on grounds of economy as it was recognised that there was a great reluctance among some Children's Officers to delegate care, and it was not clear that the voluntary sector had the wherewithal to provide for large numbers of additional children. The Select Committee also noted that, if the voluntary organisations became known as providers of residential care for the state, the charitable public would be less willing to donate to the voluntary societies anyway. Unwittingly the voluntary societies had become a yardstick not for setting standards of child care, but rather as a measurement of economic efficiency. The Select Committee wished to see a forum established where the local authorities and voluntary societies could share their experiences and knowledge.

Within the sphere of child care the financial contribution that the voluntary societies made has not been acknowledged and has remained largely hidden. The societies provided subsidised care for those children accepted into care by local authorities and placed in voluntary homes. Also, by accepting children referred to them by parents themselves they may well have relieved the burden of care from the local authority children's committees (although the extent to which this is true depends upon the admission policies of the voluntary societies and local authorities being broadly similar). A further hidden financial contribution that the voluntary societies provided was staff training. Both the NCH and Barnardo's trained staff, many of whom went on to work in the public sector. At a local and national level then, by providing subsidised child care, voluntary activity made a significant contribution.[46]

Conclusion

An energetic and healthy voluntary sector had many advantages even within an extensive welfare state. Voluntary organisations could complement or supplement state provision, they could pioneer new areas of need, and provide advice or assistance in areas considered to be controversial. As far as the voluntary children's societies were concerned, they aimed to set a high standard of child care for the state to follow, acting as a 'watchdog' against the public sector. It may have been that, as residential child care was deemed by the 1948 Act to be the least-favoured method of care and therefore, in some minds, controversial, the government was happy to let this form of provision remain partly in voluntary sector hands. While the voluntary sector supplemented and duplicated the work of the local authorities, this did not result in empty beds within local authority homes with consequently higher costs. On the contrary, the knowledge that the local authorities had voluntary homes to fall back on allowed them to reduce their residential provision to a minimum. Here the voluntary sector acted unwittingly as a safety net to the state.

The early 1950s was a time of negotiation for the voluntary sector. By 1953 it became clear that many local authorities preferred to provide their own residential care rather than refer cases to the voluntary homes. Within the NCH there had been some moves towards providing a new specialised service for distinct groups of children (for example the residential special school at Edgworth) but the society wanted to retain its interest in 'normal' work where it was felt that the religious ethos of its care would make an important contribution. In January 1954 the NCACH invited Miss Rosling from the Home Office Children's Department to talk to the central council. Her view seemed to be that there was no future role for the voluntary societies in 'normal' child-care work. Miss Rosling urged the voluntary societies to become involved instead in work that the local authorities could not do, for instance 'prevention'. It seemed that the voluntary residential care of children would die a natural death.

However, the local authorities were not able to discontinue the use of voluntary homes altogether and the presence of voluntary home accommodation allowed local authority provision to be kept to a minimum. The picture is further complicated by the influence that local councillors and local politics could wield; for example the county council in Kent relied quite heavily upon voluntary residential provision, and the children's committee chairman had to justify to the council why the committee was not making even greater use of voluntary provision. There were several reasons for this reliance. First, the Kent children's committee included representatives of Barnardo's, who pressed the cause of voluntary child care. Secondly, the financial benefits of utilising the voluntary societies were appreciated by economically minded councillors. Thirdly, voluntary societies were, historically, well represented in Kent and the council had a tradition of using these homes before the enactment of the 1948 Children Act. Other authorities, for example Preston, appear to have used the voluntary homes as a 'safety net', enabling them to make the most economical use of their own local authority homes which were maintained at full occupancy, with any additional children being accommodated in voluntary homes. In the 1950s and 1960s Preston seems to have maintained a residential capacity of approximately 30 beds which appear to have been always fully occupied.[47] The number of children maintained by the Preston children's committee in voluntary homes over this period then fluctuated between 15 and 45. This need to accommodate an excess number of children in the voluntary homes did not seem to convince the children's committee of a need to increase its own provision.

A study of the voluntary children's homes in this period reveals that a complex pattern of relationships was forming between the voluntary agencies and central and local government. While suspicion often remained between local authority children's committees and the voluntary sector, there was evidence of a greater willingness to try to co-ordinate child-care work, and a recognition on the part of the voluntary societies of the need to broaden the services they offered. Organisations such as Barnardo's and the NCH were involved in complex negotiations with central and local government, and could manipulate a situation to their own advantage by changing the profile of the children they provided for and placing a branch home under the authority of a different central government department (as the NCH did at Edgworth), or by seeking representation on the local authority children's committees (as Barnardo's did in Kent). However, tension continued to exist between the voluntary children's societies and the Home Office as there seemed to be a conviction among some civil servants that residential care would become almost a thing of the past. The spirit of 'friendly rivalry' envisaged by the Curtis report proved to be largely illusory. The insecurities felt by those involved, exacerbated by a lack of effective direction from the Home Office, ensured that the relationship between the local authorities and the societies was fraught with difficulty.

Notes

1. See, for example, G. Finlayson, *Citizen, State and Social Welfare in Britain, 1830–1990*, Oxford, Oxford University Press, 1994; F. Prochaska, *The Voluntary Impulse: Philanthropy in Modern Britain*, London, Faber and Faber, 1988; M. Brenton, *The Voluntary Sector in British Social Services*, London, Longman, 1985.

2. See A. Digby, *British Welfare Policy: Workhouse to Workfare*, London, Faber and Faber, 1989; R. Lowe, *The Welfare State in Britain since 1945*, London, Macmillan, 1993.

3. Wolfenden Committee, *The Future of Voluntary Organisations*, London, Croom Helm, 1978, p. 20.

4. G. Finlayson, 'A Moving Frontier: Voluntarism and the State in British Social Welfare 1911–49', *Twentieth Century British History* 1(2), 1990, pp. 183–206 (185).

5. Finlayson, 'A Moving Frontier', p. 185.

6. N. Deakin, 'The Perils of Partnership: The Voluntary Sector and the State', in *An Introduction to the Voluntary Sector*, ed. J. Davies Smith, C. Rochester and R. Hedley, London, Routledge, 1995, p. 43.

7. Quoted in H. Cunningham, *The Children of the Poor*, Oxford, Blackwell, 1991, p. 224.

8. See for example *The Future of Child Guidance in Relation to War Experience: Proceedings of a Conference*, London, 1941; M. Cole and R. Padley, *Evacuation Survey*, London, Routledge, 1940; L. Rendel, *The Insecure Child*, Caldecott Community, Hyde Heath, 1943.

9. See R. A. Parker, 'Gestation of Reform: The Children Act of 1948', in *Approaches to Welfare*, ed. P. Bean and S. MacPherson, London, Routledge and Kegan Paul, 1983, p. 197. Parker notes that in 1943 an informal committee within the Ministry of Health feared that as many as 10,000 children would be unable to return to their homes for various reasons after the war and that provision would have to be made for their care. The numbers proved to be much smaller, and in 1948 the local authority children's departments took responsibility for around 1,500 children displaced by the war. Rendel, writing in 1943, had estimated the scale of the problem to be faced after the war by emphasising the figures for 1942–43 for cases of divorce (7,645 children); 'illegitimacy' (36,686); deserted or criminally neglected children (31,934) (Rendel, *The Insecure Child*, pp. 3–4).

10. See, for example, R. Holman, 'Fifty Years Ago: The Curtis and Clyde Reports', *Children and Society* 10, 1996, pp. 197–209.

11. *The Report of the Care of Children Committee*, cmnd 6922, London, HMSO, 1946, pp. 38–39.

12. Lady Allen of Hurtwood, *Whose Children?*, London, The Favil Press, 1945, p. 31. See also Public Records Office (hereafter PRO) MH 102/1617, Memorandum from Lady Allen to Home Office Children's Branch, 9 February 1948.

13. Allen, *Whose Children?*, p.11.

14. See S. Fielding, P. Thompson and N. Tiratsoo, *England Arise!*, Manchester, Manchester University Press, 1995.

15. Fielding et al., *England Arise!*, p. 218.

16. Quoted in Finlayson, *Citizen, State and Social Welfare*, p. 281.

17. University of Liverpool Special Collections and Archives (hereafter ULSCA) D239/B1/2/9, Council Minutes, April 1946. For a short time Barnardo's participated in the 'Advisory Council to Preserve the Voluntary Spirit', with Herbert Morrison as President. Barnardo's soon resigned from the organisation because of its 'strong political bias'.

18. PRO MH102/1615, Minutes of meeting, 6 February 1948.

19. The NCH and Barnardo's had both voluntarily sought increased inspection by 1943. The NCH invited the Board of Education to inspect and recommend changes to the organisation in 1936 and Barnardo's had asked the Home Office to review the work of the society in 1942 following criticism from parents.

20. M. Allen and M. Nicholson, *Memoirs of an Uneducated Lady*, London, Thames and Hudson, 1975, p. 189.

21. *Report of the Care of Children Committee*, London, HMSO, 1946, p. 133.

22. *Care of Children Committee*, p. 160.

23. ULSCA D239/B1/13, Minutes of Council meeting, December 1942. The original member societies of the NCACH were Dr Barnardo's Homes, the National Children's Home, the Church of England Waifs and Strays Society, the Jewish Board of Guardians, the Catholic Children's Rescue Society, Shaftesbury's Home and Arethusa.

24. ULSCA D239/B1/13, Minutes of Council meeting, May 1944. In May 1944 the NCACH agreed to employ Dyson, Bell and Co. to act on their behalf as parliamentary agents.

25. ULSCA D239/C1/5/2, Minutes of the NCACH North East Region, 18 March 1948.

26. Hansard, Parliamentary Debates (House of Lords) Fifth Series, vol. 153, col. 936, 10 February 1948. See also PRO MH102/1615, Minutes of meeting between Mr Ross (Home Office), Mr Kirkpatrick and Mr Potter (NCACH), 6 February 1948. The NCACH strongly disagreed with Beveridge's plea for children in the care of voluntary societies to be made wards of state as this, it was argued, would impinge upon parental rights. It was claimed that most of the children in the voluntary homes were there by the voluntary agreement of the parents and so the parents retained parental rights.

27. Hansard, Parliamentary Debates (House of Lords) Fifth Series, vol. 153, col. 937, 10 February 1948.

28. Hansard, Parliamentary Debates (House of Lords) Fifth Series, vol. 153, col. 937, 10 February 1948.

29. Hansard, Parliamentary Debates (House of Lords) Fifth Series, vol. 153, col. 939, 10 February 1948.

30. ULSCA D239/C1/5/5, Home Office Circular, 16/50.

31. ULSCA D541/J27/1/6, Letter from Mr Jacka to Mr Morgan, Ministry of Education, 16 October 1950.

32. ULSCA D541/J27/1/6, Minutes of meeting between Mr Jacka and Mr Sutton (Ministry of Education, Inspectorate), 18 December 1950.

33. ULSCA D239/C1/5/5, Meeting of the NCACH, 29 January 1954. In 1954 the Home Office authorised an average weekly rate of £4 10s (for children under the age of five) and £3 5s (for children over five) as the amount which local authorities could pay voluntary homes for children in local authority care placed in the home.

34. Grants paid to the voluntary societies for improvements to premises or equipment were

1949–1950	£7,743
1950–1951	£20,255
1951–1952	£11,430
1952–1953	£30,000

Sixth Report of the Select Committee on Estimates, London, HMSO, 1952, p. x.

35. ULSCA D239/C1/4/3, General Superintendent's Annual Report to the Council, 1952. The NCH also found that most of its 'local authority' referrals came from the Home Counties.

36. ULSCA D239/C1/4/3, Annual Report to Council, 1952.

37. Although the paid executive staff of Barnardo's were becoming increasingly influential during the period of this study, final responsibility for policy remained with the voluntary council of the organisation.

38. ULSCA D239/C1/4/1. In 1949 it was noted that because of the overcrowding in the branch homes Barnardo's had been unable to accept the 'flood' of applications from local authorities in the wake of the Children Act 1948. However, the society had children referred from 49 different local authorities, with the largest number of referrals from Middlesex (47 children), Kent (22), Worcestershire (15) and Essex (14). The figures for 'local authority' admissions were: 1949, 207 children; 1951, 297 children; 1952, 258 children; 1953, 255 children. In 1951 'local authority' children represented approximately one in five of the children admitted.

39. ULSCA D239/B1/15, Meeting of Council October 1953. The council noted in 1953 that 'the present position was that there was no waiting list except for physically handicapped children and for special schools ... throughout the last fifteen years, there had hitherto always been a waiting list ... the present accommodation problem in the homes was such that the total number of vacancies amounted to four homes.'

40. ULSCA D239/C2/4/a/1, Report of the General Administration Department, 1950. This was a particular problem with Worcester County Council, which removed children that it had placed with Barnardo's without reference to senior Barnardo's staff, despite repeated requests for consultation.

41. The average cost of providing residential care in Barnardo's (taking all types of home into consideration) had risen from £217 p.a. in 1950 to £256 p.a. in 1952.

42. The voluntary income of Barnardo's grew from £361,692 in 1945 to £802,787 in 1953.

43. The voluntary income of the NCH grew from £308,623 in 1945 to £377,935 in 1953.

44. In 1952 £34,129 was redirected from the 'reconstruction fund' to meet 'ordinary expenditure'.

45. The estimated average weekly cost of maintaining a child in a local authority home was said to be:

	England and Wales	Scotland
1950–1951	£4 12s 1d	£4 13s 4d
1951–1952	£4 18s 8d	£5 3s 6d
1952–1953	£5 5s 1d	£5 9s 11d

The Select Committee compared this to Barnardo's where the average weekly cost for all the types of homes the society managed was £3 6s 4d, and the NCH where the cost in the 'ordinary' branches was £3 2s 2d. *Sixth Report of the Select Committee on Estimates*, pp. xxii–xxiv.

46. For example, on 30 November 1949 the voluntary organisations took full responsibility for 28,760 children, compared with 55,255 children in the care of local authorities (of whom 5,968 had been placed by local authorities in voluntary homes).

47. See the annual returns of local authority children's departments to the Home Office Children's Department. These statistics give the numbers of children and the type of accommodation provided for them as on 31 March each year, and so cannot give a complete picture of how local authorities were providing for the children.

12

Mental Incapacity, Ill-Health and Poverty: Family Failure in Post-War Britain

Pat Starkey

The problems posed for local authorities by numbers of poor families were brought to public attention by the account of their wartime activities published by members of Pacifist Service Units (PSU) based in Liverpool, Manchester and Stepney during the Second World War.[1] The efforts of PSU were rewarded by support from public figures and its establishment as a permanent peacetime voluntary social work agency, renamed Family Service Units (FSU). Its work attracted the attention of mental health agencies and Medical Officers of Health, partly as a consequence of the creation of a tripartite structure for the new National Health Service that vested responsibility for environmental health with local departments of public health, so that dirty homes and children were classified as medical problems. This chapter will suggest that the close association between PSU/FSU and public health doctors meant that poor and poorly functioning families were pathologised, frequently in terms of the intellectual inadequacy or mental illness of the parents.[2] Children were evidence of parental failure and, in the case of those families who came to be labelled 'problem families', of a syndrome which was generally assumed to have a defined aetiology and prognosis. Little attempt was made to develop a critique of the economic and social conditions which contributed to the families' situation.

The professionalisation of social work, the large increase in the numbers of those who called themselves social workers, and new methods of dealing with family difficulties weakened the influence of public health doctors after the mid-1950s. To some extent, therefore, changes in methods of helping those who came to be designated problem families may be understood as an aspect of the rise and fall – the working out of struggles and ambitions – of two professions, medicine and social work.[3] It was a function of the increased professionalisation of social work, which was in part the result of a wider acknowledgement of its role in post-war Britain and a consequent increase in the number of courses designed to equip social workers for their task. Newly confident of their task and status, social workers wrested from public health doctors the care of families deemed to be at risk because of parental incompetence or neglect.[4]

I

The imminence of war in 1939 prompted efforts to remove the most vulnerable from situations of potential danger to places of safety; this decanting of inner-city populations to rural and suburban neighbourhoods drew public attention to the poor conditions in some urban areas. Contemporaries who remarked on the physical condition of evacuated children in the late summer of that year found much to shock them. Accounts of the House of Commons debate on evacuation include descriptions of situations characterised by poverty, deprivation and degradation. They also demonstrate the class and regional loyalties of Members of Parliament from both the reception areas and the inner-city constituencies. While MPs from the shires lamented the dirty clothes and unsavoury personal habits of some of the children billeted on homes in their areas, their colleagues from poorer districts defended their constituents against the more extreme charges. One Glasgow MP, anxious to stress the difficulties of everyday life in the Gorbals and to contrast them with the facilities enjoyed by the more fortunate, remarked that some of those forlorn and deracinated urban children newly arrived in the countryside had come from dwellings in his constituency in which country people would not keep their cattle.[5]

In recent years commentators have challenged some of the more colourful descriptions of evacuees. John Macnicol has argued that they had their origins in highly exaggerated cultural differences,[6] an observation elaborated by Harry Hendrick who has asserted that the evacuation process allowed the 'unashamed unveiling of rural and small town middle class prejudice, manifest in malevolent criticism of incontinence, infestation, inadequate clothing' and, significantly perhaps, lack of gratitude.[7] In spite of his misgivings about the objective accuracy of some of the reports, Hendrick does admit that the conditions described so unforgivingly were not entirely fictitious.[8] Certainly, members of the Liverpool Pacifist Service Unit believed in their existence and the 1943 report of the Women's Group on Public Welfare, prompted by the evacuation process,[9] reinforced their impressions of situations they had encountered. Some Liverpool children were lousy and dirty. They were poor school attenders. Many of them did have an inadequate diet. Their clothes were few and in poor condition. And the dwellings in which they and their families lived were ill-equipped, insanitary, and in very poor repair. In the aftermath of the damage caused by the Blitz in May 1941, such families were difficult to rehouse. Many had four or five children, some had eight or ten; in a city whose housing stock had been severely reduced by bombing, there were few dwellings large enough for them. The lifestyle of others was such that they were unlikely to be welcomed, even as temporary lodgers, into the homes of respectable families. Large and anti-social families, therefore, remained concentrated in emergency accommodation for much longer than their smaller and better-behaved neighbours and became the focus of the young pacifists' attention.[10] Once the slow process of rehousing was complete, the Pacifist Service Unit expanded its programme of support to poor families and began to accept referrals from both voluntary agencies and statutory bodies. Education, welfare and public health departments, as well as individual relieving officers, invited them to visit families exhibiting serious difficulties. Charitable agencies, such as the Discharged Prisoners' Aid Society, also requested help.[11]

But how did PSU workers understand the task in which they were engaged? It appears that their understanding was informed by two linked ideas – first that of inherited mental ill health and second, as a consequence, that of the parent as a danger to the child. Case notes kept on their clients reveal a conceptualisation of these families informed in part by the eugenism which had been a central tenet of pre-war social science orthodoxy, giving rise to a degree of pessimism about their future prospects. Few 'of those who have known really bad conditions' were deemed to be capable of 'reaching and maintaining ... the standards of a normal home'.[12] One commentator on PSU's work noted that only one in ten families showed sustained improvement after assistance had been withdrawn.[13] Failure was attributed, neither to poverty nor to those environmental elements for which they could not be held responsible – such as the inadequate maintenance of rented housing – but to personal inadequacy.[14]

Lack of confidence in the parents' ability to effect much improve-ment in their plight led to forms of treatment which underlined their incapacity and had the potential to create considerable dependency. PSU methods were based on what they came to call intensive family casework. This involved regular visiting – sometimes as frequently as two or three times daily – and close supervision of the family's arrange-ments for many aspects of its life – especially of household chores and the management of the children. The degree of supervision was a unique feature of PSU's work. No other agency, voluntary or statutory, was able to offer intensive care comparable to that given by the Manchester and Liverpool units, which used the dedication of their young and idealistic resident workers to provide a 24-hour service; people in need were encouraged to call at the unit house and could expect that their problems would receive a sympathetic hearing and an attempt at resolution. Nor was any other agency prepared to engage in the sort of hands-on domestic work that PSU undertook. Intensive casework included helping families to clean and de-louse themselves, their children and their homes as well as giving assistance with basic decoration and maintenance. Attention was also paid to children's educational needs. On occasion, reluctant school attenders were collected in the morning and escorted to the classroom. Sometimes, selected children were welcomed for short stays in the unit house in order to relieve urgent family difficulties.[15]

In addition to the pessimism which led to such vigilance, there was a degree of confusion about the nature and extent of family failure. While they were predisposed to consider primarily the physical conditions in which client families lived, and the lack of cleanliness which characterised their domestic organisation, unit workers also noted – with a surprise equal to that of middle-class observers witnessing the return of evacuees from the delights of country life to the dangerous chaos but emotional stability of the city[16] – that many children seemed happy and well adjusted and that they enjoyed good relationships with their parents. Evidence of what might be called abuse is rare. But parents were rarely given credit for providing adequate emotional support to their children nor was serious consideration given to the fact that their difficulties in domestic management may have owed as much to environmental as to personal shortcomings. There was little discussion as to the limits of the improvement which could be achieved with individual families whose primary problem was poverty, or of the possible effects of a change in social organisation and a redistribution of resources.

Frequent visiting, in order to offer practical assistance and support, became the essential component of the PSU approach. In addition, units exploited contacts among the wider pacifist community and local billeting officers, making it possible to offer both families and unaccompanied children the benefit of a holiday in the country. One version of this was what was called 'applied evacuation', a process which involved the removal of children from poor home conditions for what might be termed therapeutic reasons. This was sometimes for months at a time, during which time it was expected that their mothers would improve their standards of home management. It was claimed that the period of separation was good for all parties.[17]

Happy endings, engineered by the efforts of the unit, mask an insensitivity to the conditions in which some families had to live. Failure was perceived to lie in the deficiency in the maternal functions of providing a clean and healthy home and exerting adequate control over the children. Success was attributed to the evacuation organised for the children and measured in terms of what the workers saw as improved parental control and better domestic organisation. The assessment neglected any consideration of the children's ability to adapt to different situations, and failed to take into account the difficulties for them attendant on the process of removal from one environment to another. No worker recorded the suspicion that a child exhibiting newly acquired habits of obedience might just have been expressing his or her fear of being sent away again, or that some children might have thought that they were being punished by being made to live separately from their parents. Children became little more than pieces of evidence; on the one hand, they witnessed to parental failure and, on the other, demonstrated the wisdom under-lying the treatment prescribed for the family.

There was, however, no agreement among the workers about this form of evacuation. Some opposed it while others believed that temporary separation from an unhealthy environment was the only way to enable some children to experience a standard of life better than that in their own homes.[18] But on the whole – and not surprisingly – PSU was eager to claim success for its methods and to record such achievements in newsletters sent to its supporters. While the positive effects of separation from inadequate parents were stressed, it was also claimed that children's mental and physical development might improve as a result of their exposure to rural surroundings. In keeping with the propaganda campaign in support of evacuation waged by the Board of Education and Ministry of Health,[19] a comparison was made between rural and urban life which idealised all aspects of the former while emphasising the unhealthy features of life in the town. One set of notes records:

> The value to children of periods in the country is strikingly illustrated ... by a boy of eleven whose parents are separated and who was living with his mother and younger sisters in extreme poverty. He was out of control and rarely attended school, running wild in the streets, uncouth, uncivil, showing respect for no-one. The unit arranged for his evacuation to a camp school ... where the children enjoy an open-air life in huts. He has been away only four months but the regular and balanced meals, proper sleep and fresh air have brought about a great improvement. He is fitter and mentally brighter, and his manners and general attitude to other people have been transformed ... Other children have been sent for varying periods to hostels catering for difficult children and several have gone to a remarkable farm-training colony for young people, which is run mainly by pacifists, and where astonishing improvements have taken place in the children, mentally and physically.[20]

So up-beat an evaluation was well in line with popular belief, but contrary to objective assessment, even at the time.[21] Contemporary studies did not necessarily support the contention that time spent in the country as evacuees resulted in the improved physical and emotional health of children. As John Welshman has shown, although the School Medical Officer for Oxfordshire claimed that evacuees had put on weight, and his colleague in Oxford asserted confidently that country life was more attractive to children than the more restricted life in towns, such impressionistic claims were not borne out by serious studies of evacuated children. A London County Council investigation suggested that a period of evacuation did not cause any significant difference in the rate of growth of the children concerned, and this counter to popular opinion was confirmed by research carried out for the Ministry of Health.[22] Lucy Faithfull, who was involved with evacuee children during the war, noted that those who stayed with their parents through the Blitz were 'taller, despite missing school meals, were heavier and were emotionally better balanced' than those who were separated from them.[23]

Not all units became involved in evacuation. Each developed in response to local needs and conditions, and work with families was influenced both by the accident of circumstances and the unit's and its supporters' preoccupations. In Stepney, some PSU members put time and energy into working with pre-school children who spent their days playing unsupervised in the streets and on bomb sites.[24] Supplied with toys and equipment by the local Peace Pledge Union and the Save the Children Fund, the unit opened a nursery and used methods of child-management learned by those of their number who had worked in Anna Freud's nursery in Hampstead, and who continued to attend the lectures given there.[25] Freud's ideals formed the basis of the unit's approach to the children's activities. The terms in which their behaviour was described and explained, as well as the workers' justification for methods of discipline which eschewed the violence to which some children had been accustomed at home, was acknowledged to owe a great deal to Freud's methods. Their approach differed significantly from that being employed in the other key units of Manchester and Liverpool, which, although equally committed to non-violence, saw the solution of family problems primarily in terms of improvement in standards of housewifery and parental control achieved by close supervision.

Nevertheless, whatever the treatment, the underlying cause for the difficulties in which some families found themselves was understood in quasi-medical terms. Such partial understanding as the young pacifists possessed was increased as a result of their contacts with the Provisional National Council for Mental Health (PNCMH). The PNCMH had a complex history. Three bodies concerned with mental health – the National Council for Mental Hygiene, the Central Association for Mental Welfare and the Child Guidance Council – had combined in 1939 as the Mental Health Emergency Committee and had become the PNCMH in 1942.[26] Mental health training for social workers appears to have been an activity of one of its parent bodies which was taken on by the Provisional National Council for Mental Health. The Central Association for Mental Welfare had been constituted as a result of the 1913 Mental Deficiency Act, passed in part as a consequence of eugenist pressure,[27] and was successor to the National Association for the Welfare of the Feebleminded. Its most important work was done through local voluntary committees whose task was to refer to the appropriate authorities those in their areas deemed to be mentally defective and in need of institutionalisation.[28] It also organised courses and conferences on mental deficiency for doctors and trained the first social workers in mental health.[29] It was in the exercise of this educational function that contact was first made with PSU in February 1944. The PNCMH, anxious that the work of PSU should continue, suggested that the organisation might be able to provide training for Stepney PSU caseworkers.[30] An approach was made to the Manchester unit a few weeks later, and subsequently to the Liverpool unit. That all three offers were made in so short a time suggests that the move was centrally orchestrated – although made through local agents – and directed specifically at PSU. The Council's Liverpool representative informed the caseworkers that the Council was looking for people 'of the right type, adapted to work done by the Council'.[31] By April 1944 a short course had been designed to meet their needs and the first batch, made up of workers from all three units, was in London receiving training.[32] Coming from a variety of backgrounds, most PSU caseworkers lacked formal training in any type of social work. Although they were anxious to take every available opportunity to extend their knowledge and improve their practice,[33] their inexperience meant that to a large extent they were working in isolation and without any critical framework by which to evaluate either their own contribution or the literature they read. Their enthusiasm for the PNCMH course is indicative of the extent to which they had been influenced by prevailing orthodoxies and mental health concerns. Medical explanations for the situations they had encountered gave them a particular understanding of the plight of problem families and encouraged them to understand their difficulties in terms which stressed inherited weaknesses.[34] For example, his time with the Provisional National Council in 1944 prompted one of their number to write:

> I realise how little I knew of the behaviour problems arising from mental aberration and I know that I am better equipped already to deal with many of the problems arising in PSU work... I believe that undoubtedly in PSU we have been approaching the casework problems from the standpoint of the psychiatric social worker, but of course within the limits of our knowledge and experience... the problems we are encountering [on a PNCMH placement] are closely related to the problems we have met in the last three years, sometimes even of a comparable degree... often closely resembling the type of case we have been handling so nearly that names spring to one's mind spontaneously... already I am sure that we have obtained a refreshingly new outlook on problems of mental deficiency neuroses and psychoses which appear so regularly in PSU casework.[35]

II

When war ended, the ambitions of many PSU workers, whose original intentions had been just to offer service to those in need for the duration of the hostilities, had been modified. A peacetime career in some form of welfare work had become an attractive option for many of them. In spite of their lack of professional training, PSU workers had gained an enviable reputation for pioneering work with families considered hopeless by other agencies. The account of their wartime activities, published in 1945,[36] brought them to wider public notice and enabled them to create a role for themselves in the process of post-war urban reconstruction. Pacifism as an essential qualification for membership was abandoned and the Manchester and Liverpool units, together with a new unit in the Kensington and Paddington area of west London, were reconstituted as Family Service Units (FSU) in 1948. The unit in Stepney, which had been forced to close because of shortage of staff and the 'disruption caused by flying bombs',[37] re-opened after the war but declined to join the new organisation. It continued its work with families under the aegis of the Peace Pledge Union until it finally became part of FSU in 1953.[38]

In the immediate post-war period, local authority departments almost fell over themselves in attempts to persuade the new organisation to establish branches in their areas. Prominent among them were departments of public health, whose principal officers, the Medical Officers of Health, understood the potential of what FSU had to offer to the task of rehabilitating families giving rise to concern.[39] Many had already established links with Pacifist Service Units in their areas. The close association which Medical Officers of Health fostered with PSU/FSU served to reinforce the definition of the poor family in difficulties in medical terms. Articles in professional journals such The Medical Officer,[40] The Lancet,[41] the British Medical Journal[42] and Public Health[43] during the 1940s and early 1950s stressed the part played by parental, generally maternal, incompetence, resulting in many cases from inherited mental incapacity. Although ambivalent about its conceptual basis, FSU workers were already predisposed to a biologically deterministic understanding of family failure, although the humanitarian impulses which had led them to adopt a pacifist stance during the war, and their articulation of a view which purported to see worth in every person, gave rise to an ambivalence which prevented the adoption of an overtly eugenist platform.

Nevertheless, they were influenced by supporters such as David Caradog Jones, a lecturer at the University of Liverpool, a member of the Eugenics Society and a regular contributor to its journal, whose social survey of Merseyside, published in the early 1930s, argued for the existence of a social problem group within which most of those he characterised as 'criminals, paupers, unemployables and defectives' were to be found.[44] Their failure to attract normally intelligent persons led, in Caradog Jones's view, to inter-marriage and to the congregation of anti-social families, below average physically and mentally, in slum districts.[45] In many respects, his descriptions both informed and chimed with PSU/FSU workers' understanding of their experience.

Caradog Jones believed the achievement of a healthy society to be impossible without serious attention being paid to the quality of person from whom it was recruited.[46] Similar sentiments were expressed by several Medical Officers of Health. Among the most vocal were those in Liverpool, one of whom argued in 1947 that inadequate wives and mothers were responsible for families with 'Stone Age standards in an age of steel'.[47] His colleague in Rotherham agreed. Problem families owed their plight to mothers who exhibited 'low mental standards' and 'an almost complete inability to improve'. His preferred remedy, not notable for its originality, was to prevent 'mentally defective' women from producing children, either by sterilising or by segregating them. If mental defectives were adequately dealt with, he opined, then progress could be made towards the solution of the slum problem.[48] His views on surgical intervention did not command wide support, but his determination to deal with the issue of the problem family led him to find funding sufficient to establish and staff a Family Service Unit in Bristol, where he took up a post in the department of public health after the war. The unit became an arm of his department and was used to exercise close supervision over families on the Southmead estate whose chronic problems appeared to be insoluble.[49] Most other Medical Officers stopped short of incorporating FSU into their own departments, although the Bradford public health department provided the funding for the unit established in that city.[50] But many were enthusiastic supporters of their local FSUs, gave them varying amounts of financial support and referred families to their care. In the decade after the end of the war, FSU achieved an influence out of all proportion to its size, and its size was limited only by its inability to recruit and train staff sufficient to meet the requests of local authorities.

Its activities were also received with acclaim by some – but not all – other voluntary agencies, who invited its advice about work with families.[51]

Apart from FSU's work and that done by the Eugenics Society,[52] there had been little research into problem families and, with the exception of rare children's departments, such as Dudley in the late 1940s where Barbara Kahan was Children's Officer, few statutory bodies were equipped to deal with them. Kahan deliberately employed a PSU 'trained' worker to do preventive work with poorly functioning families. When she moved to Oxfordshire in 1951, she repeated the process and employed another ex-PSU worker.[53] She argued that a family caseworker could justify his employment because by keeping just one family of three children out of care he would have saved the children's committee the cost of his salary.[54] Later in the 1950s, the Children's Officers of the London County Council and Oxford City Council also employed preventive workers,[55] the LCC choosing to send its worker to FSU for training.[56] While FSU's methods were taken up by some statutory agencies, voluntary organisations were slower to emulate them. Some agencies were only too pleased to distance themselves. One of FSU's nearest comparators, the Family Welfare Association, was anxious to point out that it cared for families with problems while FSU looked after problem families.[57]

III

FSU focused on the family as an entity and worked mostly with parents. That, therefore, raises questions about its views of the children of problem families. Case notes of the 1940s and 1950s demonstrate that it paid relatively little attention to children in their own right. For FSU, their relative lack of importance stemmed from an understanding of poverty informed by a public health model of the problem family whose key feature was incompetent parenting. Such parents were dangerous to their children, who became evidence of parental inadequacy. Just by existing, many of them were walking proof of their parents' inability to employ effective contraception. They were a threat to those members of the middle class who feared being overrun by undesirables. They were often dirty and failed to conform to recognised standards of behaviour. Taken together, the characteristics such children displayed served to underline and reinforce the diagnosis of parental incompetence and to increase fears of hereditary weakness. In spite of the degree of ambivalence about eugenics entertained by a number of its members, the emphasis on parental irresponsibility linked with notions of congenital inadequacy meant that Family Service Units were slow to develop a critique of the social and economic factors responsible for creating those poor conditions which they, along with other social workers, were to come to see as crucial to the understanding of family difficulties.

The label 'problem families' which came into currency in the early 1940s was used widely by PSU and its successor organisation, as well as by members of the medical and welfare professions. Its employment by Medical Officers of Health and health visitors, together with clinical explanations for the phenomenon of the problem family, lent it a quasi-medical authority. But by the mid-1950s, the appeal of a public health explanation for the problem family had begun to wane, although the language of disease persisted in the routine use of terms such as 'diagnosis', 'treatment' and 'prognosis'. Moreover, the pessimism associated with the original definition persisted in some quarters. Catherine Wright, Assistant Medical Officer of Health for Sheffield, argued in 1955 that the prognosis for 'fully developed' problem families was either 'a limping existence, brooded over by case conferences and propped up by as many as seven to ten agencies', or neglect of the children leading to family break-up.[58] She believed the incidence of the problem family to be a 'transmissible disease' requiring preventive medicine, and argued that individual members of such families should be considered as potential 'carriers'. As infected persons, they should be registered with the medical services in the same way as those who were handicapped or tuberculous.[59] Similar language was used by contemporaries professionally concerned with the psychological welfare of children. For some, the emphasis was not on children as victims of inherited disease but on children as transmitters of modern plagues which posed a grave threat to social health. John Bowlby, for example, expressed the view that deprived children were 'the sources of social infection as real and serious as are carriers of diphtheria and typhoid'.[60] This, too, reflected on parental competence, with the implicit assumption that children cannot deprive themselves but are the victims of bad parenting, particularly bad mothering.

Treatment of the problem family was influenced by methods which stressed the importance of mental health. Although commentators in

the late 1940s and early 1950s were already urging an approach to
the solution of family problems which took account of the structural
and social components in individual distress, and arguing that there
could be no sound practice of casework without an understanding of
the principles and function of social reform, community organisation
and social groupwork,[61] it was psychodynamic work which became
the dominant mode of intervention. This was influenced to a great
extent by work done at the Family Discussion Bureau established in
London in 1948 and taken over by the Tavistock Institute in 1956 as
the Institute of Marital Studies.[62] The Tavistock continued its
crucial role in extending the influence of psychodynamic methods by
diverting resources for social work education from the training of
psychiatric social workers alone to the provision of full-time courses
for small groups from any recognised branch of casework.[63] FSU
workers enrolled for courses at the Tavistock,[64] as well as on psychiatric
social work courses at the London School of Economics,[65] and at the
universities of Leeds, Liverpool and Manchester.[66]

Although it maintained that it had a distinctive approach, FSU
was both a product of its time and part of a wider process of
experimentation in social work method. Influenced by the growing
esteem accorded to psychodynamic methods and affected by changing
views on the nature of childhood, the organisation began consciously
to distance itself from a deterministic understanding of the problem
family and to move towards a psychiatric social work methodology.
In terms of identifying causal factors for family problems, it made
little difference. It still accorded scant importance to environmental
factors because psychodynamic methods worked from the basic
premise that the individual's difficulties were located within herself
and her relationships. As David Jones, a worker in the Liverpool PSU
and first National Secretary of Family Service Units, remarked when
reflecting on Barbara Wootton's criticisms of post-war social work,
this was indicative of a tension within individual social workers:

> Social workers weren't all psychiatric and therapeutic. Social workers were
> concerned with social reform and social change ... Most social workers I knew
> were aware of the importance of social conditions and what their consequences
> were. However, what they did ... tended to divide these concerns ... they might
> be very political in their private life ... but very professional, almost very narrow,
> in their work. They didn't bring the two together in the work situation. Some
> of the people who might be regarded as the archetypes of the psychoanalytic,
> psychiatric approach in social work, to my knowledge were clearly left-wing
> politically.[67]

Although the assumption that social concern equated with left-wing views may say more about Jones than about some of his colleagues, his comment does indicate a dichotomy between personal political and social belief and professional practice. His views would have received the approval of Tom Simey, Professor of Social Administration at the University of Liverpool, and Richard Titmuss, his counterpart at the London School of Economics. Both believed that by focusing on the internal world of the client, intensive, psycho-dynamic casework was in danger of 'ignoring both wider social problems and administrative realities'.[68] It was, however, 1970 before a study of clients' perceptions led teachers of social work to argue that, 'In their preoccupation with psychological matters, social workers have tended to develop an occupational blindness to economic realities'.[69]

Meanwhile the importance of mental ill-health as an ingredient in the construct of the problem family continued to be explicit. The Liverpool FSU's *Annual Report for 1955–56* noted that of the 105 cases on its books during the previous years, 22 had spent time in mental hospitals or were ascertained mental defectives; 17 children had been treated at Child Guidance clinics and 29 children were attending or had attended special schools. Even these figures, the report concluded, underestimated the amount of emotional disturbance in families.[70] The following year, the Kensington and Paddington unit reported that of the 20 families with whom the unit had been working for more than two years, 15 were characterised by the mental ill-health of both parents.[71] And in 1960, the unit noted that about a quarter of FSU families had at least one parent who had been diagnosed as mentally ill.[72] FSU's description of its clients in a document associated with the setting up of a Combined Casework Unit in Hackney in 1962 noted that,

> Most of the families are 'problem families', having difficulties in many areas of their lives but particularly in financial management and child care. In all cases parents have deep-seated personality problems which make it difficult for them to establish satisfactory relationships with others or to profit from the social services available in the community.[73]

Little had changed since the Liverpool FSU, in an account of the first ten years of its work, stated, 'Our clients are ill. Some more than others.'[74]

In the wake of work done by John Bowlby[75] and his successors, comparisons have sometimes been drawn between the work of the major children's charities – which concentrated on child rescue, the removal of children from what were deemed to be dangerous homes and, in some cases, the prosecution of parents for neglect – and Family Service Units – which stressed the integrity of the family – generally to the advantage of the latter's reputation. There can be little doubt that FSU was responsible for focusing attention on the plight of poorly functioning families and for pioneering ways of offering them support which had a profound impact on the development of post-war social work method. But FSU was not sentimental about the family. Nor, in its early days, was it particularly concerned about the welfare of children. The integrity of the family was morally desirable. And keeping parents and children together made good economic sense. These ideals formed a substantial part of the platform on which FSU stood when arguing for greater financial help from local authorities. The arithmetic was easy. As the unit organiser in the West London unit was to argue when trying to increase the level of his local authority grant, by using methods of close supervision of inadequate parents and keeping just a handful of children out of institutional care, the unit saved the council thousands of pounds.[76]

The late 1950s were to witness increasing professional confidence on the part of social workers. Expanded opportunities for proper training, accelerating after the implementation of the central recommendations of the Younghusband Report of 1959,[77] contributed to the further weakening in influence of Medical Officers of Health. New methods of intervention were developed and some of those employed during the 1940s and 1950s were challenged as the emphasis began to shift away from intensely personal casework towards group and community work and more overtly 'political' activity. In addition, the 1963 Children and Young Persons Act, which allowed children's departments to involve themselves in preventive work and to exploit links with voluntary organisations, resulted in the relinquishing of responsibility for problem families by many departments of public health, and their transfer to local children's departments. As a result, FSU saw the replacement of Medical Officers of Health on its management committees by Children's Officers or members of their staffs[78] – in effect the replacement of medicine by social work as the dominant discipline in work with families, and the foregrounding of children within families.[79] The shift in emphasis within FSU was exemplified by its involvement in setting up the Child Poverty Action

Group in 1965 as well as the active participation of some of its units in political issues.

By the mid-1960s, few FSU social workers would have wished to associate themselves with the medicalisation of families in difficulty in the way that their predecessors' had. Emphasis came increasingly to be placed on the social context of the family, the part that group activity could play in effecting improvements in people's lives and the importance of the community as a vehicle for change and empowerment. Interventions based on a form of self-help, through the use of group and community work, gradually replaced the traditionally more directive approach of the social worker who, in the early days of the organisation, had acted as the confidante, intimate support, supervisor and mentor of many needy families, in order to ensure the implementation of policies which were in accord with the concerns of Medical Officers of Health.

Acknowledgements

This chapter is part of a larger project on Family Service Units, the research for which was made possible by the award of an ESRC grant (no: R000234593).

Notes

1. T. Stephens, *Problem Families. An Experiment in Social Rehabilitation*, London, Pacifist Service Units, 1945. See also P. Starkey, *Families and Social Workers. The Work of Family Service Units, 1940–1985*, Liverpool, Liverpool University Press, 2000, pp. 8ff.

2. It was assumed that problem families were not always poor, but that difficulties were more easily concealed 'when such a family is on the middle or upper rungs of the social ladder' because money could be used to provide domestic help and 'periods of institutional treatment'. I. Barclay, 'Postcript', in Stephens, *Problem Families*, p. 67.

3. H. Hendrick, *Child Welfare: England 1872–1989*, London and New York, Routledge, 1994, p. 242.

4. J. Welshman, 'In Search of the "Problem Family": Public Health and Social Work in England and Wales 1940–1970', *Social History of Medicine* 9, 1996, p. 465.

5. Parliamentary Papers. House of Commons Debates, 14 September 1939, cols. 802ff.

6. J. Macnicol, 'The Evacuation of Schoolchildren', in *War and Social Change. British Society in the Second World War*, ed. H. L. Smith, Manchester, Manchester University Press, 1986, p. 20. See also J. Welshman, 'Evacuation and Social Policy during the Second World War: Myth and Reality', *Twentieth Century British History* 9, 1998, pp. 28ff.

7. Hendrick, *Child Welfare: England 1872–1989*, p. 194.

8. Hendrick, *Child Welfare: England 1872–1989*, p. 194. A first-hand account by a volunteer of the experience of escorting children to evacuation areas can be found in P. Willmott, *A Singular Woman: The Life of Geraldine Aves, 1898–1986*, London, National Institute for Social Work, 1992, pp. 58ff.

9. Women's Group on Public Welfare, *Our Towns. A Close-Up. A Study Made During 1939–1942 With Certain Recommendations by the Hygiene Committee of the Women's Group on Public Welfare*, Oxford, Oxford University Press, 1943.

10. Report of the Manchester PSU mobile section, 4–12 May 1941. University of Liverpool, Special Collections and Archives (hereafter, ULSCA) D495(LI)M8/3. Minutes of the Liverpool PSU meeting, 16 May 1941. ULSCA D495(L1)M1/2.

11. See, for example, minutes of the Liverpool PSU committee, 29 October 1942, 3 December 1942, 11 February 1943. ULSCA (LI)M1/2.

12. Stephens, *Problem Families*, p. 64.

13. R. Wofinden, 'Homeless Children: A Survey of Children in the Scattered Homes, Rotherham', *The Medical Officer* 77, 1947, p. 186. Women's Group on Public Welfare, *The Neglected Child and His Family. A Study Made in 1946–47 of the Problem of the Child Neglected in His Own Home, Together With Certain Recommendations by a Sub-Committee of the Women's Group for Public Welfare*, Oxford, Oxford University Press, 1948, p. 100. See also E. E. Irvine, 'Research into Problem Families: Theoretical Considerations Arising From Dr Blacker's Investigations', *British Journal of Psychiatric Social Work* 2, 1951–54, p. 32.

14. Stephens, *Problem Families*, p. 60. For further discussion, see Starkey, *Families and Social Workers*, pp. 45ff.

15. Stephens, *Problem Families*, passim.

16. Macnicol, 'The Evacuation of Schoolchildren', p. 26.

17. PSU Newsletter, May 1944. ULSCA D495(HQ)PSU/7. See also P. Starkey, 'The Feckless Mother: Women, Poverty and Social Workers in Wartime and Post-War England', *Women's History Review* 9, 2000, pp. 539ff.

18. The wish to counteract what were perceived to be the bad influences in the child's home was not unique to FSU but found also in voluntary child-care agencies. S. Mencher, 'Factors Affecting the Relationship of the Voluntary and Statutory Child-Care Services in England', *Social Service Review* 32, 1958, p. 29.

19. Macnicol, 'The Evacuation of Schoolchildren', p. 14.

20. PSU Newsletter, May 1944. ULSCA D495(HQ)PSU/7.

21. Macnicol, 'The Evacuation of Schoolchildren', pp. 19–20.

22. Welshman, 'Evacuation and Social Policy', pp. 44ff.

23. Quoted in B. Holman, *The Corporate Parent. Manchester Children's Department 1948–71*, London, National Institute for Social Work, 1996, p. 118. Lucy Faithfull was later to become Children's Officer for the City of Oxford.

24. Stepney PSU, *Nursery Report*, nd but from internal evidence it is clear that it was produced some time after 1942. ULSCA D495(HQ)PSU/7.

25. One Pacifist Service Unit had been based there. It withdrew its services in October 1944. Minutes of the PSU national committee, 21 October 1944. ULSCA D495(HQ)PSU/1.

26. G. Jones, *Social Hygiene in Twentieth-Century Britain*, London, Croom Helm, 1986, p. 137.

27. Jones, *Social Hygiene*, pp. 31–33, 88. See also G. Searle, *Eugenics and Politics in Britain, 1900–1914*, Leyden, Noordhoff, 1976, ch. 9; P. Mazumdar, *Eugenics, Human Genetics and Human Failings: The Eugenics Society, its Sources and its Critics in Britain*, London, Routledge, 1992, pp. 23–24.

28. The Central Association for Mental Health had a branch in Liverpool, and both the Liverpool Ladies' Association for the Training of Girls and the West Derby Board of Guardians had been members of the Association in the late 1920s. Wellcome Institute for the History of Medicine, CMAC:SA/EUG/D53

29. Jones, *Social Hygiene*, p. 27.

30. Liverpool PSU, casework report, nd. ULSCA D495(LI)M5/1.

31. Minutes of the Liverpool PSU committee, 19 April 1944. ULSCA D495(LI)M1/5.

32. Minutes of the Liverpool PSU committee, 19 April 1944. ULSCA D495(LI)M1/5.

33. A. Cohen, *The Revolution in Post-War Family Casework: The Story of Pacifist Service Units and Family Service Units*, Lancaster, Lancaster University Centre for North-West Studies, 1998, p. 32. Individual members appear to have attended lectures given to other groups; for example one attended a lecture on psychopathic behaviour given to the Liverpool Child Guidance Clinic in February 1945. ULSCA D495(HQ)PSU/7. PSU members in Liverpool had also followed a part-time course organised for them at the University Settlement. Minutes of the Liverpool PSU committee, 17 February 1943. ULSCA D495(LI)M1/3. They had also discussed their work with local doctors. One of these, Dr Muriel Barton-Hall of the Liverpool Psychiatric Clinic, had delivered a course of lectures on Psychiatry and the Social Problem Group to the Liverpool PSU in 1944. Minutes of the Liverpool PSU committee, 1 March 1944. ULSCA D495(LI)M5/1. See also talks given to unit members on aspects of casework, 1944–46. ULSCA D495(LI)M17/1.

34. Minutes of the Liverpool PSU committee, 21 June 1944. ULSCA D495(LI)M1/5.

35. Brief report on work and presumed prospects with Provisional National Council for Mental Health, 19 June 1944. ULSCA D495(HQ)PSU7

36. Stephens, *Problem Families*.

37. Stephens, *Problem Families*, p. 69.

38. Report to Liverpool FSU executive committee, November 1953. ULSCA D495(LI)M12/2.

39. Requests were received from Sheffield and York, minutes of the FSU national executive committee, 27 May 1949. ULSCA D495(HQ)M2/2; minutes of the FSU national committee, 18 November 1949 ULSCA D495(HQ)M2/2; minutes of the FSU national executive committee, 7 March 1950. ULSCA D495(HQ)M2/2; minutes of the FSU national executive committee, 12 June 1950. ULSCA D495(HQ)M2/2; from Oldham and from Birmingham, minutes of the FSU national executive committee, 24 November 1950. ULSCA D495(HQ)M2/2;

from Leicester, Swansea, Devon and Nottingham, minutes of the FSU national executive committee, 17 January 1951, 28 February 1951. ULSCA D495(HQ)M2/2; from Bradford, minutes of the FSU national executive committee, 19 April 1951. ULSCA D495(HQ)M2/2; and from Newcastle, report of Liverpool FSU executive committee, July to September 1958. ULSCA D495(LI)M2.

40. See, for example, B. Andrews and J. S. Cookson, 'Problem Families – A Practical Approach', *The Medical Officer* 88, 1952; C. F. Brockington, 'Problem Families', *The Medical Officer* 78, 1947; A. Elliott, 'Problem Families in Kent', *The Medical Officer* 100, 1958; J. G. Howells and M. Davies, 'The Intelligence of Children in Problem Families', *The Medical Officer* 98, 1957; A. Querido, 'The Problem Family in the Netherlands', *The Medical Officer* 75, 1946; S. Savage, 'Rehabilitation of Problem Families', *The Medical Officer* 75, 1946; J. Scott, 'Problem Families in London', *The Medical Officer* 100, 1958; C. O. Stallybrass, 'Problem Families', *The Medical Officer* 75, 1946; R. Wofinden, 'Homeless Children'; idem, 'Unsatisfactory Families', *The Medical Officer* 94, 1955; C. Wright, 'Problem Families', *The Medical Officer* 94, 1955.

41. C. F. Brockington, 'Homelessness in Children: Causes and Prevention', *Lancet* 2, 1946; M. Sheridan, 'Neglectful Mothers', *Lancet* 2, 1959.

42. S. Savage, 'Intelligence and Infant Mortality in Problem Families', *British Medical Journal* 2, 1946; M. Sheridan, 'The Intelligence of 100 Neglectful Mothers', *British Medical Journal* 1, 1956.

43. R. Wofinden, 'Problem Families', *Public Health* 57, 1944.

44. D. Caradog Jones, *The Social Survey of Merseyside*, Liverpool, Liverpool University Press, 1934, III, pp. 546–47. Caradog Jones's observations had antecedents. Charles Booth had described 'the submerged tenth' believed to be at the base of any urban society. Quoted in Women's Group on Public Welfare, *Our Towns*, p. xiii; *The Report of the Mental Deficiency Committee* had referred to 'a group which may be described as the subnormal or social problem group, representing approximately 10 per cent of the whole population in 1929', *Report of the Interdepartmental Committee on Mental Deficiency*, 1925–29, Wood Report, Cmnd 3545, HMSO, 1929, pt. III; and E. J. Lidbetter had identified a 'race of subnormals' in a study of an area in East London. E. J. Lidbetter, *Heredity and the Social Problem Group*, London, Edward Arnold, 1933, p. 18.

45. Caradog Jones, *Social Survey*, III, pp. 546–47.

46. Caradog Jones, *Social Survey*, III, pp. 546–47.

47. C. O. Stallybrass, 'Problem Families', *Social Work* 4, 1947, p. 30.

48. Wofinden, 'Problem Families', p. 138; idem, 'Homeless Children', p. 185.

49. See P. Starkey, 'The Medical Officer of Health, the Social Worker and the Problem Family: The Case of Family Service Units, 1943–1968', *Social History of Medicine* 11, 1998, pp. 421–41.

50. Minutes of the FSU national executive committee, 1 February 1952. ULSCA D495(HQ)M2.

51. The Liverpool Personal Service Society believed that the organisation was doing more harm than good and attempted to stop its activities. Minutes of the PSU national committee, 3 September 1942, and minutes of the PSU executive committee extraordinary meeting, 6 September 1942. ULSCA D495(HQ)PSU/1. See also Cohen, *The Revolution in Post-War Family Casework*, p. 24.

52. For example, C. Blacker, *Problem Families – Five Enquiries*, London, Eugenics Society, 1952.

53. Personal communication with Barbara Kahan, May 1990; cf. J. Packman, *The Child's Generation*, Oxford, Blackwell, 2nd edn, 1981, pp. 60ff.

54. Quoted in Packman, *The Child's Generation*, p. 55.

55. Packman, *The Child's Generation*, p. 55.

56. Minutes of Kensington and Paddington FSU committee, 15 October 1957, ULSCA D495(WL)M1; Kensington and Paddington FSU, *Annual Report for 1957–58*, ULSCA D495(WL)M1.

57. J. Lewis, *The Voluntary Sector, the State and Social Work in Britain*, London and New York, Routledge, 1995, pp. 120–22.

58. C. Wright, 'Problem Families. A Review and Some Observations', *The Medical Officer* 94, 1955, p. 381.

59. Wright, 'Problem Families', pp. 382, 383. See also Savage, 'Rehabilitation of Problem Families', p. 252; Brockington, 'Problem Families', p. 75.

60. J. Bowlby, *Child Care and the Growth of Love*, Harmondsworth, Penguin, 1953, p. 181.

61. V. Cormack, 'Principles of Casework', *Social Work* 4, 1947, p. 69.

62. E. E. Irvine, 'Renaissance in British Casework', *Social Work* 13, 1956, p. 189; see also R. Chambers, 'Professionalism in Social Work', in *Social Science and Social Pathology*, ed. B. Wootton, London, George Allen and Unwin, 1959, p. 359, and E. Younghusband, *Social Work in Britain 1950–1975*, London, George Allen and Unwin, 1978, II, p. 121

63. Irvine, 'Renaissance in British Casework', p. 192; Younghusband, *Social Work in Britain 1950–1975*, II, p. 23.

64. Minutes of the Liverpool FSU committee, 7 July 1954. ULSCA D495(LI)M2.

65. Minutes of the Liverpool FSU executive committee, 4 June 1956. ULSCA D495(LI)M3/2; Liverpool FSU executive committee reports, 1 July to 30 September 1956 and 1 April to 30 June 1958. ULSCA D495(LI)M2.

66. Minutes of the FSU national executive committee, 26 October 1962, 22 May 1963, 17 March 1965, 20 July 1966, 12 March 1968. ULSCA D495(HQ) M2/5.

67. Cohen, *The Revolution in Post-War Family Casework*, p. 77.

68. Lewis, *The Voluntary Sector, the State and Social Work*, p. 117.

69. J. Mayer and N. Timms, *The Client Speaks. Working Class Impressions of Casework*, London, Routledge and Kegan Paul, p. 141.

70. Liverpool FSU, *Annual Report for 1955–56*. ULSCA D495(LI)M2.

71. Kensington and Paddington FSU, *Annual Report for 1956–57*. ULSCA D495(WL)M1.

72. Kensington and Paddington FSU, *Annual Report for 1960–61*. ULSCA D495(WL)M1.

73. Basis of the operation of the Combined Casework Unit, 23 February 1962. ULSCA D495(HQ)B1–B3/4.

74. *Liverpool FSU 1948–1958*, ULSCA D495(LI)M2.

75. J. Bowlby, *Maternal Care and Mental Health*, Geneva, World Health Organisation, 1951.

76. Kensington and Paddington FSU, *Annual Report for 1954–55*. ULSCA D495(WL)M1.

77. Ministry of Health, *Report of the Working Party on Social Workers in the Local Authority Social Services*, Younghusband Report, HMSO, 1959.

78. Minutes of the FSU Fieldwork Organisers' Meeting, 20–21 September 1965. ULSCA D495(HQ)M3/1. See Starkey, 'The Medical Officer of Health, the Social Worker and the Problem Family', p. 435.

79. Some commentators believe this process to have been completed by the implementation of the recommendations of the Seebohm committee in 1971. See Welshman, 'In Search of the "Problem Family"'.

FALKIRK COUNCIL
LIBRARY SUPPORT
FOR SCHOOLS

Notes on Contributors

Lynn Abrams teaches history at the University of Glasgow. She has published widely on the history of marriage and divorce in Germany and on child welfare and the family in Scotland including *The Orphan Country: Children of Scotland's Broken Homes, 1845 to the Present Day* (Edinburgh, 1998).

Jane Brown is a research fellow in the Criminology and Socio-Legal Research Unit, University of Glasgow. She has a particular interest in studying sensitive topics and researching the views of young people.

Michele Burman teaches criminology and research methods at the University of Glasgow, where she is also Director of the Criminology and Socio-Legal Research Unit. She has a long-standing research interest in troubled and troublesome girls.

Patrick A. Dunae is a member of the History Department at Malaspina University College in Nanaimo, British Columbia. He has written and edited several books on emigration and education history. His articles have appeared in *Victorian Studies*, *Histoire sociale/Social History* and the *International History Review*. His book on the Fairbridge child emigrants to British Columbia is forthcoming.

Julie Grier is a research student at the University of Liverpool and has completed a PhD thesis on the relationship of the state and the voluntary sector in the sphere of child welfare.

Molly Ladd-Taylor is Associate Professor of History at York University in Toronto, Canada. Her publications include *Mother-Work: Women, Child Welfare and the State, 1890–1930* (1995); *'Bad'*

Mothers: The Politics of Blame in Twentieth-Century America (1997); and 'Saving Babies and Sterilising Mothers: Eugenics and Welfare Politics in the Inter-War United States', *Social Politics* (1997).

Jon Lawrence is Senior Lecturer in History at the University of Liverpool. His extensive publications on modern British history include *Speaking for the People: Party, Language and Popular Politics in England, 1867–1914* (1998) and *Party, State and Society: Electoral Behaviour in Britain Since 1820* (with Miles Taylor, 1997). He is currently working on attitudes to violence in British society in the aftermath of the First World War.

Lydia Murdoch is an Assistant Professor of History at Vassar College. She is currently working on a book tentatively titled *Imagined Orphans: Poor Families, the Home, and Child Welfare in England, 1870–1918*.

Tamara Myers is an Assistant Professor of History at the University of Winnipeg, Canada, and a member of the Montreal History Group. Her work on juvenile justice in Quebec has been published in the *Canadian Historical Review*. She is currently working on a monograph which examines female delinquency in Montreal in the first half of the twentieth century.

Kathleen Paul is Associate Professor of History at the University of South Florida. She has written extensively on questions of race and citizenship in post-war Britain, notably in her book *Whitewashing Britain: Race and Citizenship in the Post-War Era* (Ithaca, NY, Cornell University Press, 1997), and in articles for *International Labor and Working Class History* (1996), *Journal of British Studies* (1995) and *Contemporary Record* (1992). She is currently working on a monograph dealing with twentieth-century child migration within the British Empire/Commonwealth.

Geoffrey Sherington holds a personal chair in the history of education and is Dean of the Faculty of Education, University of Sydney, Australia. He has written extensively on the history of education in Britain and Australia and also on the history of British child and youth migration. His publications include *English Education, Social Change and War* (Manchester University Press, 1981), *Australia's Immigrants* (Allen and Unwin, 1990) *Youth in Australia* (1995) and *Fairbridge: Empire and Child Migration* (Woburn Press, 1998). He is currently continuing studies of British child migration and beginning research on the history of comprehensive schools since the Second World War.

Pat Starkey is a lecturer in the School of History and Assistant Director of the School of Combined Honours at the University of Liverpool. Her research interests are in the history of charity and voluntary organisations in the nineteenth and twentieth centuries, and in women's history. Her recent publications include 'The Medical Officer of Health, the social worker and the problem family, 1943-1968: the case of Family Service Units', *Social History of Medicine*, 11 (1998); 'The feckless mother. Women, poverty and social workers in 1940s England', *Women's History Review*, 9 (2000); and *Families and Social Workers: The Work of Family Service Units, 1940–1985* (Liverpool, 2000).

John Stewart is Senior Lecturer in British Political History in the School of Humanities, Oxford Brookes University. He is the author of *'The Battle for Health': A Political History of the Socialist Medical Association, 1930–1951* (Aldershot, Ashgate, 1999) and of many articles in journals including *Twentieth Century British History*, *Agricultural History Review*, *Children and Society*, *Medical History*, *Journal of Medical Biography*, *Scottish Historical Review* and *Annals of Science*. He is currently working on a history of Scottish social welfare in the twentieth century.

Shurlee Swain is Senior Lecturer in History at Australian Catholic University and a Senior Research Associate in the History Department at the University of Melbourne. She has published widely in the area of child welfare history; her latest book, *Confronting Cruelty: Historical Aspects of Child Abuse* is to be published by Melbourne University Press in February 2002.

Kay Tisdall presently holds a joint post as Lecturer in Social Policy (University of Edinburgh) and Director of Policy and Research (Children in Scotland, the national umbrella agency for organisations working with children and their families).

Index

Page numbers in *italics* refer to figures.

financial contributions of 249
funding 248
regionalisation 247
relationship with the state 1944–53
  10, 234, 246–8, 250, 251
Second World War child care 240
see also Girls' Village Home, Ilford
Barnett, Henrietta 154–5
barrack schools
  age factors 159–60, 161
  criticisms 7, 149, 151–61
  disease 160
  girls 153, 154, 156–60
  hygiene 160
  male dominated nature 152–3, 158–9
  North Surrey District School *152*
  replacement by family cottages 147–
  8, 155–6, 166
Bear, G. G. 37
belonging
  cultural 213
  and the family 8, 195, 200, 201,
  204, 206, 211, 212
Beveridge, Lord 241–2
Big Brother scheme 65
Björkqvist, K. 37
Black Isle 202
Blitz 258, 261
Board of Education 235, 236, 261
boarding out 8, 147, 155, 196–213
  access to blood family records 196,
  200–1, 202, 204, 205, 207–8,
  209–10, 212, 213
  and Barnardo's 245–6, 247
  blending in 199–200
  case histories 201–11, 212
  child abuse 202, 203
  cultural issues 213
  Curtis committee's recommendation
  of 237
  feelings of loss 212
  and forced familial separation 8,
  196–7, 199–200, 207, 212
  and identity 8, 197, 200, 201, 205,
  206, 207–10, 212, 213
  Select Committee on Estimates
  recommendation of 248–9

three-act model of 212–13
  see also foster care
Boards of Guardians 56, 57, 70, 152
Boer War 176, 179
Booth, William 161
Bowlby, John 200, 267, 269–70
boys
  runaway 18
  violent behaviour 37, 47
Boys Garden City 240
Bradford, England 265
Bristol, England 265
Britain
  child rescue movement 102–3, 105
  post-war child welfare legislation 10,
  234–51
  post-war family failure 9–10, 256–71
  state–voluntary sector relationship
  234–51
  see also British child emigration;
  England; Scotland; Wales
British child emigration 2–6
  aftercare 69, 74, 95–6, 126
  to Australia 3–6, 53–78, 85–6, 101,
  112–15, 121–40
  pre-First World War 55, 56–7,
  60, 62, *66*, 67, 69, 70–1
  inter-war period 55, 57–9, *58*,
  60–1, 62–3, *63*, 67–8, 71–3
  post-Second World War 6, 55,
  59, 64–5, 74–6, 113–14, 121–40
  to Canada 53, 60, 82–97, 123, 129
  Canadian prohibition of 4, 82, 86,
  87, 123
  cessation 137, 139–40
  as child rescue 112–13, 115–16
  compensation claims 101
  culture shock 114–15
  employment opportunities 65–7,
  69–71, 72, 73, 74, 77, 124
  Fairbridge Society 3–5, 54–78, *58*,
  63, *66*, 82–97, 122, 123, 132–3,
  135
  funding 113–14
  history of 122–3
  and identity 54, 73, 76–7
  perceptions of 126

FALKIRK COUNCIL
LIBRARY SUPPORT
FOR SCHOOLS